Gathering of the Greatest Quotes

*Over 3650 Daily Inspirational and
Motivational Quotations from the
Most Famous People of the Whole World*

Darleen Mitchell

TABLE OF CONTENT

Introduction

Words have great power, quotes of great people -even more.

I hope you enjoy this magnificent collection of quotes and will refer to it for many years. It is a source of comfort, perspective, and entertainment; it brings happiness, not just to you, but to everyone around you.

You can read these pages every day like a normal book and inspire yourself positively, or you can cut out the one that speaks to you and hang them on the wall, where this quote will be visible all day for you and people in your home. So, start to change your attitude about life and get happy!

Darleen Mitchell

Abraham Lincoln

Abraham Lincoln (February 12, 1809 – April 15, 1865) **was** a self-taught lawyer, legislator and vocal opponent of slavery was elected 16th president of the United States in November 1860, shortly.

***

Most folks are about as happy as they make their minds up to be.

***

It has been my experience that folks who have no vices have very few virtues.

***

No man has a good enough memory to be a successful liar.

***

Human action can be modified to some extent, but human nature cannot be changed.

***

Love is the chain to lock a child to its parent.

***

Those who look for the bad in people will surely find it.

***

There are no bad pictures; that's how your face looks sometimes.

***

You can tell the greatness of a man by what makes him angry.

***

Common looking people are the best in the world: that is the reason the Lord makes so many of them.

***

He has a right to criticize, who has the heart to help.

***

Tact: the ability to describe others as they see themselves.

***

A woman is the only thing I am afraid of that I know will not hurt me.

***

A farce or comedy is best played; a tragedy is best read at home.

***

My great concern is not whether you have failed, but whether you are content with your failure.

***

Upon the subject of education, not presuming to dictate any plan or system respecting it, I can only say that I view it as the most important subject which we as a people can be engaged in.

***

For people who like that kind of a book that is the kind of book, they will like.

***

I am rather inclined to silence, and whether that be wise or not, it is at least more unusual nowadays to find a man who can hold his tongue than to find one who cannot.

***

If I were two-faced, would I be wearing this one?

***

Perhaps a man's character was like a tree and his reputation like its shadow; the shadow is what we think of it, the tree is the real thing.

***

You can fool some of the people all of the time, and all of the people some of the time, but you cannot fool all of the people all of the time.

***

I am a slow walker, but I never walk back.

***

I don't like that man. I must get to know him better.

***

When you reach the end of your rope, tie a knot and hang on.

***

You have to do your growing no matter how tall your grandfather was.

***

Adhere to your purpose, and you will soon feel as well as you ever did. On the contrary, if you falter, and give up, you will lose the power of keeping any resolution and will regret it all your life.

***

It often requires more courage to dare to do right than to fear to do wrong.

***

And in the end, it is not the years in your life that count, it's the life in your years.

***

You cannot escape the responsibility of tomorrow by evading it today.

***

Better to remain silent and be thought a fool than to speak out and remove all doubt.

***

Leave nothing for tomorrow which can be done today.

***

Be sure you put your feet in the right place, then stand firm.

***

We can complain because rose bushes have thorns, or rejoice because thorn bushes have roses.

***

Every man's happiness is his responsibility.

***

If I am killed, I can die but once; but to live in constant dread of it, is to die over and over again.

∗∗∗

Nearly all men can stand adversity, but if you want to test a man's character, give him power.

∗∗∗

I would rather be a little nobody, then to be an evil somebody.

∗∗∗

I will prepare, and someday my chance will come.

∗∗∗

I have been driven many times upon my knees by the overwhelming conviction that I had nowhere else to go. My wisdom and that of all about me seemed insufficient for that day.

∗∗∗

Always bear in mind that your resolution to success is more important than any other thing.

∗∗∗

That some achieve great success, is proof to all that others can achieve it as well.

∗∗∗

I'm a success today because I had a friend who believed in me and I didn't have the heart to let him down.

***

I have a congenital aversion to failure.

***

I happen temporarily to occupy this big White House. I am living witness that any one of your children may look to come here as my father's child has.

***

Things may come to those who wait, but only the things left by those who hustle.

***

I am not bound to win, but I am bound to be true. I am not bound to succeed, but I am bound to live by the light that I have. I must stand with anybody that stands right, and stand with him while he is right, and part with him when he goes wrong.

***

All that I am or ever hope to be, I owe to my angel mother.

***

The greatest fine art of the future will be the making of a comfortable living from a small piece of land.

***

We live amid alarms; anxiety beclouds the future; we expect some new disaster with each newspaper we read.

***

Human nature will not change. In any future great national trial, compared with the men of this, we shall have as weak and as strong, as silly and as wise, as bad and as good.

***

There are no accidents in my philosophy. Every effect must have its cause. The past is the cause of the present, and the present will be the cause of the future. All these are links in the endless chain stretching from the finite to the infinite.

***

The best way to predict your future is to create it.

***

What is to be, will be, and no prayers of ours can arrest the decree.

***

Let every American, every lover of liberty, every good wisher to his posterity, swear by the blood of the Revolution, never to violate in the least particular, the laws of the country; and never to tolerate their violation by others.

***

Fourscore and seven years ago our fathers brought forth on this continent a new nation, conceived in liberty and dedicated to the proposition that all men are created equal.

***

I claim not to have controlled events but confess plainly that events have controlled me.

***

I know not how to aid you, save in the assurance of one of mature age, and much severe experience, that you cannot fail, if you resolutely determine, that you will not.

***

The best thing about the future is that it comes one day at a time.

***

I have not permitted myself, gentlemen, to conclude that I am the best man in the country; but I am reminded, in this connection, of a story of an old Dutch farmer who remarked to a companion once that 'it was not best to swap horses while crossing streams.

***

I have stepped out upon this platform that I may see you and that you may see me, and in the arrangement, I have the best of the bargain.

***

The demon of intemperance ever seems to have delighted in sucking the blood of genius and generosity.

***

Books serve to show a man that those original thoughts of his aren't very new after all.

***

This is a world of compensations, and he who would be no slave must consent to have no slave. Those who deny freedom to others, deserve it not for themselves; and, under a just God, cannot long retain it.

***

I would not be a slave, so I would not be a master. This expresses my idea of democracy.

***

Whenever I hear anyone arguing for slavery, I feel a strong impulse to see it tried on him.

***

In giving freedom to the slave, we assure freedom to the free — honorable alike in what we give, and what we preserve. We shall nobly save, or meanly lose, the last best hope of earth.

***

You think slavery is right and should be extended; while we think slavery is wrong and ought to be restricted. That I suppose is the rub. It certainly is the only substantial difference between us.

***

The one victory we can ever call complete will be that one which proclaims that there is not one slave or one drunkard on the face of God's green earth.

***

Slavery is founded in the selfishness of man's nature — opposition to it, in his love of justice.

***

All I ask for the negro is that if you do not like him, let him alone. If God gave him but little, that little let him enjoy.

✳✳✳

I leave you, hoping that the lamp of liberty will burn in your bosoms until there shall no longer be a doubt that all men are created free and equal.

✳✳✳

If slavery is not wrong, nothing is wrong.

✳✳✳

No man is good enough to govern another man, without that other's consent. I say this is the leading principle–the sheet anchor of American republicanism.

✳✳✳

Let us at all times remember that all American citizens are brothers of a common country, and should dwell together in the bonds of fraternal feeling.

✳✳✳

I can see how it might be possible for a man to look down upon the earth and be an atheist, but I cannot conceive how a man could look up into the heavens and say there is no God.

***

It may seem strange that any men should dare to ask a just God's assistance in wringing their bread from the sweat of other men's faces, but let us judge not that we are not judged. The prayers of both could not be answered; that of neither has been explained fully. The Almighty has His purposes.

***

I have never studied the art of paying compliments to women; but I must say that if all that has been said by orators and poets since the creation of the world in praise of women were applied to the women of America, it would not do them justice for their conduct during this war. I will close by saying, God bless the women of America!

***

My concern is not whether God is on our side; my greatest concern is to be on God's side, for God is always right.

***

The will of God prevails. In great contests, each party claims to act by the will of God. Both may be, and one must be, wrong. God cannot be for and against the same thing at the same time. In the present civil war, it is quite possible that God's purpose is something different from the use of either party –

and yet the human instrumentalities, working just as they do, are of the best adaptation to effect His purpose.

✳✳✳

No man is poor who has a Godly mother.

✳✳✳

I care not for a man's religion whose dog and cat are not the better for it.

✳✳✳

Let us have faith that right makes might, and in that faith, let us, to the end, dare to do our duty as we understand it.

✳✳✳

The United States government must not undertake to run the Churches. When an individual, in the Church or out of it, becomes dangerous to the public interest he must be checked.

✳✳✳

Any people anywhere, being inclined and having the power, have the right to rise, and shake off the existing government, and form a new one that suits them better. This is a most valuable – a most sacred right – a right, which we hope and believe, is to liberate the world.

The legitimate object of government is 'to do for the people what needs to be done, but which they cannot, by individual effort, do at all, or do so well, for themselves.'

✳✳✳

A house divided against itself cannot stand. I believe this government cannot endure permanently half-slave and half-free. I do not expect the Union to be dissolved – I do not expect the house to fall – but I do expect it will cease to be divided. It will become all one thing or all the other.

✳✳✳

This country, with its institutions, belongs to the people who inhabit it. Whenever they shall grow weary of the existing government, they can exercise their constitutional right of amending it, or their revolutionary right to dismember it or overthrow it.

✳✳✳

I desire to conduct the affairs of this administration so that if at the end, when I come to lay down the reins of power, I have lost every other friend on earth, I shall at least have one friend left, and that friend shall be down inside of me.

✳✳✳

Don't interfere with anything in the Constitution. That must be maintained, for it is the only safeguard of our liberties. And not to Democrats alone do I make this appeal, but to all who love these great and true principles.

***

The ballot is stronger than the bullet.

***

Public sentiment is everything. With public sentiment, nothing can fail; without it, nothing can succeed.

***

What is conservatism? Is it not adherence to the old and tried, against the new and untried?

***

Elections belong to the people. It's their decision. If they decide to turn their back on the fire and burn their behinds, then they will have to sit on their blisters.

***

I cannot make it better known than it already is that I strongly favor colonization.

***

Discourage litigation. Persuade your neighbors to compromise whenever you can. Point out to them how the nominal winner is often a real loser – in fees, expenses, and a waste of time. As a peacemaker, the lawyer has a superior opportunity of being a good man. There will still be business enough.

***

America will never be destroyed from the outside. If we falter and lose our freedoms, it will be because we destroyed ourselves.

***

The love of property and consciousness of right and wrong have different places in our organization, which often makes a man's course seem crooked, his conduct a riddle.

Albert Einstein

Albert Einstein (March 14, 1879- April 18, 1955).
Theoretical physicist, one of the founders of modern
theoretical physics, winner of the Nobel Prize in
Physics in 1921, social activist and humanist. He
lived in Germany, Switzerland and the United States.
Honorary Doctor of about 20 leading universities in
the world, a member of many Academies of Sciences.

Any intelligent fool can make things bigger, more
complex, and more violent. It takes a touch of genius
-- and a lot of courage -- to move in the opposite
direction.

✳✳✳

Imagination is more important than knowledge.

✳✳✳

Gravitation is not responsible for people falling in
love.

✳✳✳

I want to know God's thoughts; the rest are details.

✳✳✳

The hardest thing in the world to understand is
income tax.

***

Reality is merely an illusion, albeit a very persistent
one.

***

The only real valuable thing is intuition.

***

A person starts to live when he can live outside
himself.

***

I am convinced that He (God) does not play dice.

***

God is subtle, but he is not malicious.

***

The weakness of attitude becomes the weakness of
character.

***

I never think of the future. It comes soon enough.

***

The eternal mystery of the world is its
comprehensibility.

***

Sometimes one pays most for the things one gets for nothing.

***

Science without religion is lame. Religion without science is blind.

***

мAnyone who has never made a mistake has never tried anything new.

***

Great spirits have often encountered violent opposition from weak minds.

***

Everything should be made as simple as possible, but not simpler.

***

Common sense is the collection of prejudices acquired by age eighteen.

***

Science is a wonderful thing if one does not have to earn one's living at it.

***

The secret to creativity is knowing how to hide your sources.

***

The only thing that interferes with my learning is my education.

***

God does not care about our mathematical difficulties. He integrates empirically.

***

The whole of science is nothing more than a refinement of everyday thinking.

***

Technological progress is like an ax in the hands of a pathological criminal.

***

Peace cannot be kept by force. It can only be achieved by understanding.

***

The most incomprehensible thing about the world is that it is comprehensible.

***

We can't solve problems by using the same kind of thinking we used when we created them.

***

Education is what remains after one has forgotten everything he learned in school.

***

The important thing is not to stop questioning. Curiosity has its reason for existing.

***

Do not worry about your difficulties in Mathematics. I can assure you mine are still greater.

***

Equations are more important to me because politics is for the present, but an equation is something for eternity.

***

If A is a success in life, then A equal's x plus y plus z. Work is x; y is playing, and z is keeping your mouth shut.

***

Two things are infinite: the universe and human stupidity; and I are not sure about the universe.

***

As far as the laws of mathematics refer to reality, they are not certain, as far as they are certain, they do not refer to reality.

***

Whoever undertakes to set himself up as a judge of Truth and Knowledge is shipwrecked by the laughter of the gods.

***

I know not with what weapons World War III will be fought, but World War IV will be fought with sticks and stones.

***

To form an immaculate member of a flock of sheep one must, above all, be a sheep.

***

The fear of death is the most unjustified of all fears, for there's no risk of accident for someone dead.

***

Too many of us look upon Americans as dollar chasers. This is a cruel libel, even if it is reiterated thoughtlessly by the Americans themselves.

Heroism on command, senseless violence, and all the loathsome nonsense that goes by the name of patriotism -- how passionately I hate them!

No, this trick won't work. How on earth are you ever going to explain regarding chemistry and physics so important a biological phenomenon as first love?

My religion consists of a humble admiration of the illimitable superior spirit who reveals himself in the slight details we can perceive with our frail and feeble mind.

Yes, we have to divide up our time like that, between our politics and our equations. But to me, our equations are far more important, for politics are only a matter of present concern. A mathematical equation stands forever.

***

The release of atom power has changed everything except our way of thinking the solution to this problem lies in the heart of humankind. If only I had known, I should have become a watchmaker.

***

Great spirits have always found violent opposition from mediocrities. The latter cannot understand it when a man does not thoughtlessly submit to hereditary prejudices but honestly and courageously uses his intelligence.

***

The most beautiful thing we can experience is the mysterious. It is the source of all true art and all science. He to whom this emotion is a stranger, who can no longer pause to wonder and stand rapt in awe, is as good as dead: his eyes are closed.

***

A man's ethical behavior should be based effectually on sympathy, education, and social ties; no religious basis is necessary. Man would indeed be in a poor way if he had to be restrained by fear of punishment and hope of reward after death.

***

The further the spiritual evolution of humanity advances, the more certain it seems to me that the path to genuine religiosity does not lie through the fear of life, and the fear of death, and blind faith, but through striving after rational knowledge.

***

Now he has departed from this strange world a little ahead of me. That means nothing. People like us, who believe in physics, know that the distinction between past, present, and future is only a stubbornly persistent illusion.

***

You see, wire telegraph is a kind of a very, very long cat. You pull his tail in New York, and his head is meowing in Los Angeles. Do you understand this? And radio operates the same way: you send signals here, they receive them there. The only difference is that there is no cat.

***

One had to cram all this stuff into one's mind for the examinations, whether one liked it or not. This coercion had such a deterring effect on me that, after I had passed the final examination, I found the consideration of any scientific problems distasteful to me for an entire year.

***

...one of the strongest motives that lead men to art and science is escaped from everyday life with its painful crudity and hopeless dreariness, from the fetters of one's ever-shifting desires. A finely tempered nature longs to escape from the personal life into the world of objective perception and thought.

***

He who joyfully marches to music rank and file has already earned my contempt. He has been given a large brain by mistake since for him the spinal cord would surely suffice. This disgrace to civilization should be done away with at once. Heroism at command, how violently I hate all this, how despicable and ignoble war is; I would rather be torn to shreds than be a part of such a base an action. It is my conviction that killing under the cloak of war is nothing but an act of murder.

***

A human being is a part of a whole, called by us universe, a part limited in time and space. He experiences himself, his thoughts and feelings as something separated from the rest a kind of optical delusion of his consciousness. This delusion is a kind of prison for us, restricting us to our desires and affection for a few persons nearest to us. Our task must be to free ourselves from this prison by widening our circle of compassion to embrace all living creatures and the whole of nature in its beauty.

Anthony Robbins

Anthony Jai Robbins (born February 29, 1960) is an American author, entrepreneur, philanthropist and life coach.

***

A real decision is measured by the fact that you've taken a new action. If there's no action, you haven't truly decided.

***

Beliefs have the power to create and the power to destroy. Human beings have the awesome ability to take any experience of their lives and create a meaning that disempowers them or one that can save their lives.

***

Commit to CANI! - Constant and Never-ending Improvement

***

For changes to be of any true value, they've got to be lasting and consistent.

***

I challenge you to make your life a masterpiece. I challenge you to join the ranks of those people who live what they teach, who walk their talk.

***

I've come to believe that all my past failure and frustration were laying the foundation for the understandings that have created the new level of living I now enjoy.

***

If you do what you've always done, you'll get what you've always gotten.

***

In essence, if we want to direct our lives, we must take control of our consistent actions. It's not what we do once in a while that shapes our lives, but what we do consistently.

***

In life, you need either inspiration or desperation.

***

It is in your moments of decision that your destiny is shaped.

***

It not knowing what to do, it's doing what you know.

***

It's not the events of our lives that shape us, but our beliefs as to what those events mean.

✳✳✳

Life is a gift, and it offers us the privilege, opportunity, and responsibility to give something back by becoming more.

✳✳✳

Live with passion!

✳✳✳

Most people have no idea of the giant capacity we can immediately command when we focus all of our resources on mastering a single area of our lives.

✳✳✳

My definition of success is to live your life in a way that causes you to feel a ton of pleasure and very little pain - and because of your lifestyle, have the people around you feel a lot more pleasure than they do pain.

✳✳✳

Once you have mastered time, you will understand how true it is that most people overestimate what they can accomplish in a year - and underestimate what they can achieve in a decade!

***

One reason, so few of us achieve what we truly want is that we never direct our focus; we never concentrate our power. Most people dabble their way through life, never deciding to master anything in particular.

***

Only those who have learned the power of sincere and selfless contribution experience life's deepest joy: true fulfillment.

***

Passion is the genesis of genius.

***

People are not lazy. They have impotent goals - that is, goals that do not inspire them.

***

Setting goals are the first step in turning the invisible into the visible.

***

Success comes from taking the initiative and following up persisting eloquently expressing the depth of your love. What simple action could you take today to produce a new momentum toward success in your life?

***

Surmounting difficulty is the crucible that forms character.

***

Take control of your consistent emotions and begin to consciously and deliberately reshape your daily experience of life.

***

The higher your energy level, the more efficient your body, the more efficient your body, the better you feel and the more you will use your talent to produce outstanding results.

***

The meeting of preparation with opportunity generates the offspring we call luck.

***

The path to success is to take massive, determined action.

***

The secret of success is learning how to use pain and pleasure instead of having pain and pleasure use you.

If you do that, you're in control of your life. If you don't, life controls you.

***

The truth is that we can learn to condition our minds, bodies, and emotions to link pain or pleasure to whatever we choose. By changing what we link pain and pleasure to, we will instantly change our behaviors.

***

The way we communicate with others and with ourselves ultimately determines the quality of our lives.

***

There is no greatness without a passion for being great, whether it's the aspiration of an athlete or an artist, a scientist, a parent, or a businessperson.

***

There is no such thing as failure. There are only results.

***

There's always a way - if you're committed.

***

There's no abiding success without commitment.

***

To effectively communicate, we must realize that we are all different in the way we perceive the world and use this understanding as a guide to our communication with others.

***

Want to learn to eat a lot? Here it is: Eat a little. That way, you will be around long enough to eat a lot.

***

We are the only beings on the planet who lead such rich internal lives that it's not the events that matter most to us, but rather, it's how we interpret those events that will determine how we think about ourselves and how we will act in the future.

***

We aren't in an information age; we are in an entertainment age.

***

We can change our lives. We can do, have, and be what we wish.

***

We will act consistently with our view of who we truly are, whether that view is accurate or not.

***

What we can or cannot do, what we consider possible or impossible, is rarely a function of our true capability. It is more likely a function of our beliefs about who we are.

***

Whatever happens, take responsibility!

***

When people are like each other, they tend to like each other.

***

You always succeed in producing a result.

***

You see, in life, lots of people know what to do, but few people do what they know. Knowing is not enough! You must take action.

***

You see, it's never the environment; it's never the events of our lives, but the meaning we attach to the events - how we interpret them - that shapes who we are today and who we'll become tomorrow.

Aristotle

The Greek philosopher **Aristotle** (384-322 B.C.) made significant and lasting contributions to nearly every aspect of human knowledge, from logic to biology too.

***

A constitution is the arrangement of magistrates in a state.

***

A friend to all is a friend to none.

***

A likely impossibility is always preferable to an unconvincing possibility.

***

All human actions have one or more of these seven causes: chance, nature, compulsions, habit, reason, passion, desire.

***

All men by nature desire knowledge.

***

Anybody can become angry – that is easy, but to be angry with the right person and to the right degree and at the right time and for the proper purpose, and in the right way – that is not within everybody's power and is not easy.

***

At his best, man is the noblest of all animals; separated from law and justice, he is the worst.

***

Change in all things is sweet.

***

The character may almost be called the most effective means of persuasion.

***

Comedy aims at representing men as worse, Tragedy as better than in actual life.

***

Courage is the first of human qualities because it is the quality which guarantees the others.

***

Criticism is something we can avoid easily by saying nothing, doing nothing, and being nothing.

***

Democracy is when the indigent, and not the men of property, are the rulers.

***

Dignity does not consist in possessing honors, but in deserving them.

***

Each man judges well the things he knows.

***

Educating the mind without educating the heart is no education at all.

***

Education is an ornament in prosperity and a refuge in adversity.

***

Equality consists in the same treatment of similar persons.

***

Even when laws have been written down, they ought not always to remain unaltered.

***

Every rascal is not a thief, but every thief is a rascal.

***

Excellence is an art won by training and habituation. We do not act because we have virtue or excellence, but we instead have those because we have worked correctly. We are what we repeatedly do. Excellence, then, is not an act but a habit.

***

Excellence is never an accident. It is always the result of high intention, sincere effort, and intelligent execution; it represents the wise choice of many alternatives – choice, not chance, determines your destiny.

***

Fear is pain arising from the anticipation of evil.

***

For what is the best choice, for each is the highest it is possible for him to achieve.

***

Friends hold a mirror up to each other; through that mirror, they can see each other in ways that would not otherwise be accessible to them, and it is this mirroring that helps them improve themselves as persons.

***

Friendship is essentially a partnership.

***

Good habits formed at youth make all the difference.

***

Happiness depends upon ourselves.

***

Happiness is activity.

***

Happiness is an expression of the soul in considered actions.

***

Happiness is the settling of the soul into its most appropriate spot.

***

He who has never learned to obey cannot be a good commander.

***

He who is to be a good ruler must have first been ruled.

***

Hope is a waking dream.

***

I count him braver who overcomes his desires than him who conquers his enemies; for the hardest victory is over self.

***

I have gained this by the philosophy that I do without being commanded what others do only from fear of the law.

***

In all things of nature, there is something of the marvelous.

***

It is during our darkest moments that we must focus on seeing the light.

***

It is easy to perform a good action, but not easy to acquire a settled habit of performing such actions.

***

It is not enough to win a war; it is more important to organize peace.

***

It is possible to fail in many ways...while to succeed is possible only in one way.

**

It is the mark of an educated mind to be able to entertain a thought without accepting it.

**

It is well to be up before daybreak, for such habits contribute to health, wealth, and wisdom.

**

Knowing yourself is the beginning of all wisdom.

**

Liars when they speak the truth are not believed.

**

Love is composed of a single soul inhabiting two bodies.

**

Man is a goal seeking animal. His life only has meaning if he is reaching out and striving for his purposes.

**

Man is by nature a political animal.

***

Men acquire a particular quality by always acting in a specific way.

***

Men are swayed more by fear than by reverence.

***

Men create gods after their image, not only about their form but concerning their mode of life.

***

Misfortune shows those who are not friends.

***

Most people would instead give than get affection.

***

My best friend is the man who in wishing me well wishes it for my sake.

***

No notice is taken of a little evil, but when it increases it strikes the eye.

***

No one would choose a friendless existence on condition of having all the other things in the world.

***

Obstinate people can be divided into the opinionated, the ignorant, and the boorish.

***

Of all the varieties of virtues, liberalism is the most beloved.

Perfect friendship is the friendship of men who are good, and alike in excellence; for this wish well similar to each other qua good, and they are right in themselves.

***

Piety requires us to honor truth above our friends.

***

Pleasure in the job puts perfection in work.

***

Poetry demands a man with a special gift for it, or else one with a touch of madness in him.

***

Poetry is finer and more philosophical than history; for poetry expresses the universal, and history only the particular.

***

Poverty is the parent of revolution and crime.

***

Probable impossibilities are to be preferred to improbable possibilities.

***

Quality is not an act; it is a habit.

***

Republics decline into democracies and democracies degenerate into despotism.

***

Something is infinite if, taking it quantity by quantity, we can always take something outside.

***

Teenagers these days are out of control. They eat like pigs, they are disrespectful of adults, they interrupt and contradict their parents, and they terrorize their teachers.

***

The actuality of thought is life.

***

Art aims to represent not the outward appearance of things, but their inward significance.

***

The aim of the wise is not to secure pleasure, but to avoid pain.

***

The antidote for fifty enemies is one friend.

***

The beauty of the soul shines out when a man bears with composure one heavy mischance after another, not because he does not feel them, but because he is a man of high and heroic temper.

***

The difference between a learned man and an ignorant one is the same as that between a living man and a corpse.

***

The energy of the mind is the essence of life.

Every rascal is not a thief, but every thief is a rascal.

***

Excellence is an art won by training and habituation. We do not act rightly because we have virtue or excellence, but we rather have those because we have acted rightly. We are what we repeatedly do. Excellence, then, is not an act but a habit.

***

The distinction is never an accident. It is always the result of high intention, sincere effort, and intelligent execution; it represents the wise choice of many alternatives – choice, not chance, determines your destiny.

***

Fear is pain arising from the anticipation of evil.

***

For what is the best option, for each is the highest it is possible for him to achieve.

***

No one would choose a friendless existence on condition of having all the other things in the world.

***

Obstinate people can be divided into the opinionated, the ignorant, and the boorish.

***

Of all the varieties of virtues, liberalism is the most beloved.

Perfect friendship is the friendship of men who are good, and alike in excellence; for these wish well similar to each other qua good, and they are good in themselves.

***

Piety requires us to honor truth above our friends.

***

Pleasure in the job puts perfection in work.

***

Poetry demands a man with a special gift for it, or else one with a touch of madness in him.

***

Poetry is finer and more philosophical than history; for poetry expresses the universal, and history only the particular.

***

Poverty is the parent of revolution and crime.

***

Probable impossibilities are to be preferred to improbable possibilities.

***

Quality is not an act; it is a habit.

✳✳✳

Republics decline into democracies and democracies degenerate into despotism.

✳✳✳

Something is infinite if, taking it quantity by quantity, we can always take something outside.

✳✳✳

Teenagers these days are out of control. They eat like pigs, they are disrespectful of adults, they interrupt and contradict their parents, and they terrorize their teachers.

✳✳✳

The actuality of thought is life.

✳✳✳

Art aims to represent not the outward appearance of things, but their inward significance.

✳✳✳

The aim of the wise is not to secure pleasure, but to avoid pain.

✳✳✳

The antidote for fifty enemies is one friend.

✳✳✳

The beauty of the soul shines out when a man bears with composure one heavy mischance after another, not because he does not feel them, but because he is a man of high and heroic temper.

✳✳✳

The difference between a learned man and an ignorant one is the same as that between a living man and a corpse.

✳✳✳

The educated differ from the uneducated as much as the living from the dead.

✳✳✳

The energy of the mind is the essence of life.

✳✳✳

The gods too are fond of a joke.

✳✳✳

The greatest thing by far is to be a master of metaphor; it is the one thing that cannot be learned from others, and it is also a sign of genius since a good metaphor implies an intuitive perception of the similarity of the dissimilar.

***

The happy life is regarded as life in conformity with virtue. It is a life which involves effort and is not spent in amusement.

***

The ideal man bears the accidents of life with dignity and grace, making the best of circumstances.

***

The least initial deviation from the truth is multiplied later a thousand-fold.

***

The perfect political community is one in which the middle class is in control, and outnumbers both of the other classes.

***

The one exclusive sign of thorough knowledge is the power of teaching.

***

The one exclusive sign of thorough knowledge is the power of teaching.

***

The proof that you know something is that you can teach it.

✳✳✳

The roots of education are bitter, but the fruit is sweet.

✳✳✳

The secret to humor is surprise.

✳✳✳

The society that loses its grip on the past is in danger, for it produces men who know nothing but the present, and who are not aware that life had been, and could be, different from what it is.

✳✳✳

The true and the approximately true are apprehended by the same faculty; it may also be noted that men have a sufficient instinct for what is true, and usually, do arrive at the truth. Hence the man who makes a good guess at truth is likely to make a good guess at probabilities.

✳✳✳

The ultimate value of life depends upon awareness and the power of contemplation rather than upon mere survival.

***

The worst form of inequality is to try to make unequal things equal.

***

There is no great genius without some touch of madness.

***

This is the reason why mothers are more devoted to their children than fathers: it is that they suffer more in giving them birth and are more certain that they are their own.

***

Those who educate children well are more to be honored than they who produce them; for these only gave them life, those the art of living well.

***

Through discipline comes freedom.

***

To be conscious that we are perceiving or thinking is to be conscious of our existence.

***

To love someone is to identify with them.

***

To the query, what is a friend? His reply was A single soul dwelling in two bodies.

***

To write well, express yourself like common people, but think like a wise man. Or, think as wise men do, but speak as the ordinary people do.

***

We cannot learn without pain.

***

We live in deeds, not years; in thoughts, not breaths; in feelings, not in figures on a dial. We should count time by heart throbs. He most lives who thinks most, feels the noblest, acts the best.

***

We make war that we may live in peace.

***

We must be neither cowardly nor rash but courageous.

***

We praise a man who feels angry on the right grounds and against the proper persons and also in the right manner at the right moment and for the right length of time.

Whosoever is delighted in solitude is either a wild beast or a god.

* * *

Why is it that all those who have become eminent in philosophy, politics, poetry, or the arts are clearly of an atrabilious temperament and some of them to such an extent as to be affected by diseases caused by black bile?

* * *

Wicked men obey from fear; good men, from love.

* * *

Wishing to be friends is quick work, but friendship is a slow-ripening fruit.

* * *

Wit is educated insolence.

* * *

You will never do anything in the world without courage. It is the greatest quality of the mind next to honor.

Arthur Clarke

Sir Arthur Charles Clarke (16 December 1917 – 19 March 2008) was a British science fiction writer, science writer, and futurist, inventor.

***

The best efforts of human scientists in this direction seemed comparable to those of Stone Age men trying to break through the amour of a bank vault with flint axes.

***

I can never look now at the Milky Way without wondering from which of those banked clouds of stars the emissaries are coming.

***

We have abolished space here on the little Earth; we can never abolish the space that yawns between the stars.

***

Communication technologies are necessary, but not sufficient, for us humans to get along with each other.

***

The danger of asteroid or comet impact is one of the best reasons for getting into space.

***

One of the great tragedies of humankind is that morality has been hijacked by religion. So now people assume that religion and morality have a necessary connection. But the basis of morality is very simple and doesn't require religion at all.

***

My favorite definition of an intellectual: Someone who has been educated beyond his/her intelligence.

***

I am an optimist. Anyone interested in the future has to be. Otherwise, he would simply shoot himself.

***

Every revolutionary idea seems to evoke three stages of the reaction. They may be summed up by the phrases: (1) It's completely impossible. (2) It's possible, but it's not worth doing. (3) I said it was a good idea all along.

***

Sometimes I think we're alone in the universe, and sometimes I think we're not. In either case, the idea is quite staggering.

***

Now I'm a scientific expert; that means I know nothing about absolutely everything.

***

One of the biggest roles of science fiction is to prepare people to accept the future without pain and to encourage a flexibility of mind. Politicians should read science fiction, not westerns and detective stories.

***

This is the first age that's ever paid much attention to the future, which is a little ironic since we may not have one.

***

All human plans [are] subject to ruthless revision by Nature, or Fate, or whatever one preferred to call the powers behind the Universe.

***

I would defend the liberty of consenting adult creationists to practice whatever intellectual perversions they like in the privacy of their own homes, but it is also necessary to protect the young and innocent.

***

There were some things that only time could cure. Evil men could be destroyed, but nothing could be done with good men who were deluded.

✳✳✳

Science can destroy religion by ignoring it as well as by disproving its tenets.

✳✳✳

Sometimes when I'm in a bookstore or library, I am overwhelmed by all the things that I do not know. Then I am seized by a powerful desire to read all the books, one by one.

✳✳✳

Science fiction is something that happens - but usually, you wouldn't want it to. Fantasy is something that happen - though often you only wish that it could.

✳✳✳

Never attribute to malevolence what is merely due to incompetence.

✳✳✳

I don't believe in God, but I'm very interested in her.

✳✳✳

The creation of wealth is certainly not to be despised, but in the long run, the only human activities worthwhile are the search for knowledge and the creation of beauty. This is beyond argument; the only point of debate is which comes first.

***

When in doubt, say nothing and move on.

***

The rash assertion that 'God made man in His own image' is ticking like a time bomb at the foundation of many faiths, and as the hierarchy of the universe is disclosed to us, we may have to recognize this chilling truth: if there are any gods whose chief concern is man, they cannot be very important gods.

***

The hypothesis you refer to as God, though not disprovable by logic alone, is unnecessary for the following reason. If you assume that the universe can be quote explained unquote as the creation of an entity known as God, he must be of a higher degree of organization than his product. Thus, you have more than doubled the size of the original problem, and have taken the first step on a diverging infinite regress. William of Ockham pointed out as recently as your fourteenth century that entities should not be multiplied unnecessarily. I cannot, therefore, understand why this debate continues.

***

Human judges can show mercy. But against the laws of nature, there is no appeal.

***

If children have interests, then education happens.

***

A faith that cannot survive a collision with the truth is not worth many regrets.

***

It must be wonderful to be seventeen and to know everything.

***

It was the mark of a barbarian to destroy something one could not understand.

***

The more wonderful the means of communication, the more trivial, tawdry, or depressing its contents seemed to be.

***

The Information Age offers much to humankind, and I would like to think that we will rise to the challenges it presents. But it is vital to remember that information — in the sense of raw data — is not knowledge, that knowledge is not wisdom, and that wisdom is not foresight. But information is the first essential step to all of these.

As our species is in the process of proving, one cannot have superior science and inferior morals. The combination is unstable and self-destroying.

Arthur Schopenhauer

Arthur Schopenhauer (22 February 1788 – 21 September 1860) was a German philosopher, most famous for his work The World as Will and Representation (1819).

***

A man can do what he wants, but not want what he wants.

***

After your death, you will be what you were before your birth.

***

Friends and acquaintances are the surest passports to fortune.

***

Great men are like eagles, and build their nest on some lofty solitude.

***

Happiness consists in frequent repetition of pleasure.

***

Honor has not to be won; it must only not be lost.

***

It is a clear gain to sacrifice pleasure to avoid pain.

***

Just remember, once you're over the hill you begin to pick up speed.

***

Life is a constant process of dying.

***

Martyrdom is the only way a man can become famous without ability.

***

Mostly it is a loss which teaches us about the worth of things.

***

Music is the melody whose text is the world.

***

The more unintelligent a man is, the less mysterious existence seems to him.

***

The two enemies of human happiness are pain and boredom.

To live alone is the fate of all great souls.

Every miserable fool who has nothing at all of which he can be proud adopts as a last resource pride in the nation to which he belongs.

Talent hits a target no one else can hit; Genius hits a target no one else can see.

They tell us that suicide is the greatest piece of cowardice that suicide is wrong; when it is quite obvious that there is nothing in the world to which every man has a more unassailable title than to his own life and person.

The discovery of truth is prevented more effectively, not by the false appearance things present and which mislead into error, not directly by weakness of the reasoning powers, but by preconceived opinion, by prejudice.

The doctor sees all the weakness of humanity; the lawyer all the wickedness, the theologian all the stupidity.

***

Every parting gives a foretaste of death, every reunion a hint of the resurrection.

Audrey Hepburn

Audrey Hepburn (born May 4, 1929—died January 20, 1993) was a British actress, model, dancer and humanitarian. Recognized as a film and fashion icon.

***

I don't take my life seriously, but I do take what I do – in my life – seriously.

***

I decided, very early on, to accept life unconditionally; I never expected it to do anything special for me, yet I seemed to accomplish far more than I had ever hoped. Most of the time it just happened to me without my ever seeking it.

***

I decided, very early on, just to accept life unconditionally; I never expected it to do anything special for me, yet I seemed to accomplish far more than I had ever hoped. Most of the time it just happened to me without my ever seeking it.

***

The living is like tearing through a museum. Not until later do you start absorbing what you saw, thinking about it, looking it up in a book, and remembering – because you can't take it in all at once.

There is one difference between a long life and a great dinner; at the dinner, the sweet things come last.

My own life has been much more than a fairy tale. I've had my share of difficult moments, but whatever difficulties I've gone through, I've always gotten the prize at the end.

The greatest victory has been to be able to live with me, to accept my shortcomings. I'm a long way from the human being I'd like to be. But I've decided I'm not so bad after all.

I have learned how to live...how to be in the world and of the world, and not just to stand aside and watch.

Pick the day. Enjoy it – to the hilt. The day as it comes. People as they come. The past, I think, has helped me appreciate the present – and I don't want to spoil any of it by fretting about the future.

Not to live for the day, that would be materialistic — but to treasure the day. I realize that most of us live on the skin — on the surface — without appreciating just how wonderful it is simply to be alive at all.

***

I believe, every day, you should have at least one exquisite moment.

***

Life is a party. Dress for it.

***

Giving is living. If you stop wanting to give, there's nothing more to live for.

Audrey Hepburn Quotes on Love & Relationships

***

People, even more than things, have to be restored, renewed, revived, reclaimed, and redeemed; never throw out anyone.

reputation

***

You can tell more about a person by what he says about others than you can by what others say about him.

***

I was born with an enormous need for affection, and a terrible need to give it.

***

Your heart breaks, that's all. But you can't judge, or point fingers. You have to be lucky enough to find someone who appreciates you.

***

If I get married, I want to be married.

***

The best thing to hold onto in life is each other.

***

When you have nobody, you can make a cup of tea for, when nobody needs you, that's when I think life is over.

***

We all want to be loved, don't we? Everyone looks for a way of finding love. It's a constant search for affection in every walk of life.

***

When the chips are down, you are alone, and loneliness can be terrifying. Fortunately, I've always had a chum I could call. And I love to be alone. It doesn't bother me one bit. I'm my own company.

**

I may not always be offered work, but I'll always have my family.

**

True friends are families which you can select.

**

Whatever a man might do, whatever misery or heartache your children might give you – and they give you a lot – however much your parents irritate you – it doesn't matter because you love them.

**

They say love is the best investment; the more you give, the more you get in return.

**

Nothing is impossible, the word itself says 'I'm possible'!

**

Pick the day. Enjoy it – to the hilt. The day as it comes. People as they come. The past, I think, has helped me appreciate the present – and I don't want to spoil any of it by fretting about the future.

***

I always tried to do better: I always saw a little further. I tried to stretch myself.

***

To plant a garden is to believe in tomorrow.

***

I heard a definition once: Happiness is health and a short memory! I wish I'd invented it because it is very true.

***

The most important thing is to enjoy your life, to be happy, it's all that matters.

***

I believe in pink. I believe that laughing is the best calorie burner. I believe in kissing, kissing a lot. I believe in being strong when everything seems to be going wrong. I believe that happy girls are the prettiest girls. I believe that tomorrow is another day and I believe in miracles.

***

I believe in manicures. I believe in overdressing. I believe in primping at leisure and wearing lipstick. I believe in pink. I believe happy girls are the prettiest girls. I believe that tomorrow is another day, and... I believe in miracles.

***

Success is like reaching an important birthday and finding you're the same.

***

I probably hold the distinction of being one movie star who, by all laws of logic, should never have made it. At each stage of my career, I lacked the experience.

***

I never think of myself as an icon. What is in other people's mind is not in my mind. I just do my thing.

***

There are certain shades of limelight that can wreck a girl's complexion.

***

My greatest ambition is to have a career without becoming a career woman.

***

I've been lucky. Opportunities don't often come along. So, when they do, you have to grab them.

＊＊＊

When you have found it, you should stick to it.

＊＊＊

It is too much to hope that I shall keep up my success. I don't ask for that. All I shall do is my best – and hope.

＊＊＊

Good things aren't supposed to fall into your lap. God is very generous, but He expects you to do your part first.

＊＊＊

As you grow older, you will discover that you have two hands. One for helping yourself, the other for helping others.

＊＊＊

I love people who make me laugh. I honestly think it's the thing I like most, to laugh. It cures a multitude of ills. It's probably the most important thing in a person.

＊＊＊

Why change? Everyone has his style. When you have found it, you should stick to it.

✻✻✻

For me, the only things of interests are those linked to the heart.

✻✻✻

Anyone who does not believe in miracles is not a realist.

✻✻✻

On the one hand, maybe I've remained infantile, while on the other I matured quickly because at a young age I was very aware of suffering and fear.

✻✻✻

It's that wonderful old-fashioned idea that others come first and you come second. This was the whole ethic by which I was brought up. Others matter more than you do, so don't fuss, dear; get on with it.

✻✻✻

For beautiful eyes, look for the good in others; for beautiful lips, speak only words of kindness; and for poise, walk with the knowledge that you are never alone.

✻✻✻

The beauty in a woman is not in the clothes she wears, the figure that she carries, or the way she combs her hair. The beauty of a woman is seen in her eyes because that is the doorway to her heart; the place where love resides. True beauty in a woman is reflected in her soul. It's the caring and that she lovingly gives the passion that she shows and the beauty of a woman only grows with passing years.

✳✳✳

Elegance is the only beauty that never fades. A woman can be beautiful as well as intellectual. It's that wonderful old-fashioned idea that others come first and you come second. This was the whole ethic by which I was brought up. Others matter more than you do, so 'don't fuss, dear; get on with it.'

✳✳✳

Sex appeal is something that you feel deep down inside. It's suggested rather than shown. I'm not as well-stacked as Sophia Loren or Gina Lollobrigida, but there is more to sex appeal than just measurements. I don't need a bedroom to prove my womanliness. I can convey just as much sex appeal, picking apples off a tree or standing in the rain.

✳✳✳

The beauty of a woman is seen in her eyes because that is the doorway to her heart, the place where love resides.

✳✳✳

Look, whenever I hear or read, I'm beautiful, I don't understand it ... I'm certainly not beautiful in any conventional way. I didn't make my career in beauty.

***

The beauty of a woman is not in a facial mole, but true beauty in a woman is reflected in her soul. It is the caring that she lovingly gives, the passion that she knows.

***

A woman can be beautiful as well as intellectual.

***

Make-up can only make you look pretty on the outside, but it doesn't help if you're ugly on the inside. Unless you eat the make-up.

***

And the beauty of a woman, with passing years, only grows!

***

My look is attainable. Women can look like Audrey Hepburn by flipping out their hair, buying the large sunglasses, and the little sleeveless dresses.

***

I'm not beautiful. My mother once called me an ugly duckling. But, listed separately, I have a few good features.

There are more important things than outward appearance. No amount of makeup can cover an ugly personality.

Dress like you are already famous.

Bill Gates

William Henry Gates III (born October 28, 1955)
is an American business magnate, investor, author,
philanthropist, and humanitarian. He is best known
as the principal founder of the Microsoft
Corporation.

✱✱✱

Your most unhappy customers are your greatest
source of learning.

✱✱✱

This is a fantastic time to be entering the business
world because business is going to change more in
the next ten years than it has in the last 50.

✱✱✱

Whether it's Google or Apple or free software, we've
got some fantastic competitors, and it keeps us on
our toes.

✱✱✱

If you give people tools, [and they use] their natural
ability and their curiosity, they will develop things in
ways that will surprise you very much beyond what
you might have expected.

✱✱✱

Intellectual property has the shelf life of a banana.

✳✳✳

There's only one trick in software, and that is using a piece of software that's already been written.

✳✳✳

It's not manufacturers trying to rip anybody off or anything like that. Nobody is getting rich writing software that I know of.

✳✳✳

Great organizations demand a high level of commitment by the people involved.

✳✳✳

About three million computers get sold every year in China, but people don't pay for the software. Someday they will, though. As long as they are going to steal it, we want them to steal ours. They'll get addicted, and then we'll somehow figure out how to collect sometime in the next decade.

✳✳✳

Make it just like a Mac.

✳✳✳

At Microsoft, there are lots of brilliant ideas, but the image is that they all come from the top — I'm afraid that's not quite right.

***

The first rule of any technology used in a business is that automation applied to an efficient operation will magnify the efficiency. The second is that automation applied to an inefficient operation will magnify the inefficiency.

***

I choose a lazy person to do a hard job. Because a lazy person will find an easy way to do it.

***

In three years, every product my company makes will be obsolete. The only question is whether we will make them obsolete or somebody else will.

***

We're responsible for the creation of the PC industry. The whole idea of compatible machines and lots of software. that's something we brought to computing. And so, it's a responsibility for us to make sure that things like security don't get in the way of that dream.

***

People always fear change. People feared electricity when it was invented, didn't they?

***

Every day was saying, 'How can we keep this customer happy?' How can we get ahead in innovation by doing this because if we don't, somebody else will?

***

It's easier for our software to compete with Linux when there's piracy than when there's not.

***

Microsoft has had clear competitors in the past. It's a good thing we have museums to document that.

***

If something is expensive to develop, and somebody's not going to get paid, it won't get developed. So, you decide: Do you want the software to be written, or not?

***

If you show people the problems and you show people the solutions they will be moved to act.

***

If you can't make it good, at least make it look good.

***

In this business, by the time you realize you're in trouble, it's too late to save yourself. Unless you're running scared all the time, you're gone.

***

Intellectual property has the shelf life of a banana.

***

Microsoft is not about greed. It's about innovation and fairness.

***

As we look ahead into the next century, leaders will be those who empower others.

***

I do think this next century, hopefully, will be about a more global view. Where you don't just think, yes, my country is doing well, but you think about the world at large.

***

Technology is just a tool. Regarding getting the kids working together and motivating them, the teacher is the most important.

***

Patience is a key element of success.

***

Success is a lousy teacher. It seduces smart people into thinking they can't lose.

***

It's fine to celebrate success, but it is more important to heed the lessons of failure.

***

If geek means you're willing to study things, and if you think science and engineering matter, I plead guilty. If your culture doesn't like geeks, you are in real trouble.

***

The best way to prepare [to be a programmer] is to write programs and to study great programs that other people have written. In my case, I went to the garbage cans at the Computer Science Center and fished out listings of their operating system.

***

Measuring programming progress by lines of code is like measuring aircraft building progress by weight.

***

Capitalism is this wonderful thing that motivates people; it causes wonderful inventions to be done. But in this area of diseases of the world at large, it's let us down.

***

To win big, you sometimes have to take big risks.

***

Don't compare yourself with anyone in this world. If you do so, you are insulting yourself.

***

Life is not fair – get used to it!

***

I don't know' has become 'I don't know yet.'

***

The world won't care about your self-esteem. The world will expect you to accomplish something BEFORE you feel good about yourself.

***

You will NOT make $60,000 a year right out of high school. You won't be a vice-president with a car phone until you earn both.

***

If you think your teacher is tough, wait till you get a boss.

***

Flipping burgers are not beneath your dignity. Your Grandparents had a different word for burger flipping – they called it opportunity.

***

If you mess up, it's not your parents' fault, so don't whine about your mistakes, learn from them.

***

Before you were born, your parents weren't as boring as they are now. They got that way from paying your bills, cleaning your clothes and listening to you talk about how cool you thought you are. So, before you save the rain forest from the parasites of your parent's generation, try delousing the closet in your room.

***

Your school may have done away with winners and losers, but life HAS NOT. In some schools, they have abolished failing grades, and they'll give you as MANY TIMES as you want to get the right answer. This doesn't bear the slightest resemblance to ANYTHING in real life.

***

Life is not divided into semesters. You don't get summers off, and very few employers are interested in helping you FIND YOURSELF. Do that on your own time.

***

Television is NOT real life. In real life, people have to leave the coffee shop and go to jobs.

***

Be nice to nerds. Chances are you'll end up working for one.

***

I had a lot of dreams when I was a kid, and I think a great deal of that grew out of the fact that I had a chance to read a lot.

***

I realized about ten years ago that my wealth has to go back to society. A fortune, the size of which is hard to imagine, is best not passed on to one's children. It's not constructive for them.

Brian Tracy

Brian Tracy (born January 5, 1944) is a Canadian-American motivational public speaker and self-development author. He is the author of over seventy books that have been translated into dozens of languages.

✳✳✳

The more credit you give away, the more will come back to you. The more you help others, the more they will want to help you.

✳✳✳

Successful people are always looking for opportunities to help others. Unsuccessful people are always asking, What's in it for me?

✳✳✳

Your decision to be, have and do something out of ordinary entails facing difficulties that are out of the ordinary as well. Sometimes your greatest asset is simply your ability to stay with it longer than anyone else.

✳✳✳

Those people who develop the ability to continuously acquire new and better forms of knowledge that they can apply to their work and their lives will be the movers and shakers in our society for the indefinite future.

No one lives long enough to learn everything they need to learn to start from scratch. To be successful, we absolutely, positively have to find people who have already paid the price to learn the things that we need to learn to achieve our goals.

***

It doesn't matter where you are coming from. All that matters are where you are going.

***

If you raise your children to feel that they can accomplish any goal or task they decide upon, you will have succeeded as a parent, and you will have given your children the greatest of all blessings.

***

Develop an attitude of gratitude, and give thanks for everything that happens to you, knowing that every step forward is a step toward achieving something bigger and better than your current situation.

***

All successful people men and women are big dreamers. They imagine what their future could be, ideal in every respect, and then they work every day toward their distant vision, that goal or purpose.

***

You cannot control what happens to you, but you can control your attitude toward what happens to you, and in that, you will be mastering change rather than allowing it to master you.

***

I've found that luck is quite predictable. If you want more luck, take more chances. Be more active. Show up more often.

***

In life you can never be too kind or too fair; everyone you meet is carrying a heavy load. When you go through your day expressing kindness and courtesy to all you meet, you leave behind a feeling of warmth and good cheer, and you help alleviate the burdens everyone is struggling with.

***

The more you seek security, the less of it you have. But the more you seek opportunity, the more likely it is that you will achieve the security that you desire.

***

The glue that holds all relationships together -- including the relationship between the leader and the led is trust, and trust is based on integrity.

***

Relationships are the hallmark of the mature person.

***

Only by contending with challenges that seem to be beyond your strength to handle at the moment you can grow more surely toward the stars.

***

Never say anything about yourself; you do not want to come true.

***

The person we believe ourselves to be will always act in a manner consistent with our self-image.

***

Teamwork is so important that it is virtually impossible for you to reach the heights of your capabilities or make the money that you want without becoming very good at it.

***

We feel good about ourselves to the exact degree we feel in control of our lives.

***

The potential of the average person is like a huge ocean unspoiled, a new continent unexplored, a world of possibilities waiting to be released and channeled toward some great good.

***

You have available to you, right now, a powerful supercomputer. This powerful tool has been used throughout history to take people from rags to riches, from poverty and obscurity to success and fame, from unhappiness and frustration to joy and self-fulfillment, and it can do the same for you.

***

You have within you right now, everything you need to deal with whatever the world can throw at you.

***

Success is predictable.

Bernard Werber

Bernard Werber (born 18 September 1961) is a
French science fiction writer, active since the 1990s.
He is chiefly recognized for having written the trilogy
Les Fourmis, the only one of his novels to have been
published in English.

***

Ants can live together in solidarity and forget
themselves in the community. In a normative
capitalist society, everyone is an egoist. In the ants'
civilization, you are part of the group; you don't live
for yourself alone.

***

Science fiction is my way of pushing the imagination
onward. It's a way to understand how the world will
look in the future.

***

The best way to renew thought is to go outside the
human imagination.

***

Can we ever really know anyone well? Let's say we
often found ourselves in each other's company and
neither of us minded.

***

We of the modern age are a bridge between the old human and the new one. We still have the mentality of the old human - a slave mentality, like the Children of Israel in Egypt: too controlled, full of fear.

***

Between what I think, what I want to say, what I believe I say, what I say, what you want to hear, what you believe to hear, what you hear, what you want to understand, what you think you understand, what you understand...They are ten possibilities that we might have some problem communicating. But let's try anyway.

***

You know people. Most of them don't hear anything. Those who hear - don't listen. A few who listen - don't understand. And those who could understand they don't care.

***

All men with great theories about women are men who are afraid of women

***

Ask the student who failed the exam if you want to know the price of the year

∗∗∗

A man reveals himself most classically when he
makes more and more stupid mistakes

∗∗∗

I love people who apologize for their mistakes

∗∗∗

I do not like people who do not know how to defend
their views

∗∗∗

If the opponent is stronger, your actions must go
beyond his comprehension

∗∗∗

If you're bald, then you're bald! Accept it as it is

∗∗∗

In life, we face only those issues that can be resolved.

Benjamin Franklin

Benjamin Franklin (January 17, 1706 - April 17, 1790) was America's scientist, inventor, politician, philanthropist, and businessman.

***

The wit of conversation consists more in finding it in others than showing a great deal yourself. He who goes out of your company pleased with his own facetiousness and ingenuity, will the sooner come into it again.

***

If you would not be forgotten, as soon as you are dead and rotten, either write things worth reading or do things worth the writing.

***

Be not sick too late, nor well too soon.

***

There are two ways of being happy — we may either diminish our wants or augment our means — either will do, the result is the same, and it is for each man to decide for himself, and do that which happens to be the easiest. If you are idle or sick or poor, however hard it may be to diminish your wants, it will be harder to augment your means.

If you are active and prosperous, or young, or in good health, it may be easier for you to augment your means than to diminish your wants. But if you are wise, you will do both at the same time, young or old, rich or poor, sick or well; and if you are wise, you will do both in such a way as to augment the general happiness of society.

***

Fear to do ill, and you need fear naught else.

***

An old young man will be a young, old man.

***

Some, to make themselves considerable, pursue learning; others grasp at wealth; some aim at being thought witty; and others are only careful to make the most of a handsome person; but what is wit, or wealth, or form, or learning, when compared with virtue? It is true we love the handsome, we applaud the learned, and we fear the rich and powerful; but we even worship and adore the virtuous.

***

A learned blockhead is a greater blockhead than an ignorant one.

***

It is a common error in friends, when they would extol their friends, to make comparisons, and to depreciate the merits of others.

***

Each year one vicious habit rooted out, in time might make the worst man good throughout.

***

A new truth is truth; an old error is an error.

***

A man of words and not of deeds is like a garden full of weeds.

***

Having lived long, I have experienced many instances of being obliged by better information or fuller consideration to change opinions, even on important subjects, which I once thought right, but found to be otherwise.

***

The way to secure peace is to be prepared for war. They that are on their guard, and appear ready to receive their adversaries, are in much less danger of being attacked, than the supine, secure, and negligent.

***

A fat kitchen makes a lean will.

***

Don't go to the doctor with every distemper, nor to the lawyer with every quarrel, nor to the pot for every thirst.

***

An ounce of prevention is worth a pound of cure.

***

The worship of God is a duty; the hearing and reading of sermons may be useful; but if men rest in hearing and praying, as too many do, it is as if a tree should value itself in being watered and putting forth leaves, though it never produced any fruit.

***

Eat to live, and not live to eat.

***

A great talker may be no fool, but he is one that relies on him.

***

When you incline to have new clothes, look first well over the old ones, and see if you cannot shift with them another year, either by scouring, mending, or even patching if necessary. Remember, a patch on your coat, and money in your pocket, is better and more credible, than a writ on your back, and no money to take it off.

***

Lost time is never found again.

***

When there is so much to be done for yourself, your family, and your country be up by peep of the day! Let not the sun look down and say, 'Inglorious here he lies!'

***

Don't misinform your Doctor nor your Lawyer.

***

To expect people to be good, to be just, to be temperate, etc., without showing them how they should become so, seems like the ineffectual charity mentioned by the apostle, which consisted in saying to the hungry, the cold and the naked, be ye fed, be ye warmed, be ye clothed, without showing them how they should get food, fire or clothing.

He's the best physician that knows the worthlessness of the most medicines.

Would you live with ease, do what you ought and not what you please?

Eat to please yourself, but dress to please others.

Man and woman have each of the qualities and tempers in which the other is deficient, and which in union contribute to the common felicity.

God heals, and the Doctor takes the Fees.

He that is known to pay punctually and exactly to the time he promises may at any time, and on any occasion, raise all the money his friends can spare.

This is sometimes of great use.

When I am employed in serving others, I do not look upon myself as conferring favors, but as paying debts. I have received much kindness from men to whom I shall never have an opportunity of making the least direct returns; and numberless mercies from God, who is infinitely above being benefited by our services. Those kindnesses from men I can, therefore, only return on their fellow-men, and I can only show my gratitude for those mercies from God by a readiness to help His other children.

Early to bed and early to rise, makes a man healthy, wealthy, and wise.

Life, like a dramatic piece, should not only be conducted with regularity, but it should finish handsomely.

God helps them who help themselves.

Men are subject to various inconveniences merely through lack of a small share of courage, which is a quality very necessary in the common occurrences of life, as well as in a battle. How many impertinences do we daily suffer from great uneasiness, because we have not courage enough to discover our dislike?

The art of getting riches consists very much in thrift. All men are not equally qualified for getting money, but it is in the power of everyone alike to practice this virtue.

***

Having been poor is no shame; being ashamed of it is.

***

If a man empties his purse into his head, no man can take it away from him. An investment in knowledge always pays the best interest.

***

Our opinions are not in our power; they are formed and governed much by circumstances that are often as inexplicable as they are irresistible.

***

Tricks and treachery are the practice of fools that don't have brains enough, to be honest.

***

After all, wedlock is the natural state of man. A bachelor is not a complete human being. He is like the odd half of a pair of scissors, which has not yet found its fellow and therefore is not even half so useful as they might be together.

***

A penny saved is a penny earned.

I would advise you to read with a pen in hand and enter in a little book short hints of what you find that is curious, or that may be useful; for this will be the best method of imprinting such particulars in your memory.

***

By the collision of different sentiments, sparks of truth are struck out, and political light is obtained. The different factions, which at present divide us, aim all at the public good; the differences are only about the various modes of promoting it.

***

Reading makes a full man, meditation a profound man, discourse a clear man.

***

There are in life real evils enough, and it is folly to afflict ourselves with imaginary ones; it is time enough when the real ones arrive.

'You may delay, but time will not.

***

Work as if you were to live a hundred years. Pray as if you were to die tomorrow.

***

Hope and faith may be more firmly built upon charity, than charity upon faith and hope.

***

If a man empties his purse into his head, no man can take it away from him. An investment in knowledge always pays the best interest.

***

One today is worth two tomorrows.

***

I look upon death to be as necessary to our constitution as sleep.

***

Life's tragedy is that we get old too soon and wise too late.

***

We shall rise refreshed in the morning.

***

We need a revolution every 200 years because all governments become stale and corrupt after 200 years.

***

The best thing to give to your enemy is forgiveness; to an opponent, tolerance; to a friend, your heart; to your child, a good example; to a father, deference; to your mother, conduct that will make her proud of you; to yourself, respect; to all others, charity.

***

Security without liberty is called prison.

***

The best of all medicines is rest and fasting.

***

When you're finished changing, you're finished.

***

Tell me, and I forget. Teach me, and I remember. Involve me, and I learn.

It seems to me, that if statesmen had a little more arithmetic, or were accustomed to calculation, wars would be much less frequent.

***

The trifling actions of a man, in my opinion, as well as the smallest features and lineaments of the face, give a nice observer some notion of his mind.

***

He who sacrifices freedom for security deserves neither.

***

I never knew a man who was good at making excuses who was good at anything else.

***

Common sense is something that everyone needs, few have, and none think they lack.

***

Rather go to bed without dinner than to rise in debt.

***

Most men die from the neck up at age twenty-five because they stop dreaming.

***

The ancients tell us what is best, but we must learn of the moderns what is fittest.

***

I don't believe in stereotypes. I prefer to hate people on a more personal basis.

***

To lengthen thy Life, lessen thy Meals.

***

Do not anticipate trouble, or worry about what may never happen. Keep in the sunlight.

***

He that thinks money will do everything may well be suspected of doing everything for money.

***

He that thinks money will do everything may well be suspected of doing everything for money.

***

Content makes poor men rich; discontentment makes rich men poor.

***

Employ your time well, if you mean to get leisure.

***

Well done is better than well said.

***

Energy and persistence conquer all things.

***

If you would know the value of money, go try to borrow some; for he that goes a-borrowing goes a-sorrowing.

***

If you would persuade, you must appeal to interest rather than intellect.

***

The eye of the master will do more work than both his hands.

***

Creditors have better memories than debtors.

***

Hide not your talents; they for use were made. What's a sun-dial in the shade?

***

When the well's dry, we know the worth of water.

***

To the generous mind, the heaviest debt is that of gratitude when it is not in our power to repay it.

***

A brother may not be a friend, but a friend will always be a brother.

***

It is the working man who is the happy man. It is the idle man who is a miserable man.

***

Words may show a man's wit but actions his meaning.

***

There is much difference between imitating a man and counterfeiting him.

***

If you know how to spend less than you get, you have the philosopher's stone.

***

No nation was ever ruined by trade.

***

Happiness consists more in small conveniences or pleasures that occur every day, than in great pieces of good fortune that happen but seldom to a man in the course of his life.

***

Happiness consists more in small conveniences or pleasures that occur every day, than in great pieces of good fortune that happen but seldom to a man in the course of his life.

***

Speak ill of no man, but speak all the good you know of everybody.

***

Educate your children to self-control, to the habit of holding passion and prejudice and evil tendencies subject to an upright and reasoning will, and you have done much to abolish misery from their future and crimes from society.

***

There are three things extremely hard: steel, a diamond, and to know one's self.

***

Where liberty is, there is my country.

***

By failing to prepare, you are preparing to fail.

***

We are all born ignorant, but one must work hard to remain stupid.

***

To be content, look back on those who possess less than yourself, not forward on those who possess more. If this does not make you content, you don't deserve to be happy.

***

He that falls in love with himself will have no Rivals.

***

Wink at small faults; remember thou hast great ones.

***

Necessity never made a good bargain.

***

In this world, nothing can be said to be certain, except death and taxes.

***

The way to be safe is never to be secure.

***

Without continual growth and progress, such words as improvement, achievement, and success have no meaning.

***

Beware of little expenses. A small leak will sink a great ship.

***

The Constitution only gives people the right to pursue happiness. You have to catch it yourself.

***

To succeed, jump as quickly at opportunities as you do at conclusions.

***

If you would not be forgotten, as soon as you are dead and rotten, either write things worth reading or do things worth the writing.

***

Be studious in your profession, and you will be learned. Be industrious and frugal, and you will be rich. Be sober and temperate, and you will be healthy. Be in general virtuous, and you will be happy.

***

Those that won't be counseled can't be helped.

Brenda Ueland

Brenda Ueland (October 24, 1891 – March 5, 1985) was a journalist, editor, freelance writer, and teacher of writing.

***

Everybody is talented because everybody who is human has something to express.

***

When Van Gogh was a young man in his early twenties, he was in London studying to be a clergyman. He had no thought of being an artist at all. he sat in his cheap little room writing a letter to his younger brother in Holland, whom he loved very much. He looked out his window at a watery twilight, a thin lamppost, a star, and he said in his letter something like this: it is so beautiful. I must show you how it looks. And then on his cheap ruled notepaper, he made the most beautiful, tender, little drawing of it.

***

But the moment I read Van Gogh's letter I knew what art was and the creative impulse. It is a feeling of love and enthusiasm for something, and in a direct, simple, passionate and true way, you try to show this beauty in things to others, by drawing it.

***

And Van Gogh's little drawing on the cheap notepaper was a work of art because he loved the sky and the frail lamppost against it so seriously that he made the drawing with the most exquisite conscientiousness and care.

***

That is why the lives of most women are so vaguely unsatisfactory. They are always doing secondary and menial things (that do not require all their gifts and ability) for others and never anything for themselves. Society and husbands praise them for it (when they get too miserable or have nervous breakdowns) though always a little perplexedly and half-heartedly and just to be consoling. The poor wives are reminded that that is why wives are so splendid -- because they are so unselfish and self-sacrificing and that is the wonderful thing about them! But inwardly women know that something is wrong. They sense that if you are always doing something for others, like a servant or nurse, and never anything for yourself, you cannot do others any good. You make them physically more comfortable. But you cannot affect them spiritually in any way at all. To teach, encourage, cheer up, console, amuse, stimulate or advise a husband or children or friends, you have to be something yourself. [...]If you would shut your door against the children for an hour a day and say;

'Mother is working on her five-act tragedy in blank verse!' you would be surprised how they would respect you. They would probably all become playwrights.

***

I learned...that inspiration does not come like a bolt, nor is it kinetic, energetic striving, but it comes into us slowly and quietly and all the time, though we must regularly and every day gives it a little chance to start flowing, prime it with a little solitude and idleness.

***

The only good teachers for you are those friends who love you, who think you are interesting, or very important, or wonderfully funny; whose attitude is: Tell me more. Tell me all you can. I want to understand more about everything you feel and know and all the changes inside and out of you. Let more come out. And if you have no such friend, -- and you want to write, --well, then you must imagine one.

***

I learned that you should feel when writing, not like Lord Byron on a mountain top, but like a child stringing beads in kindergarten - happy, absorbed and quietly putting one bead on after another.

Everybody is original if he tells the truth if he speaks from himself. But it must be from his *true* self and not from the self he thinks he *should* be.

✳✳✳

No writing is a waste of time – no creative work where the feelings, the imagination, the intelligence must work. With every sentence you write, you have learned something. It has done you good.

✳✳✳

Don't always be appraising yourself, wondering if you are better or worse than other writers. I will not Reason and Compare, said Blake; my business is to Create. Besides, since you are like no other being ever created since the beginning of Time, you are incomparable.

✳✳✳

Work freely and rollickingly as though you were talking to a friend who loves you. Mentally (at least three or four times a day) thumb your nose at all know-it-alls, jeerers, critics, doubters.

At last, I understood that writing was this: an impulse to share with other people a feeling or truth that I had.

***

If I did not wear torn pants, orthopedic shoes, frantic disheveled hair, that is to say, if I did not tone down my beauty, people would go mad. Married men would run amuck.

***

...writing is not a performance but a generosity. (about William Blake)

***

As for Blake's happiness--a man who knew him said: If asked whether I ever knew among the intellectual, a happy man, Blake would be the only one who would immediately occur to me.

***

And yet this creative power in Blake did not come from ambition. ...He burned most of his work. Because he said, I should be sorry if I had any earthly fame, for whatever natural glory a man has is so much detracted from his spiritual glory. I wish to do nothing for profit. I wish to live for art. I want nothing whatever. I am quite happy.

✳✳✳

...He did not mind dying in the least. He said that to him it was just like going into another room. On the day of his death, he composed songs to his Maker and sang them for his wife to hear. Just before he died his countenance became fair, his eyes brightened, and he burst into the singing of the things he saw in heaven.

✳✳✳

But the great artists like Michelangelo and Blake and Tolstoy--like Christ whom Blake called an artist because he had one of the most creative imaginations that ever was on earth--do not want security, egoistic or materialistic. Why it never occurs to them. Be not anxious for the morrow, and which of you being anxious can add one cubit to his stature?

✳✳✳

So, they dare to be idle, i.e., not to be pressed and duty-driven all the time. They dare to love people even when they are very bad, and they dare not to try and dominate others to show them what they must do for their good.

✳✳✳

Creative power flourishes only when I am living in the present.

***

Inspiration does not come like a bolt, nor is it kinetic energy striving, but it comes to us slowly and quietly and all the time.

***

We have come to think that duty should come first. I disagree. Duty should be a by-product. Writing, the creative effort, the use of the imagination, should come first – at least, for some part of every day of your life. It is a wonderful blessing if you use it. You will become happier, more enlightened, alive, impassioned, light-hearted and generous to everybody else. Even your health will improve. Colds will disappear and all the other ailments of discouragement and boredom.

***

Remember William Blake who said: Improvement makes straight, straight roads, but the crooked roads without improvement are roads of genius.

***

The truth is, life itself, is always startling, strange, unexpected. But when the truth is told about it, everybody knows at once that it is life itself and not made up.

***

But in ordinary fiction, movies, etc., everything is smoothed out to seem plausible--villains made bad, heroes splendid, heroines glamorous, and so on, so that no one believes a word

***

Families are great murderers of the creative impulsive, particularly husbands (about William Blake)

***

But the only way you can grow in understanding and discover whether a thing is good or bad, Blake says, is to do it. Sooner strangle an infant in its cradle than nurse unacted desires.

***

Everyone knows how people who laugh easily create us by their laughter, --making us think of funnier and funnier things.

***

Everyone is talented, original and has something important to say.

***

The only way to write well, so that people believe what we say and are interested or touched by it, is to slough off all pretentiousness and attitudinizing.

When we are listened to, it creates us, makes us unfold and expand. Ideas begin to grow within us and come to life.

I will tell you what I have learned myself. For me, along five- or six-mile walk helps. And one must go alone and every day. I have done this for many years. It is at these times I seem to get re-charged. If I do not walk one day, I seem to have on the next what van Gogh calls the meagerness. The meagerness, he said, or what is called depression. After a day or two of not walking, when I try to write, I feel a little dull and irresolute. For a long time, I thought that the dullness was just due to the asphyxiation of an indoor, sedentary life which all people who do not move around a great deal in the open air suffer from, though they do not know it.

...the best way to know the Truth or Beauty is to try to express it. And what is the purpose of existence Here or Yonder but to discover truth and beauty and express it, i.e., share it with others?

There is that American pastime known as kidding - with the result that everyone is ashamed and hangdog about showing the slightest enthusiasm or passion or sincere feeling about anything.

* * *

Of course, in fairness, I must remind you of this: that we writers are the most lily-livered of all craftsmen. We expect more, for the most peewee efforts than any other people.

* * *

At least I understood that writing was this: an impulse to share with other people a feeling or truth that I had. Not to preach to them, but to give it to them if they cared to hear it.

* * *

I found that many gifted people are so afraid of writing a poor story that they cannot summon the nerve to write a single sentence for months. The thing to say to such people is: See how *bad* a story you can write. See how dull you can be. Go ahead. That would be fun and interesting. I will give you ten dollars if you can write something thoroughly dull from beginning to end! And of course, no one can.

* * *

Now before going to a party, I tell myself to listen with affection to anyone who talks to me, to be in their shoes when they talk, to try to know them without my mind pressing against theirs, or arguing, or changing the subject. No. My attitude is: 'Tell me more.' This person is showing me his soul. It is a little dry and meager and full of grinding talk just now, but presently he will begin to think, not just automatically to talk. He will show his true self. Then he will be wonderfully alive.' ...Creative listeners are those who want you to be recklessly yourself, even at your very worst, even vituperative, bad-tempered. They are laughing and just delighted with any manifestation of yourself, bad or good. For true listeners know that if you are bad-tempered, it does not mean that you are always so. They don't love you just when you are nice; they love all of you.

**

Think of yourself as an incandescent power, illuminated and perhaps forever talked to by God and his messengers.

**

In the same way, there is much, much in all of us, but we do not know it. No one ever calls it out in us, unless we are lucky enough to know intelligent, imaginative, sympathetic people who love us and have the magnanimity to encourage us, to believe in us, by listening, by praise, by appreciation, by laughing. If you are going to write, you must become aware of this richness in you and come to believe in it and know it is there so that you can write opulently with self-trust. Once you become aware of it, have faith in it, you will be all right. But it is like this: if you have a million dollars in the bank and don't know, it doesn't do you any good.

✳✳✳

A great musician once told me that one should never play a single note without hearing it, feeling that it is true, thinking it beautiful.

✳✳✳

I want to assure you with all earnestness, that no writing is a waste of time, – no creative work where the feelings, the imagination, the intelligence must work. With every sentence you write, you have learned something. It has done you good. It has stretched your understanding.

✳✳✳

If you write, good ideas must come welling up into you so that you have something to write. If good ideas do not come at once, or for a long time, do not be troubled at all. Wait for them. Put down little ideas no matter how insignificant they are. But do not feel, anymore, guilty about idleness and solitude.

✳✳✳

no writing is a waste of time--no creative work where the feelings, the imagination, the intelligence must work.

***

By encouraging the critic in themselves (the hater), they have killed the artist (the lover).

***

The only way to find your true self is by recklessness and freedom.

***

Enthusiasm! This is the sign that the creative fountain is in you.   Enthusiasm is the All in All, said Blake. I must tell you this often.]

***

But here is an important thing: you must practice not perfunctorily but with all your intelligence and love,

***

You will never know what your husband looks like unless you try to draw him, and you will never understand him unless you try to write his story.

***

The true self is always in motion - like music, a river of life, changing, moving, failing, suffering, learning, shining.

✳✳✳

inspiration does not come like a bolt, nor is it kinetic energy striving, but it comes to us slowly and quietly and all the time

✳✳✳

The only way to become a better writer is to become a better person

✳✳✳

I want to assure you with all earnestness that no writing is a waste of time--no creative work where the feelings, the imagination, the intelligence must work. With every sentence you write, you have learned something.

✳✳✳

Your motto: Be Bold, be Free, be Truthful

✳✳✳

...everybody is talented, original and has something important to say.

✳✳✳

Why Women who do too much housework should neglect it for their writing.

Bob Marley

Robert Nesta Marley (6 February 1945 – 11 May 1981) was a Jamaican singer-songwriter

***

I believe in death, neither in the flesh nor in spirit.

***

When one door is closed, don't you know, another is open.

***

Don't gain the world and lose your soul. Wisdom is better than silver and gold***

***

In this great future, you can't forget your past.

***

A hungry mob is an angry mob.

***

All dese governments and this and that, these people that say they're here to help, why they say you cannot smoke the herb? Herb... herb is a plant, you know? And when I check it, I can't find any reason.   All they say is, 'it makes you rebel.' Against what?

***

As a man sow, shall he reap? And I know that talk is cheap. But the heat of the battle is as sweet as the victory.

***

Babylon is everywhere. You have wrong, and you have right. Wrong is what we call Babylon, wrong things. That is what Babylon is to me. I could have born in England; I could have born in America; it makes no difference where me born because there is Babylon everywhere.

***

One good thing about music—when it hits you, you feel no pain.

***

Better to die to fight for freedom than be a prisoner all the days of your life.

***

Don't trust people whose feelings change with time. Trust people whose feelings remain the same, even when the time changes.

***

Every day the bucket a-go a well, one day the bottom a-go drop out.

✳✳✳

Every time I plant a seed, He says kill it before it grows, he says kill it before they grow.

✳✳✳

Everything is political. I will never be a politician or even think political. I deal with life and nature. That is the greatest thing to me.

✳✳✳

Free speech carries with it some freedom to listen.

✳✳✳

Have no fear for atomic energy, cause none of them can stop the time.

✳✳✳

I don't know how to live good. I only know how to suffer.

✳✳✳

I've been here before and will come again, but I'm not going this trip through.

✳✳✳

If you're white and you're wrong, then you're wrong; if you're black and you're wrong, you're wrong. People are people. Black, blue, pink, green – God make no rules about color; only society makes rules where my people suffer, and that why we must have redemption and redemption now.

***

Overcome the devils with love.

***

Live for yourself, and you will live in vain; live for others, and you will live again.

***

Love the life you live, live the life you love.

***

My feet are my only carriage.

***

My future is righteousness.

***

Put your vision to reality.

***

Some people feel the rain; others just get wet.

***

Rastafari, not a culture, it's a reality.

***

The road of life is rocky, and you may stumble too, so while you talk about me, someone else is judging you.

***

The people who were trying to make this world worse are not taking the day off. Why should I?

***

They say: only the fittest of the fittest shall survive, stay alive!

***

Cowards awaken a woman's love without loving her in return.

***

Though the road's been rocky, it sure feels good to me.

***

Truth is the light, so you never give up the fight.

***

When one door is closed, many more are open.

**

When the race gets hard to run. It means you can't take the peace.

**

When the root is strong, the fruit is sweet.

**

You can't find the right roads when the streets are paved.

**

You entertain satisfied people. Hungry people can't be entertained – or people who are afraid. You can't entertain a man who has no food.

**

Live the life you love. Love the life you live.

**

Live the life you love. Love the life you live.

**

Live the life you love. Love the life you live.

And don't expect more than she can give. Smile when she makes you happy, let her know when she makes you mad, and miss her when she's not there.

***

Conquer the devils with a little thing called love.

***

She may not be the prettiest, but...

***

He's not perfect. You aren't either, and the two of you will never be perfect. But if he can make you laugh at least once, causes you to think twice, and if he admits to being human and making mistakes, hold onto him and give him the most you can. He isn't going to quote poetry, he's not thinking about you every moment, but he will give you a part of him that he knows you could break. Don't hurt him, don't change him, and don't expect for more than he can give. Don't analyze. Smile when he makes you happy, yell when he makes you mad, and miss him when he's not there. Love hard when there is love to be had. Because perfect guys don't exist, but there's always one guy that is perfect for you.

***

I know that I'm not perfect and that I don't claim to be, so before you point your fingers make sure your hands are clean.

* * *

If puss and dog can get together, why can't we love one another?

* * *

Prayers to the devil.

* * *

If she's amazing, she won't be easy. If she's easy, she won't be amazing. If she's worth it, you won't give up. If you give up, you're not worthy. ... The truth is, everybody is going to hurt you; you gotta find the ones worth suffering for.

* * *

If you get down and quarrel every day, you're saying prayers to the devil, I say.

* * *

Love would never leave us alone.

* * *

One love, one heart, Let's get together and feel alright

**

Only once in your life, I truly believe, you find
someone who can completely turn your world
around. You tell them things that you've never
shared with another soul, and they absorb everything
you say and want to hear more. You share hopes for
the future, dreams that will never come true, goals
that were never achieved and the many
disappointments life has thrown at you. When
something wonderful happens, you can't wait to tell
them about it, knowing they will share in your
excitement. They are not embarrassed to cry with
you when you are hurting or laugh with you when
you make a fool of yourself. Never do they hurt your
feelings or make you feel like you are not good
enough, but rather they build you up and show you
the things about yourself that make you special and
even beautiful. There is never any pressure, jealousy
or competition but only a quiet calmness when they
are around. You can be yourself and not worry about
what they will think of you because they love you for
who you are. The things that seem insignificant to
most people such as a note, song or walk become
invaluable treasures kept safe in your heart to
cherish forever. Memories of your childhood come
back and are so clear and vivid; it's like being young
again. Colors seem brighter and more brilliant.
Laughter seems part of daily life where before it was
infrequent or didn't exist at all. A phone call or two

during the day helps to get you through a long day's work and always brings a smile to your face. In their presence, there's no need for continuous conversation, but you find you're quite content in just having them nearby. Things that never interested you before become fascinating because you know they are important to this person who is so special to you. You think of this person on every occasion and in everything you do. Simple things bring them to mind like a pale blue sky, gentle wind or even a storm cloud on the horizon. You open your heart knowing that there's a chance it may be broken one day and in opening your heart, you experience a love and joy that you never dreamed possible. You find that being vulnerable is the only way to allow your heart to feel true pleasure that's so real it scares you. You find strength in knowing you have a true friend and possibly a soul mate who will remain loyal to the end. Life seems completely different, exciting and worthwhile. Your only hope and security are in knowing that they are a part of your life.

***

My music fights against the system that teaches to live and die.

***

Overcome the devils with a thing called love.

She may not be the most popular or prettiest but if you love her and she makes you smile... what else matters?

***

The biggest coward of a man is to awaken the love of a woman without the intention of loving her.

***

The trust is, everyone is going to hurt you. You just got to find the ones worth suffering for.

***

The winds that sometimes take something we love are the same that bring us something we learn to love.   Therefore, we should not cry about something that was taken from us, but, yes, love what we have been given. Because what is really ours is never gone forever.

***

There will never be any love at all.

***

You say you love rain, but you use an umbrella to walk under it. You say you love the sun, but you seek shelter when it is shining. You say you love wind, but when it comes, you close your windows. So that's why I'm scared when you say you love me.

***

One love, one heart, one destiny.

***

Emancipate yourself from mental slavery, none but ourselves can free our mind.

***

In the abundance of water, a fool is thirsty.

***

Judge not, before you judge yourself.

***

Every man got to right to decide his destiny.

***

Alcohol makes you drunk, man. It doesn't make you meditate; it just makes you drunk. Here is more a consciousness.

***

Just because you are happy, it does not mean that the day is perfect but that you have looked beyond its imperfections.

***

Keep calm and chive on.

***

None but ourselves can free our minds.

***

You can't live in that negative way... make way for the positive day.

***

I do not have an education. I have inspiration. If I were educated, I would be a damn fool.

***

Two thousand years of history Black History could not be wiped away so easily

***

You have to be someone.

***

You can't live that negative way. You know what I mean. Make way for the positive day. Cause it's a new day...

***

You not supposed to feel down over whatever happens to you. I mean, you're supposed to use whatever happened to you as some upper, not a downer.

***

The day you stop racing is the day you win.

***

Don't give up the fight, Stand up for your rights.

***

It takes many a year, Mon, and maybe some bloodshed must be, but righteousness someday prevail.

***

The day you stop racing is the day you win the race.

***

What we struggle to make of it is our sole gift to Jah. The process of what that struggle becomes, in time, the Truth.

***

The harder the battle the sweet of Jah victory.

***

Rastafari, not a culture, it's a reality.

***

We Jah people can make it work.

***

I don't stand for the black man's side; I don't stand for the white man's side. I stand for God's side.

***

I don't stand for white or black.

***

Man can't do without God. Like you're thirsty, you have to drink water. You can't go without God.

***

Life and Jah are the same. Jah is the gift of existence. I am in some way eternal; I will never be duplicated. The singularity of every man and woman is Jah's gift. What we struggle to make of it is our sole gift to Jah. The process of what that struggle becomes, in time, the Truth.

***

I don't dip on anybody's side. I don't dip on the black man's side, not the white man's side. I dip on God's side, the one who create me and cause me to come from black and white.

***

People want to listen to a message, word from Jah. This could be passed through me or anybody. I am not a leader. Messenger. The words of the songs, not the person, is what attracts people.

***

Some people say great God come from the sky take away everything and make everybody feel high, but if you know what life is worth, you will look for yours on earth.

***

The devil doesn't have any power over me. The devil comes, and I shake hands with the devil. Devil has his part to play. Devil's a good friend, too... because when you don't know him, that's the time he can mosh you down.

***

We JAH people can make it work.

***

The greatness of a man is not in how much wealth he acquires, but in his integrity and his ability to affect those around him positively.

***

I have a BMW. But only because BMW stands for and The Wailers, and not because I need an expensive car.

***

Money can't buy life.

***

The greatness of a man is not in how much wealth he acquires, but in his integrity and his ability to affect those around him positively.

***

Your life is worth much more than gold.

***

Hey, mister music sure sounds good to me I can't refuse it what to be got to be.

***

My music fights against the system that teaches to live and die.

***

My music will go on forever. Maybe it's a fool say that, but when I know facts, I can say facts. My music will go on forever.

***

One good thing about music—when it hits you, you feel no pain.

***

Some will hate you pretend they love you now than behind they try to eliminate you.

***

Who are you to judge the life I live? I am not perfect, and I don't have to be! Before you start pointing fingers, make sure your hands are clean.

***

Life is one big road with lots of signs. So, when you are riding through the ruts, don't complicate your mind. Flee from hate, mischief, and jealousy. Don't bury your thoughts.

***

None but ourselves can free our minds.

***

Truth is the light.

***

And what has been hidden from the wise and the prudent been revealed in the mouth of the toddlers.

***

Beginnings are usually scary, and endings are usually sad, but its everything in between that makes it all worth living.

✳✳✳

Don't bury your thoughts, put your vision to reality.

✳✳✳

Don't complicate your mind.

✳✳✳

Don't worry about a thing, 'Cos every little thing is going to be alright.

✳✳✳

Emancipate yourself from mental slavery, none but ourselves can free our mind. Have no fear for atomic energy, because none of them can stop the time.

✳✳✳

Free speech carries with it some freedom to listen.

✳✳✳

Open your eyes... are you satisfied?

✳✳✳

If something can corrupt you, you're corrupted already.

***

It is better to live on the housetop than to live in a house full of confusion.

***

It's your conscience that is going to remind you; that it's your heart and nobody else's, that is the going to judge.

***

Judge not, before you judge yourself. Judge not, if you're not ready for judgment.

***

Man is a universe within himself.

***

I am a common sense man. That means when I explain things, I explain it in a very simple way; that means if I explain it to a baby, the baby will understand too, you know.

***

None but ourselves can free our minds.

***

Open your eyes; look within. Are you satisfied with the life you're living?

***

Prejudice is a chain; it can hold you. If your prejudice, you can't move, you keep prejudice for years. Never get anywhere with that.

***

So, before you point your fingers make sure your hands are clean.

***

Some people feel the rain; others get wet.

***

If I were educated, I would be a damn fool.

***

Tell the children the truth.

***

The good times of today are the sad thoughts of tomorrow.

***

Today, people struggle to find what's real. Everything has become so synthetic that a lot of people, all they want is to grasp onto hope.

***

Until the end of the world, all whys will be answered,
but now, you can only ask!

***

You can fool some people sometimes, but you can't
fool all the people all the time.

***

What important is a man should live in
righteousness, in natural love for humanity?

Confucius

Confucius (551 B.C. – 479 B.C.) was a Chinese social philosopher, whose teachings deeply influenced East Asian life and thought.

***

The man who says he can, and the man who says he cannot... Are both correct?

***

Your life is what your thoughts make it.

***

Real knowledge is to know the extent of one's ignorance.

***

The man who asks a question is a fool for a minute; the man who does not ask is a fool for life.

***

The journey with 1000 miles begins with one step.

***

Choose a job you love, and you will never have to work a day in your life.

***

You are what you think.

***

Looking at small advantages prevents great affairs from being accomplished.

***

All people are the same; only their habits differ.

***

Learn avidly. Question it repeatedly. Analyze it carefully. Then put what you have learned into practice intelligently.

***

We have two lives, and the second begins when we realize we only have one.

***

If you are the smartest person in the room, then you are in the wrong room.

***

Act with kindness but do not expect gratitude.

***

Worry not that no one knows you; seek to be worth knowing.

***

The man who moves a mountain begins by carrying away small stones.

***

When it is obvious that the goals cannot be reached, don't adjust the goals, adjust the action steps.

***

The essence of knowledge is, having it, to use it.

***

One joy dispels a hundred cares.

***

Anyone can find the switch after the lights are on.

***

When you see a good person, think of becoming like her/him. When you see someone not so good, reflect on your weak points.

***

I slept and dreamt life is a beauty. I woke and found life is a duty.

***

They must often change who would remain constant in happiness and wisdom.

***

Don't complain about the snow on your neighbor's roof when your doorstep is unclean.

***

A lion chased me up a tree, and I greatly enjoyed the view from the top.

***

Be not ashamed of mistakes and thus make them crimes.

***

The superior man is modest in his speech but exceeds in his actions.

***

Be strict with yourself but least reproachful of others and complaint is kept afar.

***

Roads were made for journeys, not destinations.

***

No matter how busy you make think you are you must find time for reading, or surrender yourself to self-chosen ignorance.

***

Think of tomorrow; the past can't be mended.

***

Respect yourself and others will respect you.

***

To be wronged is nothing unless you continue to remember it.

***

I hear, and I forget. I see, and I remember. I do, and I understand.

***

By nature, men are nearly alike; by practice, they get to be wide apart.

***

Learn as if you were not reaching your goal and as though you were scared of missing it.

***

Never contract friendship with a man that is not better than thyself.

He who knows all the answers has not been asked all the questions.

＊＊＊

Those who cannot forgive others break the bridge over which they must pass.

＊＊＊

Those who know the truth are not equal to those who love it.

＊＊＊

The superior man always thinks of virtue; the common man thinks of comfort.

＊＊＊

The superior man acts before he speaks and afterward speaks according to his action.

＊＊＊

Success depends upon previous preparation, and without such preparation, there is sure to be a failure.

＊＊＊

Only the wisest and stupidest of men never change.

***

Study the past if you would define the future.

***

Our greatest glory is not in never falling, but in rising every time, we fall.

***

Learning without thought is labor lost; thought without learning is perilous.

***

Do not impose on others what you do not desire.

***

The superior man makes the difficulty to be overcome his first interest; success only comes later.

***

If you make a mistake and do not correct it, this is called a mistake.

***

Education breeds confidence. Confidence breeds hope. Hope breeds peace.

***

A superior man is modest in his speech but exceeds in his actions.

***

To see the right and not to do it is cowardice.

***

Virtuous people often revenge themselves for the constraints to which they submit by the boredom which they inspire.

***

He who acts with a constant view to his advantage will be much murmured against.

***

The superior man is distressed by the limitations of his ability; he is not distressed by the fact that men do not recognize the ability that he has.

***

To see what is right and not to do it is want of courage or principle.

***

When anger rises, think of the consequences.

***

To know what you know and what you do not know, that is true knowledge.

✳✳✳

I want you to be everything that's you, deep at the center of your being.

✳✳✳

The object of the superior man is the truth.

✳✳✳

When you have faults, do not fear to abandon them.

✳✳✳

To go beyond is as wrong as to fall short.

✳✳✳

If you think regarding a year, plant a seed; if regarding ten years, plant trees; if regarding 100 years, teach the people.

✳✳✳

If you look into your own heart, and you find nothing wrong there, what is there to worry about? What is there to fear?

✳✳✳

It does not matter how slowly you go as long as you do not stop.

Virtue is not left to stand alone. He who practices it will have neighbors.

***

Better a diamond with a flaw than a pebble without.

***

The superior man does not, even for the space of a single meal, act contrary to virtue. In moments of haste, he cleaves to it. In seasons of danger, he cleaves to it.

***

The will to win, the desire to succeed, the urge to reach your full potential... these are the keys that will unlock the door to personal excellence.

***

Go before the people with your example, and be laborious in their affairs.

***

When we see persons of worth, we should think of equaling them; when we see persons of a contrary character, we should turn inwards and examine ourselves.

✳✳✳

If we don't know life, how can we know death?

✳✳✳

The expectations of life depend upon diligence; the mechanic that would perfect his work must first sharpen his tools.

✳✳✳

He who speaks without modesty will find it difficult to make his words good.

✳✳✳

What you do not want to be done to yourself, do not do to others.

✳✳✳

Without feelings of respect, what is there to distinguish men from beasts?

✳✳✳

You cannot open a book without learning something.

✳✳✳

A gentleman would be ashamed should his deeds not match his words.

***

When a person should be spoken with, and you don't speak with them, you lose them. When a person shouldn't be spoken with, and you speak to them, you waste your breath. The wise do not lose people, nor do they waste their breath.

***

To see and listen to the wicked is already the beginning of wickedness.

***

Wherever you go, go with all your heart.

***

Give a bowl of rice to a man, and you will feed him for a day. Teach him how to grow his rice, and you will save his life.

***

Study the past, if you would divine the future.

***

It is more shameful to distrust our friends than to be deceived by them.

***

Life is really simple, but we insist on making it complicated.

***

Silence is a true friend who never betrays.

***

By three methods we may learn wisdom: First, by reflection, which is noblest; Second, by imitation, which is easiest; and third by experience, which is the bitterest.

***

Wisdom, compassion, and courage are the three universally recognized moral qualities of men.

***

Death and life have their determined appointments; riches and honors depend upon heaven.

***

Everything has beauty, but not everyone sees it.

***

The more man meditates upon good thoughts, the better will be his world and the world at large.

***

He who learns but does not think is lost! He who thinks but does not learn is in great danger.

***

If you don't want to do something, don't impose on others.

***

It is easy to hate, and it is difficult to love. This is how the whole scheme of things works. All good things are difficult to achieve, and bad things are very easy to get.

***

The strength of a nation derives from the integrity of the home.

***

The superior man understands what is right; the inferior man understands what will sell.

***

Never give a sword to a man who can't dance.

***

We should feel sorrow, but not sink under its oppression.

***

Imagination is more important than knowledge.

***

When you know a thing, to hold that you know it; and when you do not know a thing, to allow that you do not know if – this is knowledge.

Dalai Lama XIV

His Holiness, the Dalai Lama, was born on 6 July 1935. Dalai Lama, Tibet's political leader, has strived to make Tibet an independent and democratic state from China.

***

Happiness is not something ready-made. It comes from your actions.

***

Love is the absence of judgment.

***

If you think you are too small to make a difference, try sleeping with a mosquito.

***

My religion is very simple. My religion is kindness.

***

There is a saying in Tibetan, 'Tragedy should be utilized as a source of strength.' No matter what sort of difficulties, how painful experience is, if we lose our hope, that's our real disaster.

***

Every day, think as you wake up, today I am fortunate to be alive, I have a precious human life, I am not going to waste it. I am going to use all my energies to develop myself, to expand my heart out to others; to achieve enlightenment for the benefit of all beings. I am going to have kind thoughts towards others; I am not going to get angry or think badly about others. I am going to benefit others as much as I can.

✳✳✳

Love and compassion are necessities, not luxuries. Without them, humanity cannot survive.

✳✳✳

Remember that the best relationship is one in which your love for each other exceeds your need for each other.

✳✳✳

Know the rules well so that you can break them effectively.

✳✳✳

Silence is sometimes the best answer

✳✳✳

Our prime purpose in this life is to help others. And if you can't help them, at least don't hurt them.

***

Choose to be optimistic; it feels better.

***

If a problem is fixable, if a situation is such that you can do something about it, then there is no need to worry. If it's not fixable, then there is no help in worrying. There is no benefit in worrying whatsoever.

***

Remember that sometimes not getting what you want is a wonderful stroke of luck.

***

People take different roads seeking fulfillment and happiness. Just because they're not on your road doesn't mean they've gotten lost.

***

This is my simple religion. No need for temples. No need for complicated philosophy. Your mind, your own heart is the temple. Your philosophy is simple kindness.

***

Judge your success by what you had to give up to get it.

***

If you want others to be happy, practice compassion. If you want to be happy, practice compassion.

***

When we meet real tragedy in life, we can react in two ways--either by losing hope and falling into self-destructive habits or by using the challenge to find our inner strength.

***

This is my simple religion. There is no need for temples; no need for complicated philosophy. Our brain, our own heart is our temple; the philosophy is kindness.

***

We can never obtain peace in the outer world until we make peace with ourselves.

***

If you can cultivate the right attitude, your enemies are your best spiritual teachers because their presence provides you with the opportunity to enhance and develop tolerance, patience, and understanding.

***

Only the development of compassion and understanding for others can bring us the tranquility and happiness we all seek.

***

World peace must develop from inner peace. Peace is not just the mere absence of violence. Peace is, I think, the manifestation of human compassion.

***

Look at children. Of course, they may quarrel, but generally speaking, they do not harbor ill feelings as much or as long as adults do. Most adults have the advantage of education over children, but what is the use of an education if they show a big smile while hiding negative feelings deep inside? Children don't usually act in such a manner. If they feel angry with someone, they express it, and then it is finished. They can still play with that person the following day

***

There is only one important point you must keep in your mind and let it be your guide. No matter what people call you, you are just who you are. Keep to this truth. You must ask yourself how is it you want to live your life. We live, and we die, this is the truth that we can only face alone. No one can help us, not even the Buddha. So consider carefully, what prevents you from living the way you want to live your life?

✳✳✳

Take into account that great love and great achievements involve great risk.

✳✳✳

All suffering is caused by ignorance. People inflict pain on others in the selfish pursuit of their happiness or satisfaction

✳✳✳

A truly compassionate attitude toward others does not change even if they behave negatively or hurt you.

✳✳✳

I believe compassion to be one of the few things we can practice that will bring immediate and long-term happiness to our lives. I'm not talking about the short-term gratification of pleasures like sex, drugs or gambling (though I'm not knocking them), but something that will bring true and lasting happiness. The kind that sticks.

✳✳✳

The more Love motivates you; the more Fearless and Freer your action will be.

***

Be kind whenever possible. It is always possible.

***

Old friends pass away, new friends appear. It is just like the days. An old day passes, a new day arrives. The important thing is to make it meaningful: a meaningful friend - or a meaningful day.

***

We can live without religion and meditation, but we cannot survive without human affection.

***

Hard times build determination and inner strength. Through them, we can also come to appreciate the uselessness of anger. Instead of getting angry nurture a deep caring and respect for troublemakers because by creating such trying circumstances they provide us with invaluable opportunities to practice tolerance and patience.

***

When you realize you've made a mistake, take immediate steps to correct it.

***

If we think only of ourselves, forget about other people, then our minds occupy a very small area. Inside that small area, even a tiny problem appears very big. But the moment you develop a sense of concern for others, you realize that, just like ourselves, they also want happiness; they also want satisfaction. When you have this sense of concern, your mind automatically widens. At this point, your problems, even big problems, will not be so significant. The result? Big increase in peace of mind. So, if you think only of yourself, only your happiness, the result is less happiness. You get more anxiety, more fear.

✳✳✳

There are only two days in the year that nothing can be done. One is called Yesterday, and the other is called Tomorrow. Today is the right day to Love, Belief, Do and mostly Live.

✳✳✳

In the practice of tolerance, one's enemy is the best teacher.

✳✳✳

Peace does not mean an absence of conflicts; differences will always be there. Peace means solving these differences through peaceful means; through dialogue, education, knowledge; and through humane ways.

**

A good friend who points out mistakes and imperfections and rebukes evil are to be respected as if he reveals the secret of some hidden treasure.

**

The way to change others' minds is with affection and not anger.

**

If you have a fear of some pain or suffering, you should examine whether there is anything you can do about it. If you can, there is no need to worry about it; if you cannot do anything, then there is also no need to worry.

**

Compassion is the radicalism of our time.

**

We can reject everything else: religion, ideology, all received wisdom. But we cannot escape the necessity of love and compassion... This, then, is my true religion, my simple faith. In this sense, there is no need for temple or church, for mosque or synagogue, no need for complicated philosophy, doctrine or dogma. Our own heart, our mind, is the temple. The doctrine is compassion. Love for others and respect for their rights and dignity, no matter who or what they are: ultimately these are all we need. So long as we practice these in our daily lives, then no matter if we are learned or unlearned, whether we believe in Buddha or God, or follow some other religion or none at all, as long as we have compassion for others and conduct ourselves with restraint out of a sense of responsibility, there is no doubt we will be happy.

Share your knowledge. It is a way to achieve immortality.

***

If there is no solution to the problem, then don't waste time worrying about it. If there is a solution to the problem, then don't spend time worrying about it.

***

To be kind, honest and have positive thoughts; to forgive those who harm us and treat everyone as a friend; to help those who are suffering and never to consider ourselves superior to anyone else: even if this advice seems rather simplistic, make the effort of seeing whether by following it you can find greater happiness.

***

Love and Compassion are the true religions to me. But to develop this, we do not need to believe in any religion.

***

Inner peace is the key: if you have inner peace, the external problems do not affect your deep sense of peace and tranquility...without this inner peace, no matter how comfortable your life is material, you may still be worried, disturbed, or unhappy because of circumstances.

***

Real change is within; leave the outside as it is.

***

The true hero is one who conquers his anger and hatred.

***

If scientific analysis were conclusively to demonstrate specific claims in Buddhism to be false, then we must accept the findings of science and abandon those claims.

***

If someone has a gun and is trying to kill you, it would be reasonable to shoot back with your gun.

***

Because we all share this planet earth, we have to learn to live in harmony and peace with each other and with nature. This is not just a dream, but a necessity.

***

It is under the greatest adversity that there exists the greatest potential for doing good, both for oneself and others.

***

The purpose of all the major religious traditions is not to construct big temples on the outside, but to create temples of goodness and compassion inside, in our hearts.

***

Do not let the behavior of others destroy your inner peace.

***

Open your arms to change but don't let go of your values.

***

We are visitors on this planet. We are here for one hundred years at the very most. During that period, we must try to do something good, something useful, with our lives. if you contribute to other people's happiness, you will find the true meaning of life

***

Whether our action is wholesome or unwholesome depends on whether that action or deed arises from a disciplined or undisciplined state of mind. It is felt that a disciplined mind leads to happiness and an undisciplined mind leads to suffering, and it is said that *bringing about discipline within one's mind is the essence of the Buddha's teaching.*

***

When we are motivated by compassion and wisdom, the results of our actions benefit everyone, not just our selves or some immediate convenience. When we can recognize and forgive the ignorant actions of the past, we gain strength to solve the problems of the present constructively.

***

I find hope in the darkest of days and focus in the brightest. I do not judge the universe.

***

Irrespective of whether we are believers or agnostics, whether we believe in God or karma, moral ethics is a code which everyone can pursue.

✱✱✱

Dangerous consequences will follow when politicians and rulers forget moral principles. Whether we believe in God or karma, ethics is the foundation of every religion.

✱✱✱

A disciplined mind leads to happiness, and an undisciplined mind leads to suffering.

✱✱✱

Compassion is not a religious business; it is a human business; it is not luxury; it is essential for our peace and mental stability; it is essential for human survival.

✱✱✱

The creatures that inhabit this earth--be they human beings or animals--are here to contribute, each in its particular way, to the beauty and prosperity of the world.

✱✱✱

Where ignorance is our master, there is no possibility of real peace.

If you can, help others; if you cannot do that, at least do not harm them.

**

I defeat my enemies when I make them my friends.

**

Sometimes when I meet old friends, it reminds me of how quickly time passes. And it makes me wonder if we've utilized our time properly or not. Proper utilization of time is so important. While we have this body, and especially this amazing human brain, I think every minute is something precious. Our day-to-day existence is very much alive with hope, although there is no guarantee of our future. There is no guarantee that tomorrow at this time we will be here. But we are working for that purely by hope. So, we need to make the best use of our time. I believe that the proper utilization of time is this: if you can, serve other people, other sentient beings. If not, at least refrain from harming them. I think that is the whole basis of my philosophy.

So, let us reflect what is true of value in life, what gives meaning to our lives, and set our priorities by that. The purpose of our life needs to be positive. We weren't born with the purpose of causing trouble, harming others. For our life to be of value, I think we must develop basic good human qualities—warmth, kindness, compassion. Then our life becomes meaningful and more peaceful—happier.

***

You must not hate those who do wrong or harmful things; but with compassion, you must do what you can to stop them — for they are harming themselves, as well as those who suffer from their actions

***

Whether one is rich or poor, educated or illiterate, religious or nonbelieving, man or woman, black, white, or brown, we are all the same. Physically, emotionally, and mentally, we are all equal. We all share basic needs for food, shelter, safety, and love. We all aspire to happiness, and we all shun suffering. Each of us has hopes, worries, fears, and dreams. Each of us wants the best for our family and loved ones. We all experience pain when we suffer loss and joy when we achieve what we seek. On this fundamental level, religion, ethnicity, culture, and language make no difference.

***

Although you may not always be able to avoid difficult situations, you can modify the extent to which you can suffer by how you choose to respond to the situation

***

Someone else's action should not determine your response.

***

A genuine, affectionate smile is very important in our day-to-day lives.

***

We need to learn how to want what we have NOT to have what we want to get steady and stable Happiness

***

Every single being, even those who are hostile to us, is just as afraid of suffering as we are, and seeks happiness in the same way we do. Every person has the same right as we do to be happy and not to suffer. So, let's take care of others wholeheartedly, of both our friends and our enemies. This is the basis for true compassion.

***

To remain indifferent to the challenges we face is indefensible. If the goal is noble, whether or not it is realized within our lifetime is largely irrelevant. What we must do therefore is to strive and persevere and never give up.

***

When we feel love and kindness toward others, it not only made others feel loved and cared for, but it helps us also to develop inner happiness and peace.

***

The various features and aspects of human life, such as longevity, good health, success, happiness, and so forth, which we consider desirable, are all dependent on the kindness and a good heart.

***

Life is as dear to a mute creature as it is to man. Just as one wants happiness and fears pain, just as one wants to live and not die, so do other creatures.

***

It is not enough to be compassionate; we must act.

***

An open heart is an open mind.

***

I have found that the greatest degree of inner tranquility comes from the development of love and compassion. The more we care for the happiness of others, the greater is our sense of well-being. Cultivating a close, warmhearted feeling for others automatically puts the mind at ease. It is the ultimate source of success in life.

***

I believe all suffering is caused by ignorance. People inflict pain on others in the selfish pursuit of their happiness or satisfaction. True happiness comes from a sense of inner peace and contentment, which in turn must be achieved through the cultivation of altruism, love and compassion and elimination of ignorance, selfishness, and greed.

***

When you talk, you are only repeating what you already know. But if you listen, you may learn something new.

***

Human use, population, and technology have reached that certain stage where mother Earth no longer accepts our presence with silence.

***

Anger or hatred is like a fisherman's hook. It is very important for us to ensure that we are not caught by it

***

When life becomes too complicated, and we feel overwhelmed, it's often useful to stand back and remind ourselves of our overall purpose, our overall goal. When faced with a feeling of stagnation and confusion, it may be helpful to take an hour, an afternoon, or even several days to reflect on what it is that will truly bring us happiness, and then reset our priorities by that. This can put our life back in proper context, allow a fresh perspective, and enable us to see which direction to take.

✱✱✱

When you are discontent, you always want more, more, more. Your desire can never be satisfied. But when you practice contentment, you can say to yourself, 'Oh yes -- I already have everything that I need.

✱✱✱

Happiness doesn't always come from a pursuit. Sometimes it comes when we least expect it.

✱✱✱

Whether you believe in God or not does matter much, whether you believe in Buddha or not does matter so much; as a Buddhist, whether you believe in reincarnation or not does not matter so much. You must lead a good life

✱✱✱

Anger is the ultimate destroyer of your peace of mind

∗∗∗

Whether you believe in God or not does matter so much, whether you believe in Buddha or not does matter so much; as a Buddhist, whether you believe in reincarnation or not does not matter so much. You must lead a good life. And a good life does not mean just good food, good clothes, good shelter. These are not sufficient. A good motivation is what is needed: compassion, without dogmatism, without complicated philosophy; just understanding that others are human brothers and sisters and respecting their rights and human dignity.

∗∗∗

Sometimes one creates a dynamic impression by saying something, and sometimes one creates as significant an impression by remaining silent

∗∗∗

I don't know whether the universe, with its countless galaxies, stars, and planets, has a deeper meaning or not, but at the very least, it is clear that we humans who live on this earth face the task of making a happy life for ourselves. Therefore, it is important to discover what will bring about the greatest degree of happiness

Let us try to recognize the precious nature of each day.

✳✳✳

If a problem can be solved, it will be. If it cannot be solved, there is no use worrying about it.

✳✳✳

The more time you spend thinking about yourself, the more suffering you will experience.

✳✳✳

The very purpose of our life is to seek happiness.

✳✳✳

One problem with our current society is that we have an attitude towards education as if it is there to make you cleverer, make you more ingenious simply...
Even though our society does not emphasize this, the most important use of knowledge and education is to help us understand the importance of engaging in more wholesome actions and bringing about discipline within our minds. The proper utilization of our intelligence and knowledge is to effect changes from within to develop a good heart

Time passes unhindered. When we make mistakes, we cannot turn the clock back and try again. All we can do is use the present well.

***

We create most of our suffering, so it should be logical that we also can create more joy. It simply depends on the attitudes, the perspectives, and the reactions we bring to situations and our relationships with other people. When it comes to personal happiness, there is a lot that we as individuals can do

***

We human beings are social beings. We come into the world as a result of others' actions. We survive here in dependence on others. Whether we like it or not, there is hardly a moment of our lives when we do not benefit from others' activities. For this reason, it is hardly surprising that most of our happiness arises in the context of our relationships with others.

***

If I am only happy for myself, many fewer chances for happiness. If I am happy when good things happen to other people, billions of more chances to be happy!

***

I believe that the very purpose of life is to be happy. From the very core of our being, we desire contentment. In my own limited experience, I have found that the more we care for the happiness of others, the greater is our sense of well-being. Cultivating a close, warmhearted feeling for others automatically puts the mind at ease. It helps remove whatever fears or insecurities we may have and gives us the strength to cope with any obstacles we encounter. It is the principal source of success in life. Since we are not solely material creatures, it is a mistake to place all our hopes for happiness on external development alone. The key is to develop inner peace.

✱✱✱

We are but visitors on this planet. We are here for ninety or one hundred years at the very most. During that period, we must try to do something good, something useful in our lives. If you contribute to other people's happiness, you will find the true goal, the true meaning of life

✱✱✱

Pain is inevitable; suffering is optional; we have bigger houses, but smaller families. More conveniences, but less time. We know, but fewer judgments; more experts, but more problems; more medicines but less health.

***

I call the high and light aspects of my being SPIRIT and the dark and heavy aspects SOUL. The soul is at home in the deep shaded valleys. Heavy torpid flowers saturated with black grow there. The rivers flow like warm syrup. They empty into huge oceans of the soul. Spirit is a land of high, white peaks and glittering jewel-like lakes and flowers. Life is sparse and sound travels great distances. There is soul music, soul food, and soul love. People need to climb the mountain not because it is there but because the soulful divinity needs to be mated with the Spirit. Deep down we must have a real affection for each other, a clear recognition of our shared human status. At the same time, we must openly accept all ideologies and systems as a means of solving humanity's problems. No matter how strong the wind of evil may blow, the flame of truth cannot be extinguished.

***

To lead a meaningful life, you need to cherish others, pay attention to human values and try to cultivate inner peace.

***

The goal is not to be better than the other man, but your previous self.

***

Non-violence means dialogue, using our language, the human language. Discussion means compromise; respecting each other's rights; in the spirit of reconciliation, there is a real solution to conflict and disagreement. There is no hundred percent winner, no hundred percent loser—not that way but half-and-half. That is the practical way, the only way.

***

It is very rare or almost impossible that an event can be adverse from all points of view.

***

Our ancient experience confirms at every position that everything is linked together; everything is inseparable.

***

The enemy is the necessary condition for practicing patience.

***

As you breathe in, cherish yourself. As you breathe out, cherish all Beings.

***

Self-satisfaction alone cannot determine if a desire or action is positive or negative. The demarcation between a positive and a negative desire or action is not whether it gives you an immediate feeling of satisfaction, but whether it ultimately results in positive or negative consequences

***

Instead of wondering WHY this is happening to you, consider why this is happening to YOU.

***

With the realization of one's potential and self-confidence in one's ability, one can build a better world.

Dale Carnegie

Dale Breckenridge Carnegie (November 24, 1888 – November 1, 1955) was an American writer and lecturer and the developer of famous courses in self-improvement, salesmanship, corporate training, public speaking, and interpersonal skills.

***

If you can't sleep, then get up and do something instead of lying there and worrying. It's the worry that gets you, not the loss of sleep.

***

Are you bored with life? Then throw yourself into some work you believe in with all your heart, live for it, die for it, and you will find the happiness that you had thought could never be yours.

***

If you want to win friends, make it a point to remember them. If you remember my name, you pay me a subtle compliment; you indicate that I have made an impression on you. Remember my name and you add to my feeling of importance.

***

Take a chance! All life is a chance. The man who goes the furthest is generally the one who is willing to do and dare.

***

Don't be afraid to give your best to what seemingly are small jobs. Every time you conquer one it makes you that much stronger. If you do the little jobs well, the big ones tend to take care of themselves.

***

If you believe in what you are doing, then let nothing hold you up in your work. Much of the best work of the world has been done against seeming impossibilities. The thing is to get the job done.

***

It isn't what you have, or who you are, or where you are, or what you are doing that makes you happy or unhappy. It is what you think about.

***

The ideas I stand for are not mine. I borrowed them from Socrates. I swiped them from Chesterfield. I stole them from Jesus. And I put them in a book. If you don't like their rules whose would you use?

***

One of the most tragic things I know about human nature is that all of us tend to put off living. We are all dreaming of some magical rose garden over the horizon- instead of enjoying the roses blooming outside our windows today.

***

Any fool can criticize, condemn, and complain -- and most fools do.

***

Most of the important things in the world have been accomplished by people who had kept on trying when there seemed to be no help at all.

***

You can make more friends in two months by becoming interested in other people than you can in two years by trying to get other people interested in you.

***

Remember happiness doesn't depend on who you are or what you have; it depends solely upon what you think.

***

The man who goes farthest is generally the one who is willing to do and dare. The sure-thing boat never gets far from shore.

***

Success is getting what you want. Happiness is wanting what you get.

***

Those convinced against their will agree still.

***

I deal with the obvious. I present, reiterate and glorify the obvious -- because the obvious is what people need to be told.

***

The royal road to a man's heart is to talk to him about the things he treasures most.

**

There are four ways, and only four ways, in which we have contact with the world. We are evaluated and classified by these four contacts: what we do, how we look, what we say, and how we mean it.

**

Your purpose is to make your audience see what you saw, hear what you heard, feel what you felt. Relevant detail, couched in concrete, colorful language, is the best way to recreate the incident as it happened and to picture it for the audience.

**

Flaming enthusiasm, backed up by horse sense and persistence, is the quality that most frequently makes for success.

**

If you want to be enthusiastic, act enthusiastic.

**

There is only one way... to get anybody to do anything. And that is by making the other person want to do it.

**

When fate hands us a lemon, let's try to make lemonade.

**

The successful man will profit from his mistakes and try again in a different way.

David Hume

David Hume (1711—1776) is one of the world's great philosophical voices because he hit upon a key fact about human nature: that our feelings more influence us than by reason.

✳✳✳

That the sun will not rise tomorrow is no less intelligible a proposition, and implies no more contradiction, than the affirmation, that it will rise.

✳✳✳

What a peculiar privilege has this little agitation of the brain which we call 'thought.'

✳✳✳

Heaven and hell suppose two distinct species of men, the good and the bad. But the greatest part of humankind float betwixt vice and virtue.

✳✳✳

The reason is, and ought only to be the slave of the passions, and can never pretend to any other office than to serve and obey them.

✳✳✳

It's when we start working together that the real healing takes place... it's when we start spilling our sweat, and not our blood.

✳✳✳

A purpose, an intention, a design, strikes everywhere even the careless, the most stupid thinker.

***

It is... a just political maxim that every man must be supposed a knave.

***

A man acquainted with history may, in some respect, be said to have lived from the beginning of the world and to have been making continual additions to his stock of knowledge in every century.

***

A propensity to hope and joy is real riches; one to fear and sorrow real poverty.

***

Philosophy would render us entirely Pyrrhonian, were not nature too strong for it.

***

Nothing endears so much a friend as sorrow for his death. The pleasure of his company has not so powerful an influence.

***

The rules of morality are not the conclusion of our reason.

***

A wise man proportions his belief to the evidence.

***

This avidity alone, of acquiring goods and possessions for ourselves and our dearest friends, is insatiable, perpetual, universal, and directly destructive of society.

***

The chief benefit, which results from philosophy, arises indirectly, and proceeds more from its secret, insensible influence, than from its immediate application.

***

To be a philosophical skeptic is, in a scholar, the first and most essential to being a sound, believing Christian.

***

The law always limits every power it gives.

***

There is a very remarkable inclination in human nature to bestow on external objects the same emotions which it observes in itself and to find everywhere those ideas which are most present to it.

***

Be a philosopher but, amid all your philosophy be still a man.

***

Where ambition can cover its enterprises, even to the person himself, under the appearance of principle, it is the most incurable and inflexible of passions.

***

I have written on all sorts of subjects... yet I have no enemies; except indeed all the Whigs, all the Tories, and all the Christians.

***

It is not reason which is the guide of life, but custom.

***

Everything in the world is purchased by labor.

***

And what is the greatest number? Number one.

***

Custom is the great guide to human life.

***

Every wise, just, and mild government, by rendering the condition of its subjects easy and secure, will always abound most in people, as well as in commodities and riches.

***

Generally speaking, the errors in religion are dangerous; those in philosophy only ridiculous.

***

He is happy whom circumstances suit his temper, but he is more excellent who suits his temper to any circumstance.

***

It is not contrary to reason to prefer the destruction of the whole world to the scratching of my finger. It is not contrary to reason for me to choose my total ruin, to prevent the least uneasiness of an Indian, or person wholly unknown to me. It is a little contrary to reason to prefer even my own acknowledged lesser good to my greater, and have a more ardent affection for the former than the latter.

✻✻✻

The corruption of the best things gives rise to the worst.

✻✻✻

To hate, to love, to think, to feel, to see; all this is nothing but to perceive.

✻✻✻

Eloquence, at its highest pitch, leaves little room for reason or reflection, but addresses itself entirely to the desires and affections, captivating the willing hearers, and subduing their understanding.

✻✻✻

The character is the result of a system of stereotyped principals.

✻✻✻

It is seldom that liberty of any kind is lost all at once.

✻✻✻

There is not to be found, in all history, any miracle attested by a sufficient number of men, of such unquestioned good sense, education and learning, as to secure us against all delusion in themselves.

✻✻✻

Beauty, whether moral or natural, is felt, more properly than perceived.

***

The heights of popularity and patriotism are still the beaten road to power and tyranny.

***

Men are much oftener thrown on their knees by the melancholy than by the agreeable passions.

***

The advantages found in history seem to be of three kinds, as it amuses the fancy, as it improves the understanding, and as it strengthens virtue.

***

Any person seasoned with a just sense of the imperfections of natural reason will fly to revealed truth with the greatest avidity.

***

No advantages in this world are pure and unmixed.

***

Human Nature is the only science of man; and yet has been hitherto the most neglected.

***

Accuracy is, in every case, advantageous to beauty, and just reasoning to delicate sentiment. In vain would we exalt the one by depreciating the other.

✳✳✳

How could politics be a science, if laws and forms of government had not a uniform influence upon society? Where would be the foundation of morals, if particular characters had no certain or determinate power to produce particular sentiments, and if these sentiments had no constant operation on actions?

✳✳✳

If the contemplation, even of inanimate beauty, is so delightful; if it ravishes the senses, even when the fair form is foreign to us: What must be the effects of moral beauty? And what influence must it have, when it embellishes our mind and is the result of our reflection and industry?

✳✳✳

The whole [of religion] is a riddle, an enigma, an inexplicable mystery. Doubt, uncertainty, the suspense of judgment appears the only result of our most accurate scrutiny, concerning this subject.

✳✳✳

Every disastrous accident alarm us, and sets us on inquiries concerning the principles whence it arose: Apprehensions spring up with regard to futurity: And the mind, sunk into diffidence, terror, and melancholy, has recourse to every method of appeasing those secret intelligent powers, on whom our fortune is supposed entirely to depend.

✳✳✳

I shall venture to affirm, that there never was a popular religion, which represented the state of departed souls in such a light, as would render it eligible for humankind, that there should be such a state. These fine models of religion are the mere product of philosophy. For as death lies between the eye and the prospect of futurity, that event is so shocking to nature, that it must throw a gloom on all the regions which lie beyond it; and suggest to the generality of humanity the idea of Cerberus and Furies; devils, and torrents of fire and brimstone.

***

The whole of natural theology resolves itself into one simple, though somewhat ambiguous proposition, That the cause or causes of order in the universe, probably bear some remote analogy to human intelligence.

***

The proper office of religion is to regulate the heart of men, humanize their conduct, infuse the spirit of temperance, order, and obedience; and as its operation is silent, and only enforces the motives of morality and justice, it is in danger of being overlooked, and confounded with these other motives.

***

If the religious spirit is ever mentioned in any historical narration, we are sure to meet afterward with a detail of the miseries which attend it. And no period can be happier or more prosperous, than those in which it is never regarded or heard of.

***

The skeptics assert, though absurdly, that the origin of all religious worship was derived from the utility of inanimate objects, as the sun and moon, to the support and well-being of humankind.

The minds of men are mirrors to one another, not only because they reflect each other's emotions, but also because those rays of passions, sentiments, and opinions may be often reverberated, and may decay away by insensible degrees.

But there still prevails, even in nations well acquainted with commerce, strong jealousy about the balance of trade, and fear, that all their gold and silver may be leaving them. This seems to me, almost in every case, a groundless apprehension; and I should as soon dread, that all our springs and rivers should be exhausted, as that money should abandon a kingdom where there are people and industry.

Avarice, or the desire of gain, is a universal passion which operates at all times, at all places, and upon all persons.

Weakness, fear, melancholy, together with ignorance, are the true sources of superstition. Hope, pride, presumption, warm indignation, together with ignorance, are the true sources of enthusiasm.

What is easy and obvious is never valued; and even what is in itself difficult, if we come to the knowledge of it without difficulty, and without any a stretch of thought or judgment, is but little regarded.

From the apparent usefulness of the social virtues, it has readily been inferred by sceptics, both ancient and modern, that all moral distinctions arise from education, and were, at first, invented, and afterward encouraged ... in order to render men tractable, and subdue their natural ferocity and selfishness, which incapacitated them for society.

∗∗∗

.. the voice of nature and experience seems plain to oppose the selfish theory.

∗∗∗

Municipal laws are a supply to the wisdom of each; and, at the same time, by restraining the natural liberty of men, make private interest submit to the interest of the public.

∗∗∗

Between married persons, the cement of friendship is by the laws supposed so strong as to abolish all division of possessions: and often has, in reality, the force ascribed to it.

∗∗∗

In ancient times, bodily strength and dexterity, being of greater use and importance in war, was also much more esteemed and valued, than at present. ... In short, the different ranks of men are, in a great measure, regulated by riches.

∗∗∗

A man who has cured himself of all ridiculous prepossessions, and is fully, sincerely, and steadily convinced, from experience as well as philosophy, that the difference of fortune makes less difference in happiness than is vulgarly imagined; such a one does not measure out degrees of esteem according to the rent-rolls of his acquaintance. ... his internal sentiments are more regulated by the personal characters of men, than by the accidental and capricious favors of fortune.

***

In our reasonings concerning matter of fact, there are all imaginable degrees of assurance, from the highest certainty to the lowest species of moral evidence. A wise man, therefore, proportions his belief to the evidence.

***

Does a man of sense run after every silly tale of hobgoblins or fairies, and canvass the evidence particularly? I never knew anyone, that examined and deliberated about nonsense who did not believe it before the end of his inquiries.

***

A miracle is a violation of the laws of nature; and as a firm and unalterable experience have established these laws, the proof against a miracle, from the very nature of the fact, is as entire as any argument from experience can be imagined.

***

On the theory of the soul's mortality, the inferiority of women's capacity is easily accounted for: Their domestic life requires no higher faculties either of mind or body. This circumstance vanishes and becomes insignificant, on the religious theory: The one sex has an equal task to perform as the other: Their powers of reason and resolution ought also to have been equal, and both of them infinitely greater than at present.

***

If we confine ourselves to a general and distant reflection on the ills of human life, that cannot affect to prepare us for them. If by close and intense meditation we render them present and intimate to us, that is the true secret for poisoning all our pleasures and rendering us perpetually miserable.

***

Do you come to a philosopher as to a cunning man, to learn something by magic or witchcraft, beyond what can be known by common prudence and discretion?

***

The whole is a riddle, an enigma, an inexplicable mystery. Doubt, uncertainty, the suspense of judgment appear the only result of our most accurate scrutiny, concerning this subject. But such is the frailty of human reason, and such the irresistible contagion of opinion, that even this deliberate doubt could scarcely be upheld; did we not enlarge our view and opposing one species of superstition to another, set them a quarreling; while we, during their fury and contention, happily make our escape into the calm, though obscure, regions of philosophy.

***

Nothing can be more real, or concern us more, than our own sentiments of pleasure and uneasiness; and if these be favorable to virtue and unfavorable to vice, no more can be requisite to the regulation of our conduct and behavior.

***

The conduct of a man, who studies philosophy in this careless manner, is more truly skeptical than that of anyone, who feeling in himself an inclination to it, is yet so over-whelmed with doubts and scruples, as totally to reject it. A true sceptic will be diffident of his philosophical doubts, as well as of his philosophical conviction; and will never refuse any innocent satisfaction, which offers itself, upon account of either of them.

***

To invent without scruple a new principle to every new phenomenon, instead of adapting it to the old; to overload our hypothesis with a variety of this kind, are certain proofs that none of these principles is the just one, and that we only desire, by a number of falsehoods, to cover our ignorance of the truth.

***

Reason, in a strict sense, as meaning the judgment of truth and falsehood, can never, of itself, be any motive to the will, and can have no influence but so far as it touches some passion or affection. Abstract relations of ideas are the object of curiosity, not of volition. And matters of fact, where they are neither good nor evil, where they neither excite desire nor aversion, are totally indifferent, and whether known or unknown, whether mistaken or rightly apprehended, cannot be regarded as any motive to action.

***

It is still open for me, as well as you, to regulate my behavior, by my experience of past events.

***

There has been a controversy started of late, much better worth examination, concerning the general foundation of Morals; whether they be derived from Reason, or from Sentiment; whether we attain the knowledge of them by a chain of argument and induction, or by an immediate feeling and finer internal sense; whether, like all sound judgement of truth and falsehood, they should be the same to every rational intelligent being; or whether, like the perception of beauty and deformity, they be founded entirely on the particular fabric and constitution of the human species.

***

Truth is disputable; not taste: what exists in the nature of things is the standard of our judgement; what each man feels within himself is the standard of sentiment. Propositions in geometry may be proved, systems in physics may be controverted; but the harmony of verse, the tenderness of passion, the brilliance of it, must give immediate pleasure. No man reasons concerning another's beauty; but frequently concerning the justice or injustice of his actions.

***

Disbelief in futurity loosens in a great measure the ties of morality, and maybe for that reason pernicious to the peace of civil society.

***

For my part, when I enter most intimately into what I call myself, I always stumble on some particular perception or other, of heat or cold, light or shade, love or hatred, pain or pleasure. I never can catch myself at any time without a perception, and never can observe anything but the perception.

***

The mind is a kind of theater, where several perceptions successively make their appearance; pass, re-pass, glide away, and mingle in an infinite variety of postures and situations.

✳✳✳

It is harder to avoid censure than to gain applause.

✳✳✳

I never asserted such an absurd thing as that things arise without a cause.

✳✳✳

Even after the observation of the frequent conjunction of objects, we have no reason to draw any inference concerning any object beyond those of which we have had experience.

✳✳✳

Among well-bred people a mutual deference is affected, contempt for others is disguised; authority concealed; attention given to each in his turn; and an easy stream of conversation maintained without vehemence, without interruption, without eagerness for victory, and without any airs of superiority.

✳✳✳

Never literary attempt was more unfortunate than my Treatise of Human Nature. It fell dead-born from the press.

✳✳✳

It is more rational to suspect knavery and folly than to discount, at a stroke, everything that past experience has taught me about the way things actually work.

***

I may venture to affirm the rest of mankind, that they are nothing but a bundle or collection of different perceptions, which succeed each other with an inconceivable rapidity, and are in a perpetual flux and movement.

***

But I would still reply, that the knavery and folly of men are such common phenomena, that I should rather believe the most extraordinary events to arise from their concurrence, than admit of so signal a violation of the laws of nature.

***

The more instances we examine, and the more care we employ, the more assurance shall we acquire, that the enumeration, which we form from the whole, is complete and entire.

***

The gazing populace receive greedily, without examination, whatever soothes superstition and promotes wonder.

***

The Crusades - the most signal and most durable monument of human folly that has yet appeared in any age or nation.

***

It is a great mortification to the vanity of man, that his utmost art and industry can never equal the meanest of nature's productions, either for beauty or value. Art is only the under-workman, and is employed to give a few strokes of embellishment to those pieces, which come from the hand of the master.

***

Such is the nature of novelty that where anything pleases it becomes doubly agreeable if new; but if it displeases, it is doubly displeasing on that very account.

***

These arguments on each side (and many more might be produced) are so plausible, that I am apt to suspect, they may, the one as well as the other, be solid and satisfactory, and that reason and sentiment concur in almost all moral determinations and conclusions.

***

.. that which renders morality an active principle and constitutes virtue our happiness, and vice our misery: it is probable, I say, that this final sentence depends on some internal sense or feeling, which nature has made universal in the whole species.

***

We may observe that, in displaying the praises of any humane, beneficent man, there is one circumstance which never fails to be amply insisted on, namely, the happiness and satisfaction, derived to society from his intercourse and good offices.

***

In all determinations of morality, this circumstance of public utility is ever principally in view; and wherever disputes arise, either in philosophy or common life, concerning the bounds of duty, the questions cannot, by any means, be decided with greater certainty, than by ascertaining, on any side, the true interests of mankind. If any false opinion, embraced from appearances, has been found to prevail; as soon as farther experience and sounder reasoning have given us jouster notions of human affairs, we retract our first sentiment, and adjust anew the boundaries of moral good and evil.

***

He sees such a desperate rapaciousness prevail; such a disregard to equity, such contempt of order, such stupid blindness to future consequences, as must immediately have the most tragical conclusion, and must terminate in destruction to the greater number, and in a total dissolution of society to the rest.

***

.. that a rule, which, in speculation, may seem the most advantageous to society, may yet be found, in practice, totally pernicious and destructive.

***

But, historians, and even common sense, may inform us, that, however specious these ideas of perfect equality may seem, they are really, at bottom, impracticable; and were they not so, would be extremely pernicious to human society. Render possessions ever so equal, men's different degrees of art, care, and industry will immediately break that equality. Or if you check these virtues, you reduce society to the most extreme indigence; and instead of preventing want and beggary in a few, render it unavoidable to the whole community.

***

We may conclude, therefore, that, in order to establish laws for the regulation of property, we must be acquainted with the nature and situation of man; must reject appearances, which may be false, though specious; and must search for those rules, which are, on the whole, most useful and beneficial.

✳✳✳

Time is a perishable commodity.

✳✳✳

... if you insist that the inference is made by a chain of reasoning, I desire you to produce that reasoning. The connection between the two is not intuitive. There is required a medium, which may enable the mind to draw such an inference, if indeed it be drawn by reasoning and argument. What that medium is, I must confess, passes my comprehension; and it is incumbent on those to produce it, who assert that it really exists, and is the origin of all our conclusions concerning matter of fact.

✳✳✳

We find in the course of nature that though the effects be many, the principles from which they arise are commonly few and simple, and that it is the sign of an unskilled naturalist to have recourse to a different quality in order to explain every different operation.

✳✳✳

The supposition that the future resembles the past, is not founded on arguments of any kind, but is derived entirely from habit.

✳✳✳

..all arguments concerning existence are founded on the relation of cause and effect; that our knowledge of that relation is derived entirely from experience; and all our experimental conclusions proceed upon the supposition that the future will be conformable to the past. .... Without the influence of custom, we should be entirely ignorant of every matter of fact beyond what is immediately present to the memory and senses.

***

And as this is the obvious appearance of things, it must be admitted, till some hypothesis be discovered, which by penetrating deeper into human nature, may prove the former affections to be nothing but modifications of the latter. All attempts of this kind have hitherto proved fruitless, and seem to have proceeded entirely from that love of simplicity which has been the source of much false reasoning in philosophy.

***

The simplest and most obvious cause which can there be assigned for any phenomena, is probably the true one.

***

But in many orders of beauty, particularly those of the finer arts, it is requisite to employ much reasoning, in order to feel the proper sentiment; and a false relish may frequently be corrected by argument and reflection. There are just grounds to conclude, that moral beauty partakes of this latter species, and demands the assistance of our intellectual faculties, in order to give it a suitable influence on the human mind.

***

Habit may lead us to believe and expectation but not to the knowledge, and still less to the understanding, of lawful relations.

✳✳✳

As every inquiry which regards religion is of the utmost importance, there are two questions in particular which challenge our attention, to wit, that concerning its foundation in reason, and that concerning its origin in human nature.

✳✳✳

When anyone tells me that he saw a dead man restored to life, I immediately consider with myself whether it be more probable that this person should either deceive or be deceived or that the fact which he relates should really have happened. I weigh the one miracle against the other and according to the superiority which I discover, I pronounce my decision. Always I reject the greater miracle. If the falsehood of his testimony would be more miraculous than the event which he relates, then and not till then, can he pretend to command my belief or opinion.

✳✳✳

We make allowance for a certain degree of selfishness in men; because we know it to be inseparable from human nature, and inherent in our frame and constitution. By this reflexion we correct those sentiments of blame, which so naturally arise upon any opposition.

✳✳✳

All sentiment is right; because sentiment has a reference to nothing beyond itself, and is always real, wherever a man is conscious of it. But all determinations of the understanding are not right; because they have a reference to something beyond themselves, to wit, real matter of fact; and are not always conformable to that standard.

∗

All that belongs to human understanding, in this deep ignorance and obscurity, is to be skeptical, or at least cautious, and not to admit of any hypothesis whatever, much less of any which is supported by no appearance of probability.

∗

How can we satisfy ourselves without going on in infinitum? And, after all, what satisfaction is there in that infinite progression? Let us remember the story of the Indian philosopher and his elephant. It was never more applicable than to the present subject. If the material world rests upon a similar ideal world, this ideal world must rest upon some other; and so on, without end. It were better, therefore, never to look beyond the present material world.

∗

The identity that we ascribe to things is only a fictitious one, established by the mind, not a peculiar nature belonging to what we're talking about.

∗

Courage, of all national qualities, is the most precarious; because it is exerted only at intervals, and by a few in every nation; whereas industry, knowledge, civility, may be of constant and universal use, and for several ages, may become habitual to the whole people.

∗

...virtue is attended by more peace of mind than vice, and meets with a more favorable reception from the world. I am sensible, that, according to the past experience of mankind, friendship is the chief joy of human life and moderation the only source of tranquility and happiness.

***

For, besides, that many persons find too sensible an interest in perpetually recalling such topics; besides this, I say, the motive of blind despair can never reasonably have place in the sciences; since, however unsuccessful former attempts may have proved, there is still room to hope, that the industry, good fortune, or improved sagacity of succeeding generations may reach discoveries unknown to former ages.

***

Avarice, the spur of industry.

***

Nothing exists without a cause, the original cause of this universe we call God.

***

Nothing is more favorable to the rise of politeness and learning, than a number of neighboring and independent states, connected together by commerce and policy.

***

I cannot but bless the memory of Julius Caesar, for the great esteem he expressed for fat men and his aversion to lean ones.

***

Manufacturers...gradually shift their places, leaving those countries and provinces which they have already enriched, and flying to others, whether they are allured by the cheapness of provisions and labour.

∗∗∗

No human testimony can have such force as to prove a miracle, and make it a just foundation for any such system of religion.

∗∗∗

The more tremendous the divinity is represented, the more time and submissive do men become his ministers: And the more unaccountable the measures of acceptance required by him, the more necessary does it become to abandon our natural reason, and yield to their ghostly guidance and direction.

∗∗∗

The great end of all human industry is the attainment of happiness. For this were arts invented, sciences cultivated, laws ordained, and societies modeled, by the most profound wisdom of patriots and legislators. Even the lonely savage, who lies exposed to the inclemency of the elements and the fury of wild beasts, forgets not, for a moment, this grand object of his being.

∗∗∗

History is the discovering of the principles of human nature.

∗∗∗

It forms a strong presumption against all supernatural and miraculous relations, that they are observed chiefly to abound among ignorant and barbarous nations; or if a civilized people has ever given admission to any of them, that people will be found to have received them from ignorant and barbarous ancestors.

✳✳✳

It seems to me, that the only Objects of the abstract Sciences or of Demonstration is Quantity and Number, and that all Attempts to extend this more perfect Species of Knowledge beyond these Bounds are mere Sophistry and Illusion.

✳✳✳

We need only reflect on what has been proved at large, that we are never sensible of any connexion betwixt causes and effects, and that 'this only by our experience of their constant conjunction, we can arrive at any knowledge of this relation.

✳✳✳

In all matters of opinion and science ... the difference between men is ... oftener found to lie in generals than in particulars, and to be less in reality than in appearance. An explication of the terms commonly ends the controversy, and the disputants are surprised to find that they had been quarreling, while at bottom they agreed in their judgment.

✳✳✳

[priests are] the pretenders to power and dominion, and to a superior sanctity of character, distinct from virtue and good morals.

✳✳✳

Examine the religious principles which have, in fact, prevailed in the world, and you will scarcely be persuaded that they are anything but sick men's dreams.

***

... superstitions, which, being unable to defend themselves on fair ground, raise these intangling brambles to cover and protect their weakness. Chased from the open country, these robbers fly into the forest, and lie in wait to break in upon every unguarded avenue of the mind, and overwhelm it with religious fears and prejudices. ... The idea of God, as meaning an infinitely intelligent, wise and good Being, arises from reflecting on the operations of our own mind and augmenting, without limit, those qualities of goodness and wisdom.

***

And whoever is moved by Faith to assent to it, is conscious of a continued miracle in his own person, which subverts all the principles of his understanding, and gives him a determination to believe what is most contrary to custom and experience.

***

The religious hypothesis, therefore, must be considered only as a particular method of accounting for the visible phenomena of the universe: but no just reasoner will ever presume to infer from it any single fact, and alter or add to the phenomena, in any single particular.

***

But to proceed in this reconciling project with regard to the question of liberty and necessity; the most contentious question of metaphysics, the most contentious science...

***

I do not think a philosopher who would apply himself so earnestly to the explaining the ultimate principles of the soul, would show himself a great master in the very science of human nature, which he pretends to explain, or very knowing in what is naturally satisfactory to the mind of man.

***

But would we know, whether the pretended prophet had really attained a just sentiment of morals? Let us attend to his narration; and we shall soon find, that he bestows praise on such instances of treachery, inhumanity, cruelty, revenge, bigotry, as are utterly incompatible with civilized society. No steady rule of right seems there to be attended to, and every action is blamed or praised, so far only as it is beneficial or hurtful to the true believers.

***

And indeed, nothing but the most determined skepticism, along with a great degree of indolence, can justify this aversion to metaphysics. For if truth, be at all within reach of human capacity, it is certain it must lie very deep and abstruse: and to hope we shall arrive at it without pains, while the greatest geniuses have failed with the utmost pains, must certainly be esteemed sufficiently vain and presumptuous. I pretend to no such advantage in the philosophy I am going to unfold and would esteem it a strong presumption against it, was it so very easy and obvious.

***

It is certain that the easy and obvious philosophy will always, with the generality of mankind, have preference above the accurate.

***

Nothing is more dangerous to reason than the flights of the imagination, and nothing has been the occasion of more mistakes among philosophers.

***

A too great disproportion among the citizens weakens any state. Every person, if possible, ought to enjoy the fruits of his labor, in full possession of all the necessities, and many of the conveniences of life. No one can doubt, but such equality is most suitable to human nature and diminishes much less from the happiness of the rich than it adds to that of the poor.

***

All knowledge resolves itself into probability. ... In every judgment, which we can form concerning probability, as well as concerning knowledge, we ought always to correct the first judgment derived from the nature of the object, by another judgment, derived from the nature of the understanding.

***

All knowledge degenerates into probability.

***

Convulsions in nature, disorders, prodigies, miracles, though the most opposite of the plan of a wise superintendent, impress mankind with the strongest sentiments of religion.

***

The greatest crimes have been found, in many instances, to be compatible with a superstitious piety and devotion; hence it is justly regarded as unsafe to draw any inference in favor of a man's morals, from the fervor or strictness of his religious exercises, even though he himself believe them sincere.

All the sciences have a relation, greater or less, to human nature; and... however wide any of them may seem to run from it, they still return back by one passage or another. Even Mathematics, Natural Philosophy, and Natural Religion are in some measure dependent on the science of MAN; since they lie under the cognizance of men, and are judged of by their powers and faculties.

***

Look round this universe. What an immense profusion of beings, animated and organized, sensible and active! You admire this prodigious variety and fecundity. But inspect a little more narrowly these living existences, the only beings worth regarding. How hostile and destructive to each other! How insufficient all of them for their own happiness! How contemptible or odious to the spectator! The whole presents nothing but the idea of a blind Nature, impregnated by a great vivifying principle, and pouring forth from her lap, without discernment or parental care, her maimed and abortive children.

***

I do not have enough faith to believe there is no god.

***

God is an ever-present spirit guiding all that happens to a wise and holy end.

***

The many instances of forged miracles, and prophecies, and supernatural events, which, in all ages, have either been detected by contrary evidence, or which detect themselves by their absurdity, prove sufficiently the strong propensity of mankind to the extraordinary and marvelous, and ought reasonably to begat a suspicion against all relations of this kind.

***

If ... the past may be no Rule for the future, all Experience becomes useless and can give rise to no Inferences or Conclusions.

***

The unhappy of all men is he who believes himself to be so.

***

This are evident that all reasonings concerning matter of fact are founded on the relation of cause and effect, and that we can never infer the existence of one object from another, unless they are connected together, either mediately or immediately... Here is a billiard ball lying on the table, and another ball moving toward it with rapidity. They strike, and the ball which was formerly at rest now acquires a motion. This is as perfect an instance of the relation of cause and effect as any which we know, either by sensation or reflection.

***

To consider the matter aright, the reason is nothing but a wonderful and unintelligible instinct in our souls, which carries us along a certain train of ideas, and endows them with particular qualities, according to their particular situations and relations. This instinct, 'is true, arises from past observation and experience; but can anyone give the ultimate reason, why past experience and observation produces such an effect, any more than why nature alone should produce it?

* * *

All this creative power of the mind amounts to no more than the faculty of compounding, transposing, augmenting, or diminishing the materials afforded us the by senses and experience.

* * *

Curiosity, or the love of knowledge, has very limited influence and requires youth, leisure education, genius and example to make it govern any person.

* * *

[A person's] utmost art and industry can never equal the meanest of nature's productions, either for beauty or value.

* * *

If suicide be supposed a crime, it is only cowardice can impel us to it. If it be no crime, both prudence and courage should engage us to rid ourselves at once of existence when it becomes a burden. It is the only way that we can then be useful to society, by setting an example which, if imitated, would preserve everyone his chance for happiness in life, and would effectually free him from all danger or misery.

* * *

I am ready to reject all belief and reasoning and can look upon no opinion even as more probable or likely than another.

* * *

the senses alone are not implicitly to be depended on. We must correct their evidence by reason, and by considerations, derived from the nature of the medium, the distance of the object, and the disposition of the organ, in order to render them, within their sphere, the proper criteria of truth and falsehood.

***

Luxury is a word of uncertain signification and may be taken in a good as in a bad sense.

***

When any opinion leads us into absurdities, 'is certainly false; but 'tis not certain opinion is false, because 'is of dangerous consequence.

***

The anticipation of pleasure is, in itself, a very considerable pleasure.

***

Such a superiority does the pursuits of literature possess above every other occupation, that even he who attains but a mediocrity in them, merits the pre-eminence above those that excel the most in the common and vulgar professions.

***

But the most common species of love is that which first arises from beauty, and afterward diffuses itself into kindness and into the bodily appetite. Kindness or esteem, and the appetite to generation are too remote to unite easily together. The one is, perhaps, the most refined passion of the soul; the other the grossest and vulgar. The love of beauty is placed in a just medium betwixt them and partakes of both their natures: From whence it proceeds, that it is so singularly fitted to produce both.

The most pernicious of all taxes are arbitrary.

of the world and drudgery of business, seeks a pretense of reason to give itself a full and uncontrolled indulgence.

Were a stranger to drop on a sudden into this world, I would show him, as a specimen of its ills, a hospital full of diseases, a prison crowded with malefactors and debtors, a field of battle strewed with carcasses, a fleet foundering in the ocean, a nation languishing under tyranny, famine, or pestilence. To turn the gay side of life to him, and give him a notion of its pleasures; whither should I conduct him? to a ball, to an opera, to court? He might justly think, that I was only showing him a diversity of distress and sorrow.

In the sphere of natural investigation, as in poetry and painting, the delineation of that which appeals most strongly to the imagination derives its collective interest from the vivid truthfulness with which the individual features are portrayed.

It cannot reasonably be doubted, but a little miss, dressed in a new gown for a dancing-school ball, receives as complete enjoyment as the greatest orator, who triumphs in the splendor of his eloquence, while he governs the passions and resolutions of a numerous assembly.

Truth is disputable, not human taste.

**

The fact that different cultures have different practices no more refutes [moral] objectivism than the fact that water flows in different directions in different places refutes the law of gravity.

**

The bigotry of theologians is a malady which seems almost incurable.

**

When I shall be dead, the principles of which I am composed will still perform their part in the universe and will be equally useful in the grand fabric, as when they composed this individual creature. The difference to the whole will be no greater betwixt my being in a chamber and in the open air. The one change is of more importance to me than the other; but not more so to the universe.

**

I am apt to suspect the Negroes to be naturally inferior to the Whites. There scarcely ever was a civilization of their complexion, nor even any individual, eminent either in action or speculation.

**

Human happiness seems to consist of three ingredients: action, pleasure, and indolence.

**

It is with books as with women, where a certain plainness of manner and of the dress is more engaging than that glare of paint and airs and apparel which may dazzle the eye, but reaches not the affections.

∗∗∗

Apart from the representational content of an idea, there is another component: its force and vivacity, its impetus.

∗∗∗

We have no other notion of cause and effect, but that of certain objects, which have always conjoined together, and which in all past instances have been found inseparable. We cannot penetrate into the reason of the conjunction. We only observe the thing itself, and always find that from the constant conjunction the objects acquire a union in the imagination.

∗∗∗

There is nothing, in itself, valuable or despicable, desirable or hateful, beautiful or deformed; but that these attributes arise from the particular constitution and fabric of human sentiment and affection.

∗∗∗

To philosopher and historian, the madness and imbecile wickedness of mankind ought to appear ordinary events.

∗∗∗

Kitsch is a species of beauty, which, as it is florid and superficial, pleases at first; but soon palls upon the taste, and is rejected with disdain, at least rated at a much lower value.

∗∗∗

It is harder to avoid censure than to gain applause; for this may be done by one great or wise action in an age. But to escape censure a man must pass his whole life without saying or doing one ill or foolish thing.

***

Nothing is so convenient as a decisive argument ... which must at least silence the most arrogant bigotry and superstition, and free us from their impertinent solicitations. I flatter myself that I have discovered an argument ... which, if just, will, with the wise and learned, be an everlasting check to all kinds of superstitious delusion, and consequently, will be useful as long as the world endures. For so long, I presume, will the accounts of miracles and prodigies be found in all history, sacred and profane.

Dennis Waitley

Denis E. **Waitley** (born 1933), is an American motivational speaker, writer, and consultant.

***

Mistakes are painful when they happen, but years later a collection of mistakes is what is called experience.

***

If you believe you can, you probably can. If you believe you won't, you most assuredly won't. Belief is the ignition switch that gets you off the launching pad.

***

Forget about the consequences of failure. Failure is only a temporary change in direction to set you straight for your next success.

***

As long as we are persistence in the pursuit of our deepest destiny, we will continue to grow. We cannot choose the day or time when we will fully bloom. It happens in its own time.

***

Don't dwell on what went wrong. Instead, focus on what to do next. Spend your energies on moving forward toward finding the answer.

***

Expect the best, plan for the worst, and prepare to be surprised.

***

You must learn from your past mistakes, but not lean on your past successes.

***

Our limitations and success will be based, most often, on your expectations for ourselves. What the mind dwells upon, the body acts upon.

***

The reason most people never reach their goals is that they don't define them, learn about them, or even seriously consider them as believable or achievable. Winners can tell you where they are going, what they plan to do along the way, and who will be sharing the adventure with them.

***

To establish true self-esteem, we must concentrate on our successes and forget about the failures and the negatives in our lives.

***

Failure should be our teacher, not our undertaker. Failure is a delay, not defeat. It is a temporary detour, not a dead end. Failure is something we can avoid only by saying nothing, doing nothing, and being nothing.

***

It's not what you are that holds you back; it's what you think you are not.

***

Where there is life, there is hope. Where there are hopes, there are dreams. Where there are vivid dreams repeated, they become goals. Goals become the action plans, and game plans that winners dwell on in intricate detail, knowing that achievement is almost automatic when the goal becomes an inner commitment. The response to the challenges of life -- purpose -- is the healing balm that enables each of us to face up to adversity and strife.

***

When you make a mistake or get ridiculed or rejected, look at mistakes as learning experiences, and ridicule as ignorance. . .. Look at rejection as part of one performance, not as a turn down of the performer.

***

Luck happens when opportunity encounters the prepared mind.

***

мYou must consider the bottom line, but make it integrity before profits.

***

Losers make promises they often break. Winners make commitments they always keep.

***

A life lived with integrity -- even if it lacks the trappings of fame and fortune is a shining star in whose light others may follow in the years to come.

***

No man or woman is an island. To exist just for yourself is meaningless. You can achieve the most satisfaction when you feel related to some greater purpose in life, something greater than yourself.

***

Procrastination is the fear of success. People procrastinate because they are afraid of the success that they know will result if they move ahead now. Because success is heavy, carries a responsibility with it, it is much easier to procrastinate and live on the 'someday I'll' philosophy.

***

Get excited and enthusiastic about your dream. This excitement is like a forest fire -- you can smell it, taste it, and see it from a mile away.

***

Life is not accountable to us. We are accountable to live.

***

We have got to have a dream if we are going to make a dream come true.

***

Out of need springs desire, and out of desire springs the energy and the will to win.

***

Life is a do-it-yourself project.

***

Life is the movie you see through your own eyes. It makes little difference what's happening out there. It's how you take it that counts.

***

Winners take time to relish their work, knowing that scaling the mountain is what makes the view from the top so exhilarating.

***

Happiness cannot be traveled to, owned, earned, worn or consumed. Happiness is the spiritual experience of living every minute with love, grace, and gratitude.

***

The greatest gifts you can give your children are the roots of responsibility and the wings of independence.

***

Love is a daily, mutual exchange of value.

***

A smile is a light in your window that tells others that there is a caring, sharing person inside.

***

Time is an equal opportunity employer. Each human being has the same number of hours and minutes every day. Rich people can't buy more hours. Scientists can't invent new minutes. And you can't save time to spend it on another day. Even so, time is amazingly fair and forgiving. No matter how much time you've wasted in the past, you still have an entire tomorrow.

Donald Trump

Donald John **Trump** (born June 14, 1946) **is** the 45th **president of** the United States.

***

I try to learn from the past, but I plan for the future by focusing exclusively on the present. That's where the fun is.

***

The point is that you can't be too greedy.

***

A little more moderation would be good. Of course, my life hasn't exactly been one of moderation.

***

Sometimes by losing a battle, you find a new way to win the war.

***

I try to learn from the past, but I plan for the future by focusing exclusively on the present. That's where the fun is. - Donald Trump.

***

Part of being a winner is knowing when enough is enough. Sometimes you have to give up the fight and walk away, and move on to something that's more productive.

***

Experience taught me a few things. One is to listen to your gut, no matter how good something sounds on paper. The second is that you're generally better off sticking with what you know. And the third is that sometimes your best investments are the ones you don't make.

***

You have to think anyway, so why not think big?

***

Deals are my art form. Other people paint beautifully on canvas or write wonderful poetry. I like making deals, preferably big deals. That's how I get my kicks.

***

Money was never a big motivation for me, except as a way to keep score. The real excitement is playing the game.

Dr. Seuss

Theodor **Seuss** Geisel (born March 2, 1904—died September 24, 1991) was an American children's author, political cartoonist, and animator, best known for his work writing and illustrating more than 60 books.

✳✳✳

You'll miss the best things if you keep your eyes shut.

✳✳✳

Being crazy isn't enough.

✳✳✳

They say I'm old-fashioned and live in the past, but sometimes I think progress progresses too fast!

✳✳✳

Oh, the things you can find if you don't stay behind!

✳✳✳

In the places, I go there are things that I see that I never could spell if I stopped with the Z.

✳✳✳

How did it get so late so soon? Its night before its afternoon. December is here before its June. My goodness, how the time has flown. How did it get so late so soon?

✳✳✳

Fantasy is a necessary ingredient in living; it's a way of looking at life through the wrong end of a telescope.

***

Simple it's not, I am afraid you will find, for a mind-maker-upper to make up his mind.

***

I know, up on top you see great sights, but down here at the bottom, we, too, should have rights.

***

Today I shall behave as if this is the day I will be remembered.

***

I meant what I said, and I said what I meant.

***

In my world, everyone's a pony, and they all eat rainbows and poop butterflies!

***

Sometimes you will never know the value of a moment until it becomes a memory.

***

I'm telling you this cause you're one of my friends. My alphabet starts where your alphabet ends!

***

Think and wonder, wonder and think.

***

So be sure when you step, step with care and great tact. And remember that life's A Great Balancing Act. And will you succeed? Yes! You will, indeed! (98 and ¾ percent guaranteed) Kid, you'll move mountains.

✳✳✳

Only you can control your future.

✳✳✳

It's not about what it is; it's about what it can become.

✳✳✳

You're off to Great Places! Today is your day! Your mountain is waiting, So... get on your way!

✳✳✳

He who makes a beast out of himself gets rid of the pain of being a man

✳✳✳

You have brains in your head. You have feet in your shoes. You can steer yourself any direction you choose. You're on your own. And you know what you know. And YOU are the one who'll decide where to go...

✳✳✳

Don't cry because it's over. Smile because it happened.

✳✳✳

Remember me and smile, for it's better to forget than to remember me and cry.

**

It's opener there in the wide-open air.

**

You'll be on your way up! You'll be seeing great sights! You'll join the high fliers who soar to high heights.

**

Just tell yourself, Duckie, you're quite lucky!

**

With your head full of brains and your shoes full of feet, you're too smart to go down any not-so-good street.

**

Congratulations! Today is your day!

**

Think! You can think any Think that you wish!

**

Take every chance. Drop every fear. ****

**

Teeth are always in style.

**

You do not like them. So, you say. Try them! Try them! And you may!

**

And you very small persons will not have to die if you make yourselves heard! So come on, now, and TRY!

***

Today was good. Today was fun. Tomorrow is another one.

***

If you never did, you should. These things are fun and fun is good

***

From there to here, from here to there, funny things are everywhere!

***

I know it is wet and the sun is not sunny, but we can have lots of good fun that is funny.

***

It is fun to have fun, but you have to know how.

***

When he worked, he worked. But when he played, he PLAYED.

***

Day Play. We play all day. Night Fight. We fight all night.

***

People are weird. When we find someone with the weirdness that is compatible with ours, we team up and call it love.

***

You know you're in love when you can't fall asleep because the reality is finally better than your dreams.

***

I'm glad we had the times together to laugh and sing a song, seems like we just got started and then before you know it, the times we had together were gone.

***

Life's too short to wake up with regrets. So, love the people who treat you right, forgive the ones who don't and believe that everything happens for a reason. If you get a chance, take it. If it changes your life, let it. Nobody said it'd be easy; they just promised it would be worth it.

***

To the world, you may be one person, but to one person you may be the world.

***

Adults are just obsolete children and the hell with them.

***

Adults are just outdated children.

***

Children want the same things we want. To laugh, to be challenged, to be entertained, and delighted.

***

Sometimes, when I see my granddaughters make small discoveries of their own, I wish I were a child.

***

So, open your mouth, lad! For every voice count!

***

Why fit in when you were born to stand out?

***

A person's a person, no matter how small.

***

If you'd never been born, then you might be an Isn't! An Isn't has any fun at all. No, he didn't!

***

Don't give up. I believe in you all.

***

You are you. Now, isn't that pleasant?

***

I am what I am! That's a great thing to be! If I say so myself, Happy Birthday to me!

***

Be who you are and say what you feel because those who mind don't matter, and those who matter don't mind.

***

Sometimes the questions are complicated, and the answers are simple.

***

I have heard there are troubles of more than one kind. Some come from ahead, and some come from behind. But I've bought a big bat. I'm already you see. Now my troubles are going to have troubles with me!

***

It's a troublesome world. All the people who are in it are troubled with troubles almost every minute. You ought to be thankful, a whole heaping lot, for the places and people you're lucky you're not.

***

Unless someone like you cares a whole awful lot, nothing is going to get better. It's not.

***

If things start happening, don't worry, don't stew, go right along and you'll start happening too.

***

All alone! Whether you like it or not, alone is something you'll be quite a lot!

***

Everything stinks till it's finished.

***

You're in pretty good shape for the shape you are in.

***

I'm sorry to say so but, sadly it's true that bang-ups and hang-ups can happen to you.

***

Things may happen and often do to people as brainy and footsy as you.

***

I'm afraid sometimes you'll play lonely games too, games you can't win because you'll play against you.

***

When you're in a Slump, you're not in for much fun. Un-slumping yourself is not easily done.

***

You're never too old, too wacky, too wild, to pick up a book and read to a child.

***

Be awesome! Be a book nut!

***

The problem with writing a book in verse is, to be successful, it has to sound like you knocked it off on a rainy Friday afternoon. It has to sound easy. When you can do it, it helps tremendously because it's a thing that forces kids to read on. You have this unconsummated feeling if you stop.

***

'The Lorax' book was intended to be propaganda.

***

You can find magic wherever you look. Sit back and relax; all you need is a book.

***

Preachers in pulpits talked about what a great message is in the book. No matter what you do, somebody always imputes meaning into your books.

***

I stay out of politics because if I begin thinking too much about politics, I'll probably... drop writing children's books and become a political cartoonist again.

***

I am not a consecutive writer.

***

Whenever things go a bit sour in a job I'm doing, I always tell myself, 'You can do better than this.'

***

So the writer who breeds more words than he needs is doing a chore for the reader who reads.

***

The more that you read, the more things you will know. The more that you learn, the more places you'll go.

***

You have to be a speedy reader because there's so so much to read.

∗

You can get help from teachers, but you are going to have to learn a lot by yourself, sitting alone in a room.

∗

It is better to know how to learn than to know.

∗

I like nonsense; it wakes up the brain cells.

∗

If you keep your eyes open enough, oh, the stuff you will learn. Oh, the most wonderful stuff.

∗

Think left and think right and think low and think high. Oh, the thinks you can think up if only you try!

∗

There's no limit to how much you'll know, depending on how far beyond zebra you go.

∗

Words and pictures are yin and yang. Married, they produce a progeny more interesting than either parent.

∗

What it said to me is how hard the people at our school work, … All of our employees who work here are working hard to do what's right for our kids.

✳✳✳

I would not like them here or there. I would not like them anywhere. I do not like green eggs and ham. I do not like them, Sam, I Am.

✳✳✳

Christmas doesn't come from a store, maybe Christmas perhaps means a little bit more....

✳✳✳

We looked! Then we saw him. Step in on the mat! We looked! And we saw him! The Cat in the Hat!

✳✳✳

So, on beyond Z! It's high time you were shown. That you don't know. All there is to be known.

✳✳✳

Just go. Go. Go! I don't care how. You can go by foot. You can go by cow.

✳✳✳

And that is a story that no one can beat. When I say that I saw it on Mulberry Street.

✳✳✳

And turtles, of course… all the turtles are FREE. As turtles and, maybe, ALL creatures should be.

Earl Nightingale

Earl Nightingale (March 12, 1921 – March 25, 1989) was an American radio speaker and author, dealing mostly with the subjects of human nature.

***

You become what you think about.

***

Our attitude toward life determines life's attitude towards us.

***

People with goals succeed because they know where they're going.

***

Success is the progressive realization of a worthy goal or ideal

***

Open your ears before you open your mouth; it may surprise your eyes!

***

Am I motivated by what I want out of life — or am I mass-motivated?

***

Your world is a living expression of how you are using and have used your mind

***

We can let circumstances rule us, or we can take charge and rule our lives from within

***

All you need is the plan, the road map, and the courage to press on to your destination

***

We can help others in the world more by making the most of yourself than in any other way.

***

Whenever we're afraid, its because we don't know enough. If we understood enough, we would never be afraid.

***

Whatever we plant in our subconscious mind and nourish with repetition and emotion will one day become a reality

***

People are where they are because that's exactly where they want to be.

. . whether they'll admit that or not

***

Wherever there is a danger, there lurks opportunity; whenever there is an opportunity, there lurks danger. The two are inseparable. They go together.

***

A great attitude does much more than turn on the lights in our worlds; it seems to magically connect us to all sorts of serendipitous opportunities that were somehow absent before the change.

***

Spoken about Earl Nightingale by Steve King, radio announcer and good friend: Earl Nightingale never let a day go by that he didn't learn something new and, in turn, pass it on to others. It was his consuming passion.

***

We are at our very best, and we are happiest when we are fully engaged in work we enjoy on the journey toward the goal we've established for ourselves. It gives meaning to our time off and comfort to our sleep. It makes everything else in life so wonderful, so worthwhile.

***

For a person to build a rich and rewarding life for himself, there are certain qualities and bits of knowledge that he needs to acquire. There are also things, harmful attitudes, superstitions, and emotions that he needs to chip away. A person needs to chip away everything that doesn't look like the person he or she most wants to become.

***

We tend to live up to our expectations.

***

You'll find boredom where a good idea is absent.

***

Creativity is a natural extension of our enthusiasm.

***

Everything in the world we want to do or get done, we must do with and through people.

***

Get into a line that you will find to be a deep personal interest, something you enjoy spending twelve to fifteen hours a day working at, and the rest of the time thinking about.

***

Learn to enjoy every minute of your life. Be happy now. Don't wait for something outside of yourself to make you happy in the future. Think about how precious is the time you have to spend, whether it's at work or with your family. Every minute should be enjoyed and savored.

Our first journey is to find that special place for us

George Washington

George Washington (born February **22**, 1732—died December **14**, 1799) was a political leader, general, statesman, and Founding Father who served as the first President of the United States (1789–1797).

***

My mother was the most beautiful woman I ever saw. All I am I owe to my mother. I attribute all my success in life to the moral, intellectual and physical education I received from her.

***

Liberty, when it begins to take root, is a plant of rapid growth. -George Washington

***

My first wish is to see this plague of humanity, war, banished from the earth.

***

True friendship is a plant of slow growth and must undergo and withstand the shocks of adversity before it is entitled to the appellation.

***

Let us with caution indulge the supposition that morality can be maintained without religion. Reason and experience both forbid us to expect that national morality can prevail in exclusion of religious principle.

***

Labor to keep alive in your breast that little spark of celestial fire, called conscience.

✳✳✳

I have always considered marriage as the most interesting event of one's life, the foundation of happiness or misery.

✳✳✳

Be courteous to all, but intimate with few, and let those few be well tried before you give them your confidence.

✳✳✳

If we desire to avoid insult, we must be able to repel it; if we desire to secure peace, one of the most powerful instruments of our rising prosperity, it must be known, that we are at all times ready for War.

✳✳✳

I hope I shall possess firmness and virtue enough to maintain what I consider the most enviable of all titles, the character of an honest man.

✳✳✳

The foolish and wicked practice of profane cursing and swearing is a vice so mean and low that every person of sense and character detests and despises it.

✳✳✳

The alternate domination of one faction over another, sharpened by the spirit of revenge natural to party dissension, which in different ages and countries has perpetrated the most horrid enormities, is itself a frightful despotism. But this leads at length to a more formal and permanent despotism.

***

Lenience will operate with greater force, in some instances than rigor. It is, therefore, my first wish to have all of my conduct distinguished by it.

***

To be prepared for war is one of the most effective means of preserving peace. -George Washington

***

We should not look back unless it is to derive useful lessons from past errors, and to profit by dearly bought experience.

***

The basis of our political system is the right of the people to make and to alter their constitutions of government.

***

If the freedom of speech is taken away then dumb and silent, we may be led, like sheep to the slaughter.

***

The Constitution is the guide which I never will abandon.

***

There is nothing which can better deserve your patronage, then the promotion of science and literature. Knowledge is in every country the surest basis of public happiness.

***

Associate with men of good quality if you esteem your reputation.

***

Laws made by common consent must not be trampled on by individuals.

***

Someday, following the example of the United States of America, there will be a United States of Europe.

***

Religion is as necessary to reason as reason is to religion. One cannot exist without the other. A reasoning being would lose his reason, in attempting to account for the great phenomena of nature, had he not a Supreme Being to refer to; and well has it been said, that if there had been no God, humankind would have been obliged to imagine one.

***

Nothing can be more hurtful to the service, than the neglect of discipline; for that discipline, more than numbers gives one army the superiority over another.

***

Discipline is the soul of an army. It makes small numbers formidable; procures success to the weak, and esteem to all.

***

Friendship is a plant of slow growth and must undergo and withstand the shocks of adversity before it is entitled to the appellation.

***

Arbitrary power is most easily established on the ruins of liberty abused to licentiousness.

***

War – An act of violence whose object is to constrain the enemy, to accomplish our will.

***

A slender acquaintance with the world must convince every man that actions, not words, are the true criterion of the attachment of friends.

***

There can be no greater error than to expect or calculate, upon real favors from nation to nation. It is an illusion which experience must cure, which a just pride ought to discard.

***

Worry is the interest paid by those who borrow trouble.

***

My observation is that whenever one person is found adequate to the discharge of a duty... it is worse executed by two persons, and scarcely done at all if three or more are employed therein.

***

I beg you to be persuaded that no one would be more zealous than myself to establish effectual barriers against the horrors of spiritual tyranny and every species of religious persecution.

***

I am persuaded, you will permit me to observe, that the path of true piety is so plain as to require but little political direction.

***

I know of no pursuit in which more real and important services can be rendered to any country than by improving its agriculture, its breed of useful animals, and other branches of a husbandman's cares.

***

The Constitution which at any time exists, 'till changed by an explicit and authentic act of the whole People is sacredly obligatory upon all.

***

Guard against the impostures of pretended patriotism.

***

To form a new Government requires infinite care and unbounded attention; for if the foundation is badly laid the superstructure must be bad.

***

The tumultuous populace of large cities is ever to be dreaded. Their indiscriminate violence prostrates for the time all public authority, and its consequences are sometimes extensive and terrible.

***

The establishment of Civil and Religious Liberty was the Motive which induced me to the Field — the object is attained

— and it now remains to be my earnest wish & prayer, that the Citizens of the United States could make wise and virtuous use of the blessings placed before them.

***

But if we are to be told by a foreign power what we shall do, and what we shall not do, we have Independence yet to seek and have contended hitherto for very little.

Gentlemen, you will permit me to put on my spectacles, for, I have grown not only gray but almost blind in the service of my country.

***

It is better to offer no excuse than a bad one

***

Government is not reason, and it is not eloquence. It is a force! Like fire, it is a dangerous servant and a fearful master. Never for a moment should it be left to irresponsible action.

***

It should be the highest ambition of every American to extend his views beyond himself, and to bear in mind that his conduct will not only affect himself, his country, and his immediate posterity; but that its influence may be co-extensive with the world, and stamp political happiness or misery on ages yet unborn.

***

The Hand of Providence has been so conspicuous in all this, that he must be worse than an infidel that lacks faith, and more than wicked, that has not gratitude enough to acknowledge his obligations.

***

I do not mean to exclude altogether the idea of patriotism. I know it exists, and I know it has done much in the present contest. But I will venture to assert, that a great and lasting war can never be supported on this principle alone. It must be aided by a prospect of interest or some reward.

***

The foundations of our national policy will be laid in the pure and immutable principles of private morality, and the preeminence of free government be exemplified by all the attributes which can win the affections of its citizens, and command the respect of the world.

***

It is better to be alone than in bad company.

***

The preservation of the sacred fire of liberty, and the destiny of the republican model of government are justly considered deeply, perhaps as finally, staked on the experiment entrusted to the hands of the American people.

***

[Gambling] is the child of avarice, the brother of iniquity, and the father of mischief.

***

No country upon earth ever had it more in its power to attain these blessings than United America. Wondrously strange, then, and much to be regretted indeed would it be, were we to neglect the means and to depart from the road which Providence has pointed us to so plainly; I cannot believe it will ever come to pass.

***

Overgrown military establishments are under any form of government inauspicious to liberty, and are to be regarded as particularly hostile to republican liberty.

***

I hope, some day or another, we shall become a storehouse and granary for the world.

***

To contract new debts is not the way to pay old ones. -George Washington

***

The time is near at hand which must determine whether Americans are to be free men or slaves.

***

Where is the security for property, for reputation, for life, if the sense of religious obligation deserts the oaths?

***

Let us raise a standard to which the wise and honest can repair; the rest is in the hands of God.

***

Citizens by birth or choice of a common country, that country has a right to concentrate your affections. The name of American, which belongs to you, in your national capacity, must always exalt the just pride of Patriotism, more than any appellation derived from local discriminations.

✳✳✳

I anticipate with pleasing expectations that retreat in which I promise myself to realize, without alloy, the sweet enjoyment of partaking, in the midst of my fellow citizens, the benign influence of good laws under a free government, the ever favorite object of my heart, and the happy reward, as I trust, of our mutual cares, labors, and dangers.

✳✳✳

Observe good faith and justice toward all nations. Cultivate peace and harmony with all. -George Washington

✳✳✳

Jealousy, and local policy mix too much in all our public councils for the good government of the Union. In words, the confederation appears to me to be little more than a shadow without the substance.

✳✳✳

I wish from my soul that the legislature of this State could see the policy of a gradual Abolition of Slavery.

✳✳✳

I go to the chair of government with feelings, not unlike those of a culprit who is going to the place of his execution.

✳✳✳

The value of liberty was thus enhanced in our estimation by the difficulty of its attainment, and the worth of characters appreciated by the trial of adversity.

***

Mankind, when left to themselves, are unfit for their own government.

***

Few people have the virtue to withstand the highest bidder

***

We are either a United people, or we are not. If the former, let us, in all matters of general concern act as a nation, which has national objects to promote, and a national character to support. If we are not, let us no longer act a farce by pretending to it.

***

When we assumed the Soldier, we did not lay aside the Citizen.

***

The Army (considering the irritable state it is in, its suffering and composition) is a dangerous instrument to play with.

***

Your love of liberty – your respect for the laws – your habits of the industry – and your practice of the moral and religious obligations, are the strongest claims to national and individual happiness.

***

The democratical States must always feel before they can see: it is this that makes their Governments slow, but the people will be right at last.

✱✱✱

The truth will ultimately prevail where there are pains to bring it to light. -

✱✱✱

The foundation of a great Empire is laid, and I please myself with a persuasion, that Providence will not leave its work imperfect.

✱✱✱

Having now finished the work assigned me, I retire from the great theatre of Action; and bidding an Affectionate farewell to this August body under whose orders I have so long acted, I here offer my commission, and take my leave of all the employments of public life.

✱✱✱

The liberty enjoyed by the people of these states of worshiping Almighty God agreeably to their conscience, is not only among the choicest of their blessings, but also of their rights.

✱✱✱

It appears to me, then, little short of a miracle, that the Delegates from so many different States should unite in forming a system of national Government, so little liable to well founded objections.

✱✱✱

In proportion as the structure of a government gives force to public opinion, it is essential that public opinion should be enlightened.

***

Let your heart feel for the afflictions and distress of everyone, and let your hand give in proportion to your purse. -George Washington

***

'Tis our true policy to steer clear of permanent alliances with any portion of the foreign world.

***

No morn ever dawned more favorable than ours did, and no day was every more clouded than the present! Wisdom, and good examples are necessary at this time to rescue the political machine from the impending storm.

***

[A] good moral character is the first essential in a man, and that the habits contracted at your age are generally indelible, and your conduct here may stamp your character through life. It is therefore highly important that you should endeavor not only to be learned but virtuous.

***

The propitious smiles of Heaven can never be expected on a nation that disregards the eternal rules of order and right, which Heaven itself has ordained.

***

Honesty will be found on every experiment, to be the best and only true policy; let us then as a Nation be. -George Washington

***

Every post is honorable in which a man can serve his country.

***

More permanent and genuine happiness is to be found in the sequestered walks of connubial life than in the giddy rounds of promiscuous pleasure.

***

A people who are possessed of the spirit of commerce, who see and who will pursue their advantages may achieve almost anything.

***

A man's intentions should be allowed in some respects to plead for his actions.

***

I shall make it the most agreeable part of my duty to study merit, and reward the brave and deserving.

***

99% of failures come from people who make excuses. -George Washington

***

No taxes can be devised which are not more or less inconvenient and unpleasant.

✳✳✳

I hold the maxim no less applicable to public than to private affairs that honesty is the best policy.

✳✳✳

Nothing is a greater stranger to my breast or a sin that my soul more abhors, than that black and detestable one, ingratitude.

✳✳✳

Of all the animosities which have existed among humankind, those which are caused by a difference of sentiments in religion appear to be the most inveterate and distressing, and ought most to be deprecated.

✳✳✳

I was summoned by my country, whose voice I can never hear but with veneration and love.

✳✳✳

We must take human nature as we find it; perfection falls not to the share of mortals.

✳✳✳

There is a Destiny which has the control of our actions, not to be resisted by the strongest efforts of Human Nature.

✳✳✳

The government of the United States is not, in any sense, founded on the Christian religion.

I shall not be deprived ... of comfort in the worst event, if I retain a consciousness of having acted to the best of my judgment.

✳✳✳

Perseverance and spirit have done wonders in all ages.

✳✳✳

The consciousness of having discharged that duty which we owe to our country is superior to all other considerations.

✳✳✳

Happiness and moral duty are inseparably connected.

✳✳✳

The harder the conflict, the greater the triumph.

✳✳✳

A sensible woman can never be happy with a fool.

✳✳✳

The turning points of lives are not great moments. The real crises are often concealed in occurrences so trivial in appearance that they pass unobserved.

✳✳✳

I conceive a knowledge of books is the basis upon which other knowledge is to be built.

✳✳✳

To encourage literature and the arts is a duty which every good citizen owes to his country.

***

The best and only safe road to honor glory, and true dignity is justice.

***

The great rule of conduct for us, regarding foreign nations, is, in extending our commercial relations, to have with them as little political connection as possible.

***

A bad war is fought with a good mind.

***

Strive not with your superiors in argument, but always submit your judgment to others with modesty.

Immanuel Kant

Immanuel Kant (1724-1804) is one of the most influential philosophers in the history of Western philosophy.

***

Seek not the favor of the multitude; it is seldom got by honest and lawful means. But seek the testimony of few; and number, not voices, but weigh them.

***

Science is organized knowledge. Wisdom is organized life.

***

From such crooked wood as that which man is made of, nothing straight can be fashioned.

***

By a lie, a man...annihilates his dignity as a man.

***

It is not God's will merely that we should be happy, but that we should make ourselves happy

***

A person is only a person when it has the power to make sense of its surrounding.

***

So act that your principle of action might safely be made a law for the whole world.

***

Morality is not the doctrine of how we may make ourselves happy, but how we may make ourselves worthy of happiness.

***

Out of timber so crooked as that from which man is made nothing entirely straight can be carved.

***

All the interests of my reason, speculative as well as practical, combine in the three following questions: What can I know? 2. What ought I to do? 3. What may I hope?

***

There is, therefore, only one categorical imperative. It is: Act only according to that maxim by which you can at the same time will that it should become a universal law.

***

Act as if the maxim of your action were to become through your will a be general natural law.

***

Nothing is divine but what is agreeable to reason.

***

All thought must, directly or indirectly, by way of certain characters, relate ultimately to intuitions, and therefore, with us, to sensibility, because in no other way can an object be given to us.

***

Ours is an age of criticism, to which everything must be subjected. The sacredness of religion and the authority of legislation are by many regarded as grounds for exemption from the examination by this tribunal, But, if they are exempted, and cannot lay claim to sincere respect, which reason accords only to that which has stood the test of a free and public examination.

***

Enlightenment is man's emergence from his self-incurred immaturity. Immaturity is the inability to use one's understanding without the guidance of another. This immaturity is self-incurred if its cause is not lack of understanding, but lack of resolution and courage to use it without the guidance of another. The motto of enlightenment is therefore: Sapere Aude! Have the courage to use your understanding!

***

All human knowledge begins with intuitions, proceeds from thence to concepts, and ends with ideas.

***

An organized product of nature is that in which all the parts are mutually ends and means.

***

Give me matter, and I will construct a world out of it!

***

God put a secret art into the forces of Nature to enable it to fashion itself out of chaos into a perfect world system.

***

In scientific matters ... the greatest discoverer differs from the most arduous imitator and apprentices only in degree, whereas he differs in kind from someone whom nature has endowed for fine art. But saying this does not disparage those great men to whom the human race owes so much in contrast to those whom nature has endowed for fine art.

***

Nature even in chaos cannot proceed otherwise than regularly and according to order.

***

Notion without intuition is empty, intuition without notion is blind.

***

Our knowledge springs from two fundamental sources of the mind; the first is the capacity of receiving representations (receptivity for impressions), the second is the power of knowing an object through these representations (spontaneity [in the production] of concepts).

***

Reason must approach nature with the view, indeed, of receiving information from it, not, however, in the character of a pupil, who listens to all that his master chooses to tell him, but in that of a judge, who compels the witnesses to reply to those questions which he thinks fit to propose. To this single idea must the revolution be ascribed, by which, after groping in the dark for so many centuries, natural science was at length conducted into the path of certain progress.

***

The idea of the supreme being is nothing but a regulative principle of reason which directs us to look upon all connection in the world as if it originated from an all-sufficient necessary cause.

***

Two things fill the mind with ever new and increasing admiration and awe, the oftener and more steadily they are reflected on: the starry heavens above me and the moral law within me.

***

Without the sensuous faculty, no object would be given to us, without understanding no object would be thought. Thoughts without content are void, intuitions without conceptions, blind.

***

Historically the most striking result of Kant's labors was the rapid separation of the thinkers of his nation and, though less completely, of the world, into two parties; —the philosophers and the scientists.

***

We are not rich by what we possess but by what we can do without.

***

Act in such a way that you treat humanity, whether in your person or the person of any other, never merely as a means to an end, but always at the same time as an end.

***

Dare to think!

***

Look closely. The beautiful may be small.

***

For peace to reign on Earth, humans must evolve into new beings who have learned to see the whole first

***

The busier we are, the more acutely we feel that we live, the more conscious we are of life.

***

The death of dogma is the birth of morality.

***

Have patience awhile; slanders are not long-lived. Truth is the child of time; erelong she shall appear to vindicate thee.

***

Age cannot bind itself and ordain to put the succeeding one into such a condition that it cannot extend its (at best very occasional) knowledge, purify itself of errors, and progress in general enlightenment. That would be a crime against human nature, the proper destination of which lies precisely in this progress and the descendants would be fully justified in rejecting those decrees as having been made in an unwarranted and malicious manner.

***

How then is perfection to be sought? Wherein lies our hope? In education, and nothing else.

***

Genius is the ability to independently arrive at and understand concepts that would normally have to be taught by another person.

***

Thoughts without content are empty, intuitions without concepts are blind.

***

What might be said of things in themselves, separated from all related to our senses, remains for us unknown

***

Better the whole people perish than that injustice be done

***

Dignity is a value that creates irreplaceability.

***

Two things fill the mind with ever new and increasing admiration and reverence the more often, and more steadily one reflects on them, the starry heavens above me and the moral law within me.

***

To acquiesce in skepticism can never suffice to overcome the restlessness of reason.

***

The reading of all good books is like a conversation with the finest minds of past centuries.

***

Settle, for sure and universally, what conduct will promote the happiness of a rational being.

Jim Rohn

Jim Rohn (September 17, 1930 – December 5, 2009) was an American entrepreneur, author, and motivational speaker.

***

It doesn't matter which side of the fence you get off on sometimes. What matters most is getting off. You cannot make progress without making decisions.

***

Whoever renders service to many puts himself in line for greatness--great wealth, great return, great satisfaction, great reputation, and great joy.

***

For every disciplined effort, there is a multiple rewards.

***

Formal education will make you a living; self-education will make you a fortune.

***

Give whatever you are doing and whoever you are with the gift of your attention.

***

Words do two major things: They provide food for the mind and create light for understanding and awareness.

***

The worst thing one can do is not to try, to be aware of what one wants and not give in to it, to spend years in silent hurt wondering if something could have materialized--never know.

***

The major reason for setting a goal is for what it makes of you to accomplish it. What it makes of you will always be the far greater value than what you get.

***

To solve any problem, here are three questions to ask yourself: First, what could I do? Second, what could I read? And third, who could I ask?

***

Formal education will make you a living; self-education will make you a fortune.

***

Discipline is the bridge between goals and accomplishment.

***

The book you don't read can't help.

***

Success is neither magical or mysterious. Success is the natural consequence of consistently applying the fundamentals.

***

Success is nothing more than a few simple disciplines, practiced every day...

***

Success is not to be pursued; it is to be attracted by the person you become.

***

Either you run the day or the day runs you.

***

Whatever good things we build end up building us.

***

We must all suffer one of two things: the pain of discipline or the pain of regret or disappointment.

***

Take advantage of every opportunity to practice your communication skills so that when important occasions arise, you will have the gift, the style, the sharpness, the clarity, and the emotions to affect other people.

***

Effective communication is 20% what you know and 80% how you feel about what you know.

***

Some people plant in the spring and leave in the summer. If you're signed up for a season, see it through. You don't have to stay forever, but at least stay until you see it through.

***

Take care of your body. It's the only place you have to live in.

***

Don't wish it were easier; wish you were better.

***

You must take personal responsibility. You cannot change the circumstances, the seasons, or the wind, but you can change yourself. That is something you have charge of.

***

Don't say, If I could, I would. Say, If I can, I will

***

Every life form seems to strive to its maximum except human beings. How tall will a tree grow? As tall as it possibly can. Human beings, on the other hand, have been given the dignity of choice. You can choose to be all, or you can choose to be less. Why not stretch up to the full measure of the challenge and see what all you can do?

***

Indecision is the thief of opportunity.

***

You cannot change your destination overnight, but you can change your direction overnight.

John Lennon

John Winston Ono **Lennon** (9 October 1940 – 8 December 1980) was an English singer, songwriter, and peace activist who co-founded the Beatles.

***

Our society is run by insane people for insane objectives. I think maniacs are running us for maniacal ends and I think I'm liable to be put away as insane for expressing that. That's what's insane about it.

***

Love is the greatest refreshment in life.

***

I'm not going to change the way I look or the way I feel to conform to anything. I've always been a freak. So, I've been a freak all my life, and I have to live with that, you know. I'm one of those people.

***

Rituals are important. Nowadays it's hip not to be married. I'm not interested in being hip.

***

When I was five years old, my mother always told me that happiness was the key to life. When I went to school, they asked me what I wanted to be when I grew up. I wrote down 'happy.' They told me I didn't understand the assignment, and I told them they didn't understand life.

***

There are two basic motivating forces: fear and love. When we are afraid, we pull back from life. When we are in love, we open to all that life has to offer with passion, excitement, and acceptance. We need to learn to love ourselves first, in all our glory and our imperfections. If we cannot love ourselves, we cannot fully open to our ability to love others or our potential to create. Evolution and all hopes for a better world rest in the fearlessness and open-hearted vision of people who embrace life.

***

As usual, there is a great woman behind every idiot.

***

Count your age by friends, not years. Count your life by smiles, not tears.

***

Declare it. Just the same way we declare war. That is how we will have peace... we need to declare it.

***

I believe in everything until it's disproved. So, I believe in fairies, the myths, dragons. It all exists, even if it's in your mind. Who's to say that dreams and nightmares aren't as real as the here and now?

***

The living is easy with eyes closed.

***

If everyone demanded peace instead of another television set, then there'd be peace.

***

God is a concept by which we measure our pain.

***

If we cannot love ourselves, we cannot fully open to our ability
to love others or our potential to create.

***

There are two basic motivating forces: fear and love. When we
are afraid, we pull back from life.

***

Before Elvis there was nothing.

***

It matters not who you love, where you love, why you love,
when you love or how you love, it matters only that you love.

***

There's an alternative to violence. It's to stay in bed and grow
your hair.

***

I don't know which will go first- rock 'n' roll or Christianity.

***

Part of me suspects that I'm a loser, and the other part of me
thinks I'm God Almighty.

***

Everything is clearer when you're in love.

***

I believe in God, but not as one thing, not as an old man in the sky. I believe that what people call God is something in all of us. I believe that what Jesus and Mohammed and Buddha and all the rest said was right. It's just that the translations have gone wrong.

***

As in a love affair, two creative people can destroy themselves trying to recapture that youthful spirit, at twenty-one or twenty-four, of creating without even being aware of how it's happening.

***

Evolution and all hopes for a better world rest in the fearlessness and open-hearted vision of people who embrace life.

***

It's better to fade away like an old soldier than to burn out.

***

When I was about twelve, I used to think I must be a genius, but nobody's noticed. If there is such a thing as a genius…I am one, and if there isn't, I don't care.

***

We live in a world where we have to hide to make love, while violence is practiced in broad daylight.

***

You have to be a bastard to make it, and that's a fact.

***

Love is the flower you've got to let grow.

***

If everyone could be happy with themselves and the choices people around them make, the world would instantly be a better place!

***

Trying to please everybody is impossible – if you did that, you'd end up in the middle with nobody liking you. You've just got to decide what you think is your best and do it.

***

I'm not afraid of death because I don't believe in it. It's just getting out of one car, and into another.

***

Turn off your mind, relax, and float downstream.

***

I'm not a career person; I'm a gardener.

***

Love, Love, Love. All you need is love. Love is all you need.

***

All we are saying is give peace a chance.

***

There's nowhere you can be that isn't where you're meant to be...

***

If someone thinks that peace and love are just a cliché that must have been left behind in the 60s, that's a problem. Peace and love are eternal.

***

A mistake is only an error; it becomes a mistake when you fail to correct it.

***

Only by trying on other people's clothes do we find what size we are.

***

Produce your dream. If you want to save Peru, save Peru. It's quite possible to do anything, but not if you put it on the leaders and the parking meters. Don't expect Carter or Reagan or John Lennon or Yoko Ono or Bob Dylan or Jesus Christ to come and do it for you. You have to do it yourself.

***

Reality leaves a lot to the imagination.

***

We've got this gift of love, but love is like a precious plant. You can't just accept it and leave it in the cupboard or think it's going to get on by itself. You've got to keep watering it. You've got to look after it and nurture it.

***

Imagine all the people living life in peace. You may say I'm a dreamer, but I'm not the only one. I hope someday you'll join us, and the world will be as one.

✳✳✳

Music is everybody's possession. It's only publishers who think that people own it.

✳✳✳

My role in society, or any artist's or poet's role, is to try and express what we all feel. Not to tell people how to feel. Not as a preacher, not as a leader, but as a reflection of us all.

✳✳✳

There's nothing you can know that isn't known.

✳✳✳

Surrealism had a great effect on me because then I realized that the imagery in my mind wasn't insanity. Surrealism to me is the reality.

✳✳✳

One thing you can't hide – is when you're disabled inside.

✳✳✳

When you're drowning you don't think; I would be incredibly pleased if someone would notice I'm drowning and come and rescue me. You scream.

✳✳✳

The time you enjoy wasting was not wasted.

***

War is over … If you want it.

***

How can I go forward when I don't know which way I'm facing?

***

Love is a promise; love is a souvenir, once given never forgotten, never let it disappear.

***

When you do something beautiful, and nobody noticed, do not be sad. For the sun, every morning is a beautiful spectacle, and yet most of the audience still sleeps.

***

Everything will be okay in the end. If it's not okay, it's not the end.

***

Everybody loves you when you're six foot in the ground.

***

There is an alternative to war. It's staying in bed and growing your hair.

***

My defenses were so great. The cocky rock and roll hero who knows all the answers was a terrified guy who didn't know how to cry. Simple.

Creativity is a gift. It doesn't come through if the air is cluttered.

Well, I don't want to be king. I want to be real.

One thing I can tell you is you have to be free. Come together, right now, over me.

You know the way people begin to look like their dogs? Well, we're beginning to look like each other.

The thing the sixties did was to show us the possibilities and the responsibility that we all had. It wasn't the answer. It just gave us a glimpse of the possibility.

Get out there and get peace, think peace, and live peace and breathe peace, and you'll get it as soon as you like.

...Christianity will go. It will vanish and shrink. I don't know what will go first, rock 'n' roll or Christianity. We're more popular than Jesus now. Jesus was all right, but his disciples were thick and ordinary. It's them twisting it that ruins it for me.

When I cannot sing my heart, I can only speak my mind.

***

Sometimes you wonder, I mean wonder. I know we make our reality, and we always have a choice, but how much is preordained? Is there always a fork in the road, and are there two preordained paths that are equally preordained? There could be hundreds of paths where one could go this way or that way — there's a chance, and it's very strange sometimes.

***

A dream you dream alone is only a dream. A dream you dream together is a reality.

***

Peace is not something you wish for; It's something you make, something you do, something you are, and something you give away.

***

Our society is run by insane people for insane objectives. I think maniacs are running us for maniacal ends and I think I'm liable to be put away as insane for expressing that. That's what's insane about it.

***

Happiness is just how you feel when you don't feel miserable.

***

There's nothing new under the sun. All the roads lead to Rome. And people cannot provide it for you. I can't wake you up. You can wake you up. I can't cure you. You can cure you.

***

Being honest may not get you a lot of friends, but it'll always get you the right ones.

***

If you want peace, you won't get it with violence.

***

Yeah, we all shine on, like the moon, and the stars, and the sun.

***

It's weird not to be weird.

***

You either get tired fighting for peace, or you die.

***

I never went to high school reunions. My thing is, out of sight, out of mind. That's my attitude toward life. So I don't have any romanticism about any part of my past.

***

Nobody controls me. I'm uncontrollable. The only one who controls me is me, and that's just barely possible.

***

I believe Jesus was right, Buddha was right, and all of those people like that are right. They're all saying the same thing — and I believe it. I believe what Jesus said — the basic things he laid down about love and goodness — and not what people say he said.

***

Life is what happens to you while you're busy making other plans.

***

All music is a rehash. There are only a few notes. Just variations on a theme. Try to tell the kids in the Seventies who were screaming to the Bee Gees that their music was just The Beatles redone. There is nothing wrong with the Bee Gees.

***

Everything is as important as everything else.

***

I don't believe in killing whatever the reason!

***

Life is very short, and there's no time for fussing and fighting my friends.

***

We all have Hitler in us, but we also have love and peace. So why not give peace a chance for once?

***

I don't believe in yesterday, by the way.

***

What we've got to do is keep hope alive. Because without it we'll sink.

***

Art is only a way of expressing pain.

***

Time wounds all heels.

***

You're all geniuses, and you're all beautiful. You don't need anyone to tell you who you are. You are what you are.

***

It doesn't matter how long my hair is or what color my skin is or whether I'm a woman or a man.

***

I am a violent man who has learned not to be violent and regrets his violence.

***

I've never really been wanted.

***

You're just left with yourself all the time, whatever you do anyway. You've got to get down to your own God in your temple. It's all down to you, mate.

***

The more real you get, the more unreal the world gets.

***

If being an egomaniac means I believe in what I do and, in my art, or music, then in that respect, you can call me that... I believe in what I do, and I'll say it.

***

There are no problems, only solutions.

***

I put things down on sheets of paper and stuff them in my pockets. When I have enough, I have a book.

Luther Martin King Jr.

Martin Luther King Jr. (January 15, 1929 – April 4, 1968) was a social activist and Baptist minister who played a key role in the American civil rights movement from the mid-1950s until his.

***

We are not makers of history. We are made by history.

***

Lightning makes no sound until it strikes.

***

Every man must decide whether he will walk in the light of creative altruism or the darkness of destructive selfishness.

***

Science investigates; religion interprets. Science gives man knowledge, which is power; religion gives man wisdom, which is control. Science deals mainly with facts; religion deals mainly with values. The two are not rivals.

***

We must use time creatively, in the knowledge that the time is always ripe to do right.

***

There is nothing more tragic than to find an individual bogged down in the length of life, devoid of breadth.

***

Property is intended to serve life, and no matter how much we surround it with rights and respect, it has no personal being. It is part of the earth man walks on. It is not a man.

***

The function of education is to teach one to think intensively and to think critically. Intelligence plus character – that is the goal of true education.

***

We may have all come on different ships, but we're in the same boat now.

***

All labor that uplifts humanity has dignity and importance and should be undertaken with painstaking excellence.

***

An individual has not started living until he can rise above the narrow confines of his individualistic concerns to the broader concerns of all humanity.

***

Rarely do we find men who willingly engage in hard, solid thinking. There is an almost universal quest for easy answers and half-baked solutions. Nothing pains some people more than having to think.

***

Every man lives in two realms: the internal and the external. The internal is that realm of spiritual ends expressed in art, literature, morals, and religion. The external is that complex of devices, techniques, mechanisms, and instrumentalities using which we live.

✳✳✳

Shallow understanding from people of good will is more frustrating than absolute misunderstanding from people of ill will.

✳✳✳

There came a time when people get tired of being pushed out of the glittering sunlight of life's July and left standing amid the piercing chill of an alpine November.

✳✳✳

The quality, not the longevity, of one's life, is what is important.

✳✳✳

A lie cannot live.

✳✳✳

The past is prophetic in that it asserts loudly that wars are poor chisels for carving out peaceful tomorrows

✳✳✳

The limitation of riots, moral questions aside, is that they cannot win and their participants know it. Hence, rioting is not revolutionary but reactionary because it invites defeat. It involves an emotional catharsis, but it must be followed by a sense of futility.

✳✳✳

Love is the only force capable of transforming an enemy into a friend.

***

He who is devoid of the power to forgive is devoid of the power to love.

***

I believe that unarmed truth and unconditional love will have the final word in reality. This is why right, temporarily defeated, is stronger than evil triumphant.

***

There can be no deep disappointment where there is not deep love.

***

We must develop and maintain the capacity to forgive. He who is devoid of the power to forgive is devoid of the power to love. There is some good in the worst of us and some evil in the best of us. When we discover this, we are less prone to hate our enemies.

***

I have decided to stick with love. Hate is too great a burden to bear.

***

Nonviolence is an absolute commitment to the way of love. Love is not an emotional bash; it is not empty sentimentalism. It is the active outpouring of one's whole being into the being of another.

***

Man must evolve for all human conflict a method which rejects revenge, aggression, and retaliation. The foundation of such a method is love.

***

It is not enough to say we must not wage war. Loving peace and sacrifice for it are necessary.

***

If you can't fly then run, if you can't run then walk, if you can't walk then crawl, but whatever you do you have to keep moving forward.

***

Only in the darkness can you see the stars.

***

Let no man pull you so low as to hate him.

***

There comes a time when one must take a position that is neither safe nor politic nor popular, but he must take it because his conscience tells him it is right.

***

Everybody can be great ... because anybody can serve. You don't have to have a college degree to serve. You don't have to make your subject and verb agree to serve. You only need a heart full of grace. A soul generated by love.

***

No one knows why they are alive until they know what they'd die for.

✳✳✳

A man who won't die for something is not fit to live.

✳✳✳

We must build dikes of courage to hold back the flood of fear.

✳✳✳

We must accept finite disappointment but never lose infinite hope.

✳✳✳

Those who are not looking for happiness are the most likely to find it because those who are searching forget that the surest way to be happy is to seek happiness for others.

✳✳✳

Never succumb to the temptation of bitterness.

✳✳✳

No person has the right to rain on your dreams.

✳✳✳

You will change your mind; You will change your looks; You will change your smile, laugh, and ways, but no matter what you change, you will always be you.

✳✳✳

Whatever your life's work is, do it well. A man should do his job so well that the living, the dead, and the unborn could do it no better.

***

Everything that we see is a shadow cast by that which we do not see.

***

We must concentrate not merely on the negative expulsion of war but the positive affirmation of peace.

***

The art of acceptance is the art of making someone who has just done you a small favor wish that he might have done you a greater one.

***

A riot is the language of the unheard.

***

A genuine leader is not a searcher for consensus but a molder of consensus.

***

Our lives begin to end the day we become silent about things that matter.

***

The ultimate measure of a man is not where he stands in moments of comfort and convenience, but where he stands at times of challenge and controversy.

***

Nothing in all the world is more dangerous than sincere ignorance and conscientious stupidity.

***

Never, never be afraid to do what's right, especially if the well-being of a person or animal is at stake. Society's punishments are small compared to the wounds we inflict on our soul when we look the other way.

***

Forgiveness is not an occasional act; it is a constant attitude.

***

Life's most persistent and urgent question is, 'What are you doing for others?'

***

Ten thousand fools proclaim themselves into obscurity, while one wise man forgets himself into immortality.

***

When you are right you cannot be too radical; when you are wrong, you cannot be too conservative.

***

That old law about 'an eye for an eye' leaves everybody blind. The time is always right to do the right thing.

***

If I cannot do great things, I can do small things in a great way.

***

Change does not roll in on the wheels of inevitability but comes through continuous struggle.

***

We are prone to judge success by the index of our salaries or the size of our automobiles rather than by the quality of our service and relationship to humanity.

***

Whatever affects one directly, affects all indirectly. I can never be what I ought to be until you are what you ought to be. This is the interrelated structure of reality.

***

Not everybody can be famous, but everybody can be great because greatness is determined by service... You only need a heart full of grace and a soul generated by love.

***

I concluded that there is an existential moment in your life when you must decide to speak for yourself; nobody else can speak for you.

***

Almost always, the dedicated creative minority has made the world better.

***

The soft-minded man always fears change. He feels security in the status quo, and he has an almost morbid fear of the new. For him, the greatest pain is the pain of a new idea.

✳✳✳

We cannot walk alone.

✳✳✳

He who passively accepts evil is as much involved in it as he who helps to perpetuate it. He who accepts evil without protesting against it is cooperating with it.

✳✳✳

I am not interested in power for power's sake, but I'm interested in moral power, that is right, and that is good.

✳✳✳

Human progress is neither automatic nor inevitable... Every step toward the goal of justice requires sacrifice, suffering, and struggle; the tireless exertions and passionate concern of dedicated individuals.

✳✳✳

People fail to get along because they fear each other; they fear each other because they don't know each other; they don't know each other because they have not communicated with each other.

✳✳✳

The ultimate tragedy is not the oppression and cruelty by the bad people but the silence over that by the good people.

✳✳✳

I refuse to accept the view that humanity is so tragically bound to the starless midnight of racism and war that the bright daybreak of peace and brotherhood can never become a reality... I believe that unarmed truth and unconditional love will have the final word.

***

We will remember not the words of our enemies, but the silence of our friends.

***

Law and order exist to establish justice, and when they fail in this purpose, they become the dangerously structured dams that block the flow of social progress.

***

People fail to get along because they fear each other; they fear each other because they don't know each other; they don't know each other because they have not communicated with each other.

***

We must learn to live together as brothers or perish together as fools.

***

Capitalism does not permit an even flow of economic resources. With this system, a small privileged few are rich beyond conscience, and almost all others are doomed to be poor at some level. That's the way the system works. And since we know that the system will not change the rules, we are going to have to change the system.

***

Our scientific power has outrun our spiritual power. We have guided missiles and misguided men.

***

We must come to see that the end we seek is a society at peace with itself, a society that can live with its conscience.

***

I have a dream that one day little black boys and girls will be holding hands with little white boys and girls.

***

What is wrong in the world today is that the nations of the world are engaged in a bitter, colossal contest for supremacy.

***

I have a dream that my four little children will one day live in a nation where they will not be judged by the color of their skin, but by the content of their character.

***

All progress is precarious, and the solution of one problem brings us face to face with another problem.

***

History will have to record that the greatest tragedy of this period of social transition was not the strident clamor of the bad people, but the appalling silence of the good people.

***

A nation or civilization that continues to produce soft-minded men purchases its spiritual death on the installment plan.

The more there are riots, the more repressive action will take place, and the more we face the danger of a right-wing takeover and eventually a fascist society.

***

Injustice anywhere is a threat to justice everywhere.

***

No, no, we are not satisfied, and we will not be satisfied until justice rolls down like waters and righteousness like a mighty stream.

***

The hope of a secure and livable world lies with disciplined nonconformists who are dedicated to justice, peace and brotherhood.

***

The moral arc of the universe bends at the elbow of justice.

***

It may be true that the law cannot make a man love me, but it can keep him from lynching me, and I think that's pretty important.

***

Of all the forms of inequality, injustice in health care is the most shocking and inhumane.

***

Never forget that everything Hitler did in Germany was legal.

***

I submit that an individual who breaks a law that conscience tells him is unjust, and who willingly accepts the penalty of imprisonment to arouse the conscience of the community over its injustice, is, in reality, expressing the highest respect for the law.

***

The principle of self-defense, even involving weapons and bloodshed, has never been condemned, even by Gandhi.

***

We who in engage in nonviolent direct action are not the creators of tension. We merely bring to the surface the hidden tension that is already alive.

***

Nonviolence means avoiding not only external physical violence but also internal violence of spirit. You not only refuse to shoot a man, but you refuse to hate him.

***

At the center of non-violence stands the principle of love.

***

Nonviolence is a powerful and just weapon. which cuts without wounding and ennobles the man who wields it. It is a sword that heals.

***

Violence as a way of achieving racial justice is both impractical and immoral. I am not unmindful of the fact that violence often brings about momentary results. Nations have frequently won their independence in battle. But in spite of temporary victories, violence never brings permanent peace.

**

World peace through nonviolent means is neither absurd nor unattainable. All other methods have failed. Thus, we must begin anew. Nonviolence is a good starting point. Those of us who believe in this method can be voices of reason, sanity, and understanding amid the voices of violence, hatred, and emotion. We can very well set a mood of peace out of which a system of peace can be built.

**

Returning hate for hate multiplies hate, adding deeper darkness to a night already devoid of stars. Darkness cannot drive out darkness; only light can do that. Hate cannot drive out hate; only love can do that. Hate multiplies hate, violence multiplies violence, and toughness multiplies toughness in a descending spiral of destruction.

**

If the cruelties of slavery could not stop us, the opposition we now face will surely fail. Because the goal of America is freedom, abused and scorned tho' we may be, our destiny is tied up with America's destiny.

**

Freedom is never voluntarily given by the oppressor; it must be demanded by the oppressed.

**

In our glorious fight for civil rights, we must guard against being fooled by false slogans, as 'right-to-work.' It provides no 'rights' and no 'works.' Its purpose is to destroy labor unions and the freedom of collective bargaining... We demand this fraud be stopped.

***

In the process of gaining our rightful place, we must not be guilty of wrongful deeds. Let us not seek to satisfy our thirst for freedom by drinking from the cup of bitterness and hatred. We must forever conduct our struggle on the high plane of dignity and discipline. We must not allow our creative protest to degenerate into physical violence. Again, and again, we must rise to the majestic heights of meeting physical force with soul force.

***

I dare to believe that peoples everywhere can have three meals a day for their bodies, education, and culture for their minds, and dignity, equality, and freedom for their spirits.

***

If physical death is the price that I must pay to free my white brothers and sisters from a permanent death of the spirit, then nothing can be more redemptive.

***

Oppressed people cannot remain oppressed forever. The yearning for freedom eventually manifests itself.

***

I want to be the white man's brother, not his brother-in-law.

***

When we let freedom ring, when we let it ring from every village and every hamlet, from every state and every city, we will be able to speed up that day when all of God's children, black men, and white men, Jews, and Gentiles, Protestants and Catholics, will be able to join hands and sing in the words of the old Negro spiritual, 'Free at last! Free at last! Thank God Almighty, we are free at last!'

***

If any earthly institution or custom conflicts with God's will, it is your Christian duty to oppose it. You must never allow the transitory, evanescent demands of human-made institutions to take precedence over the eternal demands of the Almighty God.

***

Courage is an inner resolution to go forward despite obstacles; Cowardice is submissive surrender to circumstances. Courage breeds creativity; Cowardice represses fear and is mastered by it. Cowardice asks the question, is it safe? Expediency asks the question, is it politic? Vanity asks the question, is it popular? But conscience asks the question. And there comes a time when we must take neither safe position, nor politic, nor popular, but one must take it because it is right.

***

Take the first step in faith. You don't have to see the whole staircase; just take the first step.

***

By opening our lives to God in Christ, we become new creatures. This experience, which Jesus spoke of like the new birth, is essential if we are to be transformed nonconformists ... Only through an inner spiritual transformation do we gain the strength to fight the evils of the world vigorously in a humble and loving spirit.

***

Now there is a final reason I think that Jesus says, 'Love your enemies.' It is this: that love has within it a redemptive power. And there is a power there that eventually transforms individuals. Just keep being friendly to that person. Just keep loving them, and they can't stand it too long. Oh, they react in many ways in the beginning. They react with guilt feelings, and sometimes they'll hate you a little more at that transition period, but keep loving them. And by the power of your love, they will break down under the load. That's love, you see. It is redemptive, and this is why Jesus says, love. There's something about love that builds up and is creative. There is something about hate that tears down and is destructive. So, love your enemies.

***

The God whom we worship is not a weak and incompetent God. He can beat back gigantic waves of opposition and to bring low prodigious mountains of evil. The ringing testimony of the Christian faith is that God is able.

***

I have a dream that one day every valley shall be exalted, every hill and mountain shall be made low, the rough places will be made straight, and the glory of the Lord shall be revealed, and all flesh shall see it together.

***

The first question which the priest and the Levite asked was: 'If I stop to help this man, what will happen to me?' But... the good Samaritan reversed the question: 'If I do not stop to help this man, what will happen to him?'

***

Seeing is not always believing.

Margaret Thatcher

Margaret Thatcher (October 13, 1925- April 8, 2013) was Britain's first female prime minister (1979-1990)

***

Disciplining yourself to do what you know is right and important, although difficult, is the high road to pride, self-esteem, and personal satisfaction.

***

If you lead a country like Britain, a strong country, a country which has taken the lead in world affairs in good times and in bad, a country that is always reliable, then you have to have a touch of iron about you.

***

If you want something said, ask a man; if you want something done, ask a woman.

***

If you set out to be liked, you would be prepared to compromise on anything at any time, and you would achieve nothing.

***

To cure the British disease with socialism was like trying to cure leukemia with leeches.

***

I've got a woman's ability to stick to a job and get on with it when everyone else walks off and leaves it.

***

You and I come by road or rail, but economists travel on infrastructure.

***

Any leader has to have a certain amount of steel in them, so I am not that put out being called the Iron Lady.

***

You may have to fight a battle more than once to win it.

***

To wear your heart on your sleeve isn't a very good plan; you should wear it inside, where it functions best.

***

The truths of the Judaic-Christian tradition, are infinitely precious, not only, as I believe, because they are true, but also because they provide the moral impulse which alone can lead to that peace, in the true meaning of the word, for which we all long... There is little hope for democracy if the hearts of men and women in democratic societies cannot be touched by a call to something greater than themselves.

***

The facts of life are conservative.

***

It is not the creation of wealth that is wrong, but the love of money for its own sake.

***

Of course, it's the same old story. Truth usually is the same old story.

***

Freedom will destroy itself if it is not exercised within some moral framework, some body of shared beliefs, some spiritual heritage transmitted through the Church, the family, and the school.

***

Left-wing zealots have often been prepared to ride roughshod over due process and basic considerations of fairness when they think they can get away with it. For them, the ends always seem to justify the means. That is precisely how their predecessors came to create the gulag.

***

Plan your work for today and every day, then work your plan.

***

It may be the cock that crows, but it is the hen that lays the eggs.

***

Every family should have the right to spend their money, after tax, as they wish, and not as the government dictates. Let us extend choice, extend the will to choose and the chance to choose.

***

There are still people in my party who believe in consensus politics. I regard them as Quislings, as traitors... I mean it.

***

It's passionately interesting for me that the things that I learned in a small town, in a very modest home, are just the things that I believe have won the election.

***

When people are free to choose, they choose freedom.

***

I'm back... and you knew I was coming. On my way here, I passed a cinema with the sign 'The Mummy Returns.'

***

You don't tell deliberate lies, but sometimes you have to be evasive.

***

Look at a day when you are supremely satisfied at the end. It's not a day when you lounge around doing nothing; it's a day you've had everything to do, and you've done it.

***

I don't mind how much my Ministers talk, so long as they do what I say.

***

Power is like being a lady... if you have to tell people you are, you aren't.

***

It pays to know the enemy – not least because at some time you may have the opportunity to turn him into a friend.

***

Do you know that one of the great problems of our age is that we are governed by people who care more about feelings than they do about thoughts and ideas?

***

To those waiting with bated breath for that favorite media catchphrase, the U-turn, I have only this to say, 'You turn if you want; the lady's not for turning.

***

I always cheer up immensely if an attack is particularly wounding because I think, well, if they attack one personally, it means they have not a single political argument left.

***

No one would remember the Good Samaritan if he'd only had good intentions; he had money as well.

***

Christmas is a day of meaning and traditions, a special day spent in the warm circle of family and friends.

***

Europe was created by history. America was created by a philosophy.

***

There are significant differences between the American and European version of capitalism. The American traditionally emphasizes the need for limited government, light regulations, low taxes, and maximum labor-market flexibility. Its success has been shown above all in the ability to create new jobs, in which it is consistently more successful than Europe.

***

It's a funny old world.

***

What Britain needs is an iron lady.

***

Being prime minister is a lonely job... you cannot lead from the crowd.

***

I love the argument; I love debate. I don't expect anyone to sit there and agree with me, that's not their job.

***

No woman in my time will be prime minister or chancellor or foreign secretary – not the top jobs. Anyway, I wouldn't want to be prime minister; you have to give yourself 100 percent.

***

I am extraordinarily patient, provided I get my way in the end.

***

If you just set out to be like, you will be prepared to compromise on anything at any time and would achieve nothing.

***

For every idealistic peacemaker willing to renounce his self-defense in favor of a weapons-free world, there is at least one warmaker anxious to exploit the other's good intentions.

***

A world without nuclear weapons would be less stable and more dangerous for all of us.

***

Watch your thoughts, for they will become actions. Watch your actions, for they'll become... habits. Watch your habits for they will forge your character. Watch your character, for it will make your destiny.

***

I do not know anyone who has got to the top without hard work. That is the recipe. It will not always get you to the top but should get you pretty near.

***

I do not know anyone who has got to the top without hard work. That is the recipe. It will not always get you to the top but should get you pretty near.

***

Some Socialists seem to believe that people should be numbers in a State computer. We believe they should be individuals. We are all unequal. No one, thank heavens, is like anyone else, however much the Socialists may pretend otherwise. We believe that everyone has the right to be unequal, but to us, every human being is equally important.

***

It used to be about trying to do something. Now it's about trying to be someone.

***

They've got the usual Socialist disease — they've run out of another people's money.

***

I wasn't lucky. I deserved it.

***

My policies are based not on some economics theory, but on things I and millions like me were brought up with: an honest day's work for an honest day's pay; live within your means; put by a nest egg for a rainy day; pay your bills on time; support the police.

***

Platitudes? Yes, there are platitudes. Platitudes are there because they are true.

***

I don't think there will be a woman prime minister in my lifetime.

***

If you want to cut your own throat, don't come to me for a bandage.

***

I usually make up my mind about a man in ten seconds, and I very rarely change it.

***

The battle for women's rights has been largely won.

***

The problem with socialism is that you eventually run out of other peoples' money.

***

What is success? I think it is a mixture of having a flair for the thing that you are doing; knowing that it is not enough, that you have got to have hard work and a certain sense of purpose.

***

I too have a certain idea of America. Moreover, I would not feel entitled to say that of any other country, except my own. This is not just sentiment, though I always feel ten years younger – despite the jet-lag – when I set foot on American soil: there is something so positive, generous, and open about the people – and everything works. I also feel, though, that I have in a sense a share of America.

***

Look at a day when you are supremely satisfied at the end. It's not a day when you lounge around doing nothing; it's when you've had everything to do, and you've done it.

There is no such thing as society: there are individual men and women, and there are families.

***

People think that at the top there isn't much room. They tend to think of it as an Everest. My message is that there is tons of room at the top.

***

Constitutions have to be written on hearts, not just paper.

***

A man may climb Everest for himself, but at the summit, he plants his country's flag.

***

I never hugged him, I bombed him. — On dictator, Muammar Gaddafi

***

It is always important in matters of high politics to know what you do not know. Those who think that they know, but are mistaken, and act upon their mistakes, are the most dangerous people to have in charge.

***

Any woman who understands the problems of running a home will be nearer to understanding the problems of running a country.

***

I think we have gone through a period when too many children and people have been given to understand 'I have a problem, it is the Government's job to cope with it!' or 'I have a problem, I will go and get a grant to cope with it!' 'I am homeless, the Government must house me!' and so they are casting their problems on society and who is society? There is no such thing! There are individual men and women, and there are families, and no government can do anything except through people, and people look to themselves first... There is no such thing as society. There is a living tapestry of men and women, and people and the beauty of that tapestry and the quality of our lives will depend upon how much each of us is prepared to take responsibility for ourselves and each of us prepared to turn round and help by our efforts those who are unfortunate.

**

Standing in the middle of the road is very dangerous; you get knocked down by the traffic from both sides.

**

The choice facing the nation is between two different ways of life. And what a prize we have to fight for: no less than the chance to banish from our land the dark, divisive clouds of Marxist socialism and bring together men and women from all walks of life who share a belief in freedom.

**

I owe almost everything to my father, and it's passionately interesting for me that the things that I learned in a small town, in a very modest home, are just the things that I believe have won the election.

**

Whether it is in the United States or mainland Europe, written constitutions have one great weakness. That is that they contain the potential to have judges take decisions which should properly be made by democratically elected politicians.

✳✳✳

Oh, but you know, you do not achieve anything without trouble, ever.

✳✳✳

Pennies do not come from heaven. They have to be earned here on earth.

✳✳✳

The defense budget is one of the very few elements of public expenditure that can truly be described as essential. This point was well-made by a robust Labor Defence Minister, Denis (Now Lord) Healey, many years ago: 'Once we have cut expenditure to the extent where our security is imperiled, we have no houses, we have no hospitals, we have no schools. We have a heap of cinders.'

✳✳✳

If... many influential people have failed to understand, or have just forgotten, what we were up against in the Cold War and how we overcame it, they are not going to be capable of securing, let alone enlarging, the gains that liberty has made.

✳✳✳

Don't follow the crowd; let the crowd follow you.

✳✳✳

...The larger the slice is taken by the government, the smaller the cake available for everyone.

**

Nothing is more obstinate than a fashionable consensus.

**

Whether manufactured by black, white, brown or yellow hands, a widget remains a widget – and it will be bought anywhere if the price and quality are right. The market is a more powerful and more reliable liberating force than the government can ever be.

**

I am in politics because of the conflict between good and evil, and I believe that in the end good will triumph.

**

There can be no liberty unless there is economic liberty.

**

A week is a long time in politics.

**

To be free is better than to be unfree – always. Any politician who suggests the opposite should be treated as suspect.

**

During my lifetime most of the problems the world has faced have come, in one fashion or other, from mainland Europe, and the solutions from outside it.

***

We Conservatives hate unemployment.

***

There is much to be said for trying to improve some disadvantaged people's lot. There is nothing to be said for trying to create heaven on earth.

***

It is one of the great weaknesses of reasonable men and women that they imagine that projects which fly in the face of common sense are not serious or being seriously undertaken.

***

This lady is not for turning.

***

To me, the consensus seems to be the process of abandoning all beliefs, principles, values, and policies. So, it is something in which no one believes and to which no one objects.

***

We were told our campaign wasn't sufficiently slick. We regard that as a compliment.

***

Conservatives have excellent credentials to speak about human rights. By our efforts, and with precious little help from self-styled liberals, we were largely responsible for securing liberty for a substantial share of the world's population and defending it for most of the rest.

***

If my critics saw me walking over the Thames, they would say it was because I couldn't swim.

***

Oh, but you know, you do not achieve anything without trouble, ever.

***

Defeat? I do not recognize the meaning of the word.

***

To be successful you have to be selfish, or else you never achieve. And once you get to your highest level, then you have to be unselfish. Stay reachable. Stay in touch. Don't isolate.

***

We want a society where people are free to make choices, to make mistakes, to be generous and compassionate. This is what we mean by a moral society; not a society where the state is responsible for everything, and no one is responsible for the state.

***

The spirit of envy can destroy; it can never build.

***

I seem to smell the stench of appeasement in the air.

***

The woman's mission is not to enhance the masculine spirit, but to express the feminine; hers is not to preserve a human-made world but to create a human world by the infusion of the feminine element into all of its activities.

***

Ought we not to ask the media to agree among themselves a voluntary code of conduct, under which they would not say or show anything which could assist the terrorists' morale or their cause while the hijack lasted.

***

And what a prize we have to fight for: no less than the chance to banish from our land the dark, divisive clouds of Marxist socialism.

***

Democratic nations must try to find ways to starve the terrorist and the hijacker of the oxygen of publicity on which they depend.

***

One only gets to the top rung of the ladder by steadily climbing up one at a time, and suddenly all sorts of powers, all sorts of abilities which you thought never belonged to you—suddenly become within your possibility, and you think, Well, I'll have a go, too.

***

If it is once again one against forty-eight, then I am very sorry for the forty-eight.

***

Most women defend themselves. It is the female of the species — it is the tigress and lioness in you — which tends to defend when attacked.

∗

One of the things being in politics has taught me is that men are not reasoned or reasonable sex.

∗

I shan't be pulling the levers there, but I shall be a very good back-seat driver.

Mark Twain

Samuel Langhorne Clemens (November 30, 1835 – April 21, 1910), better known by his pen name **Mark Twain**, was the distinguished novelist, short story writer, essayist, journalist, and literary critic.

✳✳✳

Age is an issue of mind over matter. If you don't mind, it doesn't matter.

✳✳✳

Be careful about reading health books. You may die of a misprint.

✳✳✳

Clothes make the man. Naked people have little or no influence on society.

✳✳✳

I am an old man and have known a great many troubles, but most of them never happened.

✳✳✳

I am only human, although I regret it.

✳✳✳

I would have written a shorter letter, but I did not have the time.

✳✳✳

Never put off till tomorrow what you can do the day after tomorrow.

***

The only way to keep your health is to eat what you don't want, drink what you don't like, and do what you'd rather not.

***

When we remember we are all mad, the mysteries disappear, and life stands explained.

***

Worrying is like paying a debt you don't owe.

Mark Victor Hansen

Mark Victor Hansen (born January 8, 1948) is an American inspirational and motivational speaker, trainer, and author.

***

Ideas attract money, time, talents, skills, energy and other complementary ideas that will bring them into reality.

***

Dedicate yourself to the good you deserve and desire for yourself. Give yourself peace of mind. You deserve to be happy. You deserve delight.

***

I never let my subject get in the way of what I want to talk about.

***

I want to talk with people who care about things that matter that will make a life-changing difference.

***

You control your future, your destiny. What you think about comes about. By recording your dreams and goals on paper, you set in motion the process of becoming the person you most want to be. Put your future in good hands -- your own.

***

Don't wait until everything is just right. It will never be perfect. There will always be challenges, obstacles and less than perfect conditions. So what. Get started now. With each step you take, you will grow stronger and stronger, more and more skilled, more and more self-confident and more and more successful.

***

Don't think it, ink it.

***

In imagination, there's no limitation.

***

When your self-worth goes up, your net worth goes up with it.

***

True or true? Yes, or yes?

***

Imitate until you emulate; match and surpass those who launched you. It's the highest form of thankfulness.

***

Now is the only time there is. Make your now wow, your minute's miracles and your days pay. Your life will have been magnificently lived and invested, and when you die, you will have made a difference.

***

End your day by privately looking directly into your eyes in the mirror and saying, 'I love you!' Do this for thirty days and watch how you transform.

***

Your belief determines your action and your action determines your results, but first, you have to believe.

✳✳✳

The more goals you set - the more goals you get.

✳✳✳

Predetermine the objectives you want to accomplish. Think big, act big and set out to accomplish big results.

✳✳✳

With vision, every person, organization, and country can flourish. The Bible says, 'Without vision, we perish.

✳✳✳

Whatever you need more of is what you need to tithe some.

Marilyn Monroe

Marilyn Monroe (1926-1962) Model, actress, singer and arguably one of the most famous women of the twentieth century.

***

They will only care when you're gone.

***

In Hollywood, a girl's virtue is much less important than her hairdo. You're judged by how you look, not by what you are. Hollywood's a place where they'll pay you a thousand dollars for a kiss, and fifty cents for your soul. I know, because I turned down the first offer often enough and held out for the fifty.

***

I'm very definitely a woman, and I enjoy it.

***

Everybody is always tugging at you. They'd all like a sort of chunk out of you. I don't think they realize it, but it's like 'grrr do this, grr do that...'But you do want to stay intact and on two feet.

***

I have feelings too. I am still human. All I want is to be loved, for myself and my talent.

***

A woman can't be alone. She needs a man. A man and a woman support and strengthen each other. She can't do it by herself.

***

I always felt insecure and, in the way, but most of all I felt scared. I wanted to love more than anything else in the world.

***

If I'm a star, then the people made me a star.

***

Creativity has got to start with humanity, and when you're a human being, you feel, you suffer.

***

Success makes so many people hate you. I wish it weren't that way. It would be wonderful to enjoy success without seeing envy in the eyes of those around you.

***

One of the best things that ever happened to me is that I'm a woman. That is the way all females should feel.

***

Fame will go by and, so long, I've had you, Fame. If it goes by, I've always known it was fickle.

***

The most unsatisfactory men are those who pride themselves on their virility and regard sex as if it were some form of athletics at which you can win cups. It is a woman's spirit and mood a man has to stimulate to make sex interesting. The real lover is the man who can thrill you just by touching your head or smiling into your eyes or by just staring into space.

***

First, I'm trying to prove to myself that I'm a person. Then maybe I'll convince myself that I'm an actress.

***

This life is what you make it. No matter what, you're going to mess up sometimes, it's a universal truth. But the good part is you get to decide how you're going to mess it up.

***

With fame, you know, you can read about yourself, somebody else's ideas about you, but what's important is how you feel about yourself – for survival and living day to day with what comes up.

***

We are all of us stars, and we deserve to twinkle.

***

I want to grow old without facelifts... I want to have the courage to be loyal to the face I've made. Sometimes I think it would be easier to avoid old age, to die young, but then you'd never complete your life, would you? You'd never wholly know you.

***

Arthur Miller wouldn't have married me if I had been nothing but a dumb blonde.

No one ever told me I was pretty when I was a little girl. All little girls should be told they're pretty, even if they aren't.

***

I think that when you are famous, every weakness is exaggerated.

***

Respect is one of life's greatest treasures. I mean, what does it all add up to if you don't have that?

***

The nicest thing for me is sleep, then at least I can dream.

***

I won't be satisfied until people want to hear me sing without looking at me. Of course, that doesn't mean I want them to stop looking.

***

I'm one of the world's most self-conscious people. I have to struggle.

***

Fame is fickle, and I know it. It has its compensations but it also has its drawbacks, and I've experienced them both.

***

Sometimes I feel my whole life has been one big rejection.

***

I think that sexuality is only attractive when it's natural and spontaneous.

***

I restore myself when I'm alone.

***

A man is franker and sincerer with his emotions than a woman. We girls, I'm afraid, have a tendency to hide our feelings.

***

My work is the only ground I've ever had to stand on. I seem to have a whole superstructure with no foundation, but I'm working on the foundation.

***

I'm one of the world's most self-conscious people. I have to struggle.

***

I don't consider myself an intellectual. And this is not one of my aims. But I admire intellectual people.

***

I'm a failure as a woman. My men expect so much of me, because of the image they've made of me– and that I've made of myself– as a sex symbol. They expect bells to ring and whistles to whistle, but my anatomy is the same as any other woman's, and I can't live up to it.

***

Fame doesn't fulfill you. It warms you a bit, but that warmth is temporary.

***

A wise girl kisses but doesn't love, listens but doesn't believe, and leaves before she is left.

***

I don't mind living in a man's world, as long as I can be a woman in it.

***

If I play a stupid girl and ask a stupid question, I've got to follow it through, what am I supposed to do, look intelligent?

***

It's far better to be unhappy alone than unhappy with someone — so far.

***

I don't know who invented high heels, but all women owe him a lot!

***

She was a girl who knew how to be happy even when she was sad. And that's important—you know.

***

Before marriage, a girl has to make love to a man to hold him. After marriage, she has to hold him to make love to him.

***

If you're going to be two-faced at least make one of them pretty.

***

I've never fooled anyone. I've let people fool themselves. They didn't bother to find out who and what I was. Instead, they would invent a character for me. I wouldn't argue with them. They loved somebody I wasn't.

***

It's not true that I had nothing on. I had the radio on.

***

I love to do the things the censors won't pass.

***

I've been on a calendar, but never on time.

***

When it comes down to it, I let them think what they want. If they care enough to bother with what I do, then I'm already better than them.

***

I don't mind making jokes, but I don't want to look like one.

***

I knew I belonged to the public and the world, not because I was talented or even beautiful, but because I had never belonged to anything or anyone else.

✳✳✳

It's often just enough to be with someone. I don't need to touch them. Not even talk. A feeling passes between you both. You're not alone.

✳✳✳

Dogs never bite me. Just humans.

✳✳✳

I don't understand why people aren't a little more generous with each other.

✳✳✳

In spite of everything, life is not without hope.

✳✳✳

A girl doesn't need anyone that doesn't need her.

✳✳✳

The body is meant to be seen, not all covered up.

✳✳✳

All we demanded was our right to twinkle.

✳✳✳

I don't mind being burdened with being glamorous and sexual. Beauty and femininity are ageless and can't be contrived, and glamour, although the manufacturers won't like this, cannot be manufactured. Not real glamour; it's based on femininity.

✳✳✳

I don't want to make money. I want to be wonderful.

***

I don't stop when I'm tired. I only stop when I'm done.

***

All a girl wants is for one guy to prove to her that they are not all the same.

***

Ever notice how 'What the hell' is always the right answer?

***

Sex is part of nature. I go along with nature.

***

How wrong it is for a woman to expect the man to build the world she wants, rather than to create it herself.

***

Keep smiling, because life is a beautiful thing and there's so much to smile about.

***

A career is wonderful, but you can't curl up to it on a cold night.

***

What do I wear in bed? Why, Chanel No. 5, of course.

***

Boys think girls are like books. If the cover doesn't catch their eye, they won't bother to read what's inside.

✽✽✽

Just because you fail once doesn't mean you're going to fail at everything.

✽✽✽

Who said nights were for sleep?

✽✽✽

It's all make-believe.

✽✽✽

Dreaming about being an actress, is more exciting then being one.

✽✽✽

I read poetry to save time.

✽✽✽

You might as well make yourself fly as to make yourself love.

✽✽✽

That's the way you feel when you're beaten inside. You don't feel angry at those who've beaten you. You feel ashamed.

✽✽✽

Always remember to smile and look up at what you got in life.

✽✽✽

Looking back, I guess I used to play-act all the time. For one thing, it meant I could live in a more interesting world than the one around me.

∗∗∗

I am trying to find myself. Sometimes that's not easy.

∗∗∗

Maybe I'll never be able to do what I hope to, but at least I have hope.

∗∗∗

Men are always ready to respect anything that bores them.

∗∗∗

I've often stood silently at a party for hours listening to my movie idols turn into dull and little people.

∗∗∗

I am not a victim of emotional conflicts. I am a human.

∗∗∗

If I'd observed all the rules, I'd never have got anywhere.

∗∗∗

People had a habit of looking at me as if I were some mirror instead of a person. They didn't see me; they saw their lewd thoughts, then they white-masked themselves by calling me the lewd one.

∗∗∗

Millions of people live their entire lives without finding themselves. But it is something I must do.

***

For those who are poor in happiness, each time is the first time; happiness never becomes a habit.

***

Most men judge your importance in their lives by how much you can hurt them.

***

I live to succeed, not to please you or anyone else.

***

I don't forgive people because I'm weak; I forgive them because I am strong enough to know people make mistakes.

***

Please quote me right!

***

The 'public' scares me, but people I trust.

***

I have always been deeply terrified to really be someone's wife since I know from life one cannot love another, ever.

***

Beneath the makeup and behind the smile I am just a girl who wishes for the world.

***

Anything's possible, almost.

***

This is supposed to be an art form, not just a manufacturing establishment. The sensitivity that helps me to act, you see, also makes me react. An actor is supposed to be a sensitive instrument.

***

I never wanted to be Marilyn — it just happened. Marilyn's like a veil I wear over Norma Jeane.

***

It's not too much fun to know yourself too well or think you do — everyone needs a little conceit to carry them through and past the falls.

***

You never know what life is like until you have lived it.

***

This is a free and democratic country, and no one has a monopoly on anything.

***

For life: it is rather a determination not to be overwhelmed. For work: the truth can only be recalled, never invented.

***

I'm trying to find the nailhead, not just strike the blow.

***

Men are climbing to the moon, but they don't seem interested in the beating human heart.

***

If you can make a woman laugh, you can make her do anything.

***

It takes a smart brunette to play a dumb blonde.

***

Acting isn't something you do. Instead of doing it, it occurs. If you're going to start with logic, you might as well give up. You can have conscious preparation, but you have unconscious results.

***

I love a natural look in pictures. I like people with a feeling one way or another — it shows an inner life. I like to see that something is going on inside them.

***

We should all start to live before we get too old. Fear is stupid. So are regrets.

Michael Bloomberg

Michael Rubens Bloomberg (born February 14, 1942) is an American businessman, politician, author, and philanthropist.

✳✳✳

The people who are worried about privacy have a legitimate worry. But we live in a complex world where you're going to have to have a level of security greater than you did back in the olden days if you will. And our laws and our interpretation of the Constitution, I think, have to change

✳✳✳

Nobody wants a job where they don't have authority to go along with the responsibility. Quite the contrary. The more authority you give people, the better people you can attract, and the harder they're going to work, and the more loyal they are going to be.

✳✳✳

No place epitomizes the American experience and the American spirit more than New York City.

✳✳✳

The next day after I got fired, literally the next day, I started a new company.

✳✳✳

If you can't prove it's not true, then a certain number of people will glom on and say it is true.

✳✳✳

And because no matter who you are, if you believe in yourself and your dream, New York will always be the place for you.

***

We have an energy policy - we're transferring our wealth to overseas to a bunch of countries that don't have the same values as us. In some cases, they're using our money to finance terrorism against us.

***

Life is too short to spend your time avoiding failure,

***

What the Democrats have to understand is that while we do need to reform our regulation and we do need more restrictions, it is true that it is capitalism and free enterprise and companies that create jobs and wealth for every American.

***

Being an entrepreneur isn't really about starting a business. It's a way of looking at the world: seeing opportunity where others see obstacles, taking risks when others take refuge.

***

Look at all of the great strengths of America: entrepreneurial ship, work ethic, natural resources, a democracy, transparency, a willingness to be critical. Around the world, they look at us, and they say, "Why are you criticizing yourself? Why are you people arguing during the political process to elect a president or somebody else?" That's the great strength of this country.

***

I am heading straight in. I have earned my place in heaven. It's not even close.

***

Don't be afraid to assert yourself, have confidence in your abilities and don't let the bastards get you down.

***

We need people from all around the world. We need entrepreneurs; we need students that we're educating in our schools that we then throw out and we should make sure they can stay here. If we don't have the new flux of immigrants, nobody's going to create the jobs for the Americans who are currently out of work.

***

You bet I did and I enjoyed it.

***

Immigrants built America. Almost nobody that I know is any more than three generations, maybe four generations, American.

***

I've always respected those who tried to change the world for the better, rather than complain about it.

***

I have two daughters that are the loves of my life, and I want to leave them a better world, a better country, a better state, and a better city.

***

We will go forward... we will never go back.

***

In business, when you fail at something when something doesn't work, you say okay, we've learned that that's not a path to go down.

***

Every one of my position's cuts - out half the country. I'm pro-choice, I'm pro-gay rights, I'm pro-immigration, I'm against guns, I believe in Darwin.

***

I am what I am and, you know, I'm a very lucky guy.

***

The truth of the matter is: you can create a great legacy, and inspire othersrs, by giving it to philanthropic organizations.

***

I do think there are certain times we should infringe on your freedom.

***

What we shouldn't do is let people who want to come here make the decision themselves. America should be in control of its borders.

***

After hard work, the biggest determinant is being in the right place at the right time.

***

We're America, and we have to stop worrying about what happens overseas and to be optimistic, even though nobody should think we're not going to have some difficult times.

***

You must first be willing to fail — and you must have the courage to go for it anyway.

The estate taxes, on balance, are good. They get people to give money to charity, and they prevent these family dynasties which keep other people from having opportunities. It may be good for a family, but for society, it's probably not good. And I've always been in favor of having an estate tax.

✳✳✳

America is built around this premise that you can do it, and there are an awful lot of people who are unlikely to have done it who did.

✳✳✳

When it comes to public school education, we have been unwilling to measure our results. We've been unwilling to pay based on performance. We have tenure where even if you can't teach; you can't get fired. We've been unwilling to invest in new schools.

✳✳✳

Whatever you may think of the proposed mosque and community center, lost in the heat of the debate has been a basic question: Should government attempt to deny private citizens the right to build a house of worship on private property based on their particular religion?

✳✳✳

The problem of dealing with the financial industry is that you can measure it with interest rates coming down. You can measure it with the number of loans, and that sort of thing. The problem is that nobody wants to take the loans. Once the banks are willing to give it, that's only half the problem.

✳✳✳

When I came into office, people said, 'Billionaire? How do they live? What do they eat? How do they sleep?' Today, they see me on the subway coming uptown. A couple of people say hi, some people smile and nod. Some people sleep. It's not an issue.

***

Nobody should ever mistake and think that our country [USA] is weakened, or that authority is diffuse and unspecified and that we are vulnerable.

***

This is the city of dreamers and time, and again it's the place where the greatest dream of all, the American dream, has been tested and has triumphed.

***

We need our president to be successful because our futures are all tied to the success of America, which means America's government, which means, in essence, the president.

***

My father, a bookkeeper who never earned more than $11,000 a year in his life, sat there, writing out a $25 check to the NAACP. When I asked him why he said discrimination against anyone is discrimination against us all. And I never forgot that. Indeed, his philanthropy was a gift, not just to that organization, but to me.

***

If you want to know how to solve society's problems, you start with better public education.

***

Ten years have passed since a perfect blue-sky morning turned into the blackest of nights. Since then we've lived in sunshine and shadow, and although we can never unsee what happened here, we can also see that children who lost their parents have grown into young adults, grandchildren have been born, and good works and public service have taken root to honor those we loved and lost.

***

If you are honest with yourself and if you want to like what you see in the mirror, is you have to say what you believe.

***

What has changed is that people have stopped working together.

***

The public wants elected officials who have character. The public wants elected officials who are willing to stand up and say things, even if they don't agree with them.

***

The mistake that was made in the '70s is we stopped policing the streets, we stopped cleaning the streets, we stopped cleaning the graffiti off buildings, we stopped supporting our cultural institutions and building parks and schools and all those kinds of things.

***

If you have one farm worker, typically they create three jobs with higher compensation and higher skills - the people that pack, the people that ship, the people that inspect, the people that sell, that sort of thing.

***

I do not think that anybody should get paid for lousy performance. I've said that for a long time. If you work hard and you do good, you get paid well.

∗∗∗

When I care about something, I care about something. I think I have an obligation as an American too - and as a citizen, as-as a human being, to help others. Smoking is going to kill a billion people this century. I've put six hundred million dollars from my own money into trying to stop the tobacco companies from getting kids to smoke and convincing adults that it's not in their health.

∗∗∗

Getting the job done has been the basis for the success my company has achieved.

∗∗∗

Five years have come, and five years have gone, and still, we stand together as one. We come back to this place to remember the heartbreaking anniversary - and each person who died here - those known and unknown to us, whose absence is always with us.

∗∗∗

Throughout our history, every generation has expanded upon the freedoms won by their parents and grandparents. Every generation has removed some of the barriers to full participation in the American dream. And the next great barrier standing before our generation is the prohibition on marriage for same-sex couples

∗∗∗

The fact is, the most painful and tragic lesson of the 20th century was that regimes based on racial superiority and religious hatred couldn't be trusted to keep their word to the international community.

***

You can't sit there and worry about everything.

***

What goes on in Europe concerns us greatly because, if Europe comes apart, the E.U. comes apart, then you're going to have an enormous impact on America, that's a very big trading partner of ours, and people own securities around the world in this day and age.

***

Buy what's deliverable, not what could be.

***

I like the theater, dining and chasing women. Let me put it this way: I am a single, straight billionaire in Manhattan. It's like a wet dream.

***

Look, we live in a very dangerous world. We know some people want to take away our freedoms. New Yorkers probably know that as much if not more than anybody else after the tragedy of 9/11.

***

I don't know why you should be proud of something. It doesn't make you any better or worse. You are what you are.

***

Like Israel, New York City's history has been defined by immigrants who come in search of freedom and the opportunity to build a better life. And like Israel, New York City has remained a target for terrorists who seek to destroy that freedom

✳✳✳

In the game of life, when the final buzzer sounds, the only stat you carry with you is the number of assists you made.

✳✳✳

Government caters to those screaming the loudest, regardless of what they're screaming about. In business, it's exactly the opposite! You invest more in the most successful departments, and less in those that aren't performing.

✳✳✳

You know, if you look back in the 1930s, the money went to infrastructure. The bridges, the municipal buildings, the roads, those were all built with stimulus money spent on infrastructure. This stimulus bill has fundamentally gone, started with a $500 rebate check, remember. That went to buy flat-screen TVs made in China.

✳✳✳

Yes, they broke the law, but we can't deport them. Let's get over this pointing finger and do something about that; whether if - they have to pay a fine, learn to speak English, the history, you can do that. And then you have to give visas for the skills we need.

✳✳✳

I think that all money can do to get your message out. Unfortunately, we live in a world where you have to use mass media to communicate with the people, and it just costs an awful lot of money.

***

Many of America's and New York's sons and daughters are around the world fighting for the freedoms that the Statue of Liberty stands for.

***

Even though New York is the safest big city in the nation, there are still far too many illegal guns on our streets. Nearly all of them arrive from out of state - and most are sold by a small group of rogue gun dealers who refuse to obey federal laws.

***

I've always wondered if people who block each other from expressing their opinions do so because they have so little confidence in their own. To me, encountering an opposing point of view is a chance to gain a deeper understanding of the issues at stake and develop my point of view. But the first thing you've got to do is you've got to let people speak, and you've got to listen. And that's what the first amendment is all about. That's what distinguishes this country from others.

***

Millions of Americans have contributed to building a stronger Israel; I've been proud to be one of them. Last year, I went to Jerusalem to help dedicate in my father's name a new MDA medical facility which treats people of all faiths and all nationalities equally.

***

There will be ups; there will be downs, there will be sideways. I can tell you I have been hired; I have been fired, I have been lauded, I have been vilified. I've said some of the most brilliant things that just by accident appeared on my tongue, and I've said some of the dumbest things that you could imagine. But each day - even the day that I knew I was going to be fired - I looked forward to because I've always believed that tomorrow was going to be the best day of my life.

***

We're paying more for the privilege of getting sick and dying early. Once again, it makes no sense. And once again, no one in Washington is talking about how to fix it.

***

Most people won't have the opportunity to do full-time service, but those lucky enough to have monetary wealth or some spare time really can make an enormous difference. As someone who's now in the public sector, and is seeing up-close-and-personal the real impact of what we do and what we give, I can tell you: every dollar and every volunteer help, in more ways than you can count.

***

We all know that election reform takes time. That's because those who have benefited from the system are the ones who fight hardest to preserve it. So, if we're going to succeed, we need an independent coalition of citizens who believe in reform, who believe that our election laws should treat every voter equally, who believe that low levels of competition and participation are not healthy for democracy. The Independence Party is helping to build that coalition, and I am happy to join you in doing so.

***

Today, you're a piranha if you are seen having coffee with somebody from the other party in many cases.

***

The press is not doing its job of holding the candidates' feet to the fire. The tough questions are not what are you in favor of, but how are you going to get it through Congress?

***

Government by three men in a room has turned New York State into a national symbol of governmental dysfunction. Enough is enough!

***

When you go to Washington now, you can feel a sense of fear in the air - the fear to do anything, or say anything, that might affect the polls, or give the other side an advantage, or offend a special interest.

***

Our climate is changing. And while the increase in extreme weather we have experienced in New York City and around the world may or may not be the result of it, the risk that it may be - given the devastation it is wreaking - should be enough to compel all elected leaders to take immediate action.

***

I have my army in the NYPD, which is the seventh biggest army in the world.

***

Organizing around a common interest is a fundamental part of democracy. We should no more try to take away the right of individuals to collectively bargain than we should try to take away the right to a secret ballot.

***

If it wasn't for O'Flanagan's Pub on Manhattan's Upper East Side, I don't know where I would have spent my Friday nights as a young man.

***

In our democracy, near equality is no equality. The government either treats everyone the same, or it doesn't. And right now, it doesn't.

***

If you think of all the publicity about the tragedy of Virginia Tech, we have a Virginia Tech in this country every day. It's just spread across 50 states.

***

Nobody's going to elect me president of the United States.

***

One's a dog-eat-dog world, and the other one's just the opposite.

***

Ironically, it is exactly because we are a city that embraces freedom, that welcomes everyone and encourages their dreams, that New York remains on the front lines in the war on terror.

***

I have my army in the NYPD, which is the seventh biggest army in the world. I have my own State Department, much to Foggy Bottom's annoyance. We have the United Nations in New York, and so we have an entree into the diplomatic world that Washington does not have,

***

I was a Democrat before I was a Republican before I became an independent and I never changed my principles.

***

Central planning didn't work for Stalin or Mao, and it won't work for an entrepreneur either.

***

Well, we have to provide the world's best schools. We certainly don't have them, but that's our objective.

***

Is your company so small you have to do everything for yourself? Wait until you're so big that you can't. That's worse.

***

I never liked anyone who didn't have a temper. If you don't have a temper, you don't have any passion.

***

If you don't encounter setbacks in your career if you don't have doubts and disappointments, let me tell you, you're not dreaming big enough.

***

My personal view is, why don't you get out there and try to do something about the things that you don't like, create the jobs that we are lacking, rather than yell and scream. But if you want to yell and scream, we'll make sure you can do it.

***

When you come into court as a plaintiff or as a defendant, it is important that you look up at the bench and feel that that person represents you and will understand you, that that person is reflective of our community and our society.

Michael Jordan

Michael Jordan (February 17, 1963) is a former professional basketball player, successful entrepreneur and a majority owner of the Charlotte Hornets.

✳✳✳

Some people want it to happen; some wish it would happen; others make it happen.

✳✳✳

I can accept failure; everyone fails at something. But I can't accept not trying.

✳✳✳

To be successful you have to be selfish, or else you never achieve. And once you get to your highest level, then you have to be unselfish. Stay reachable. Stay in touch. Don't isolate.

✳✳✳

You have to expect things of yourself before you can do them.

✳✳✳

If you accept the expectations of others, especially negative ones, then you never will change the outcome.

✳✳✳

Talent wins games, but teamwork and intelligence win championships.

***

The good part about being famous can help people. The hard part is every day you have to be in a good mood because that is what people expect. You learn to get good at it.

***

I play to win, whether during practice or a real game. And I will not let anything get in the way of me and my competitive enthusiasm to win.

***

There is no 'i' in the team, but there is in the win.

***

Sometimes, things may not go your way, but the effort should be there every single night.

***

If you quit once it becomes a habit. Never quit!

***

Sometimes you need to get hit in the head to realize that you're in a fight.

***

I built my talents on the shoulders of someone else's talent.

***

I believe greatness is an evolutionary process that changes and evolves era to era.

**

In any investment, you expect to have fun and make money.

**

My heroes are and were my parents. I can't see having anyone else as my heroes.

**

I wasn't a work-conscious type of person. I was a player. I loved to play sports.

**

There's only one Michael Jordan.

**

I know the signs of sacredness.

**

Being Michael Jordan means acting the same as I always have.

**

I realized that if I was going to achieve anything in life, I had to be aggressive. I had to get out there and go for it.

**

I realize that I'm black, but I like to be viewed as a person, and this is everybody's wish.

**

If you're trying to achieve, there will be roadblocks. I've had them; everybody has had them. But obstacles don't have to stop you. If you run into a wall, don't turn around and give up. Figure out how to climb it, go through it, or work around it.

✳✳✳

My father used to say that it's never too late to do anything you wanted to do. And he said, 'You never know what you can accomplish until you try.

✳✳✳

To be successful you have to be selfish, or else you never achieve. And once you get to your highest level, then you have to be unselfish. Stay reachable. Stay in touch. Don't isolate.

✳✳✳

To learn to succeed, you must first learn to fail.

✳✳✳

I never looked at the consequences of missing a big shot... when you think about the consequences, you always think of a negative result.

✳✳✳

The game has its ups and downs, but you can never lose focus on your individual goals, and you can't let yourself be beaten because of lack of effort.

✳✳✳

You have competition every day because you set such high standards for yourself that you have to go out every day and live up to that.

I want to wake up every day and do whatever comes in my mind, and not feel pressure or obligations to do anything else in my life.

Live the moment for the moment.

I'm not out there sweating for three hours every day to find out what it feels like to sweat.

My attitude is that if you push me towards something that you think is a weakness, then I will turn that perceived weakness into a strength.

I've missed more than 9000 shots in my career. I've lost almost 300 games. 26 times, I've been trusted to take the game winning shot and missed. I've failed over and over and over again in my life. And that is why I succeed.

It's wrong that I don't want guys to challenge me. And the people who say that aren't in the room.

Winning isn't always championships.

Be true to the game, because the game will be true to you. If you try to shortcut the game, then the game will shortcut you. If you put forth the effort, good things will be bestowed upon you. That's true about the game, and in some ways, that's about life too.

***

You're a loser. You've always been a loser.

***

Are you going to play from the little girls' tees?

***

They don't need a ticket to watch you sitting on the bench. They can go to your house for that.

***

I've always believed that if you put in the work, the results will come. I don't do things half-heartedly. Because I know if I do, then I can expect half-hearted results.

***

Don't let them drag you down by rumors go with what you believe in.

***

Gambling is legal, and betting is legal, for what I bet.

***

I can't speak for the future. I have no crystal ball.

***

Once I made a decision, I never thought about it again.

***

It is easy to choose a path of anonymity and lead an empty life. But to strive hard and lead an impactful life, one needs a burning desire to realize dreams.

***

What is love? Love is playing every game as if it's your last!

***

The basketball court for me, during a game, is the most peaceful place I can imagine. On the basketball court, I worry about nothing. When I'm out there, no one can bother me.

***

If I had been playing for money, I would have complained a long time ago that I was underpaid.

***

I won't have any competitive instincts in any sports, other than golf. I can't see being competitive in sports anymore.

***

Never say never, because limits, like fears, are often just an illusion.

***

It is nerve-wracking watching my kids' games.

***

The minute you get away from fundamentals – whether it's proper technique, work ethic or mental preparation – the bottom can fall out of your game, your schoolwork, your job, whatever you're doing.

✳✳✳

I think the players win the championship, and the organization has something to do with it, don't get me wrong. But don't try to put the organization above the players.

✳✳✳

It's hard to say if the influx of younger players hurts the NBA, but it's impacted the league.

✳✳✳

I've never been afraid to fail.

✳✳✳

If it turns out that my best wasn't good enough, at least I won't look back and say I was afraid to try.

✳✳✳

It's heavy duty to try to do everything and please everybody. My job was to go out there and play the game of basketball as best I can. People may not agree with that. I can't live with what everyone's impression of what I should or what I shouldn't do.

✳✳✳

As athletes, we're used to reacting quickly. Here, it's 'come, stop, come, stop.' There's a lot of downtimes. That's the toughest part of the day.

✳✳✳

The game of basketball has been everything to me. My place of refuge, a place I've always gone where I needed comfort and peace. It's been the site of intense pain and the most intense feelings of joy and satisfaction. It's a relationship that has evolved, given me the greatest respect and love for the game.

✳✳✳

Always turn a negative situation into a positive situation.

In reality, I never want to grow up.

✳✳✳

There is no such thing as a perfect basketball player, and I don't believe there is only one greatest player either.

✳✳✳

I never thought a role model should be negative.

✳✳✳

The key to success is a failure.

✳✳✳

You have to expect things of yourself before you can do them.

✳✳✳

I want to be the bridge to the next generation.

✳✳✳

I own the guy guarding me.

✳✳✳

How many times have your parents told you not to do things, and the next thing you know, you do it? And you realized you shouldn't have done it.

***

I know fear is an obstacle for some people, but it is an illusion to me. Failure always made me try harder the next time.

***

If you do the work, you get rewarded. There are no shortcuts in life.

***

I want to be perceived as a guy who played his best in all facets, not just scoring. A guy who loved challenges.

***

You can practice shooting 8 hours a day, but if your technique is wrong, then all you become is very good at shooting the wrong way. Get the fundamentals down, and the level of everything you do will rise.

***

My challenge when I came back was to face the young talent, to dissect their games, and show them maybe that they needed to learn more about the game than just the money aspect.

***

Failure is acceptable. But not trying is a whole different ballpark.

***

Everybody has talent, but the ability takes hard work.

***

Best evaluation I can make of a player is to look in his eyes and see how scared they are.

***

My mother is my root, my foundation. She planted the seed that I base my life on, and that is the belief that the ability to achieve starts in your mind.

***

The best comes from the worst.

***

Champions do not become champions when they win an event, but in the hours, weeks, and months, and years they spend preparing for it. The victorious performance itself is merely a demonstration of their championship character.

***

Enjoy every minute of life. Never second-guess life.

***

I mean we all fly. Once you leave the ground, you fly. Some people fly longer than others.

***

When I lose the sense of motivation and the sense to prove something as a basketball player, it's time for me to move away from the game.

***

Learning's a gift, even when pain is your teacher.

***

People ask me if I could fly, I said, yeah.... for a little while.

***

The heart is what separates the good from the great.

***

The game is my wife. It demands loyalty and responsibility, and it gives me back fulfillment and peace.

***

Do I need my number retired throughout the league to acknowledge what I've done? No.

***

I would tell players to relax and never think about what's at stake. Just think about the basketball game. If you start to think about who is going to win the championship, you've lost your focus.

***

My body could stand the crutches, but my mind couldn't stand the sideline.

***

Just play. Have fun. Enjoy the game.

***

In college, I never realized the opportunities available to a pro athlete. I've been given a chance to meet all kinds of people, to travel and expand my financial capabilities, to get ideas and learn about life, to create a world apart from basketball.

***

I hope the millions of people I've touched have the optimism and desire to share their goals and hard work and perseverance with a positive attitude.

***

Even when I'm old and gray, I won't be able to play it, but I'll still love the game.

***

I want to be settled into somewhat of a normal life. Somewhat. I know it's never going to be completely normal.

***

Every time I feel tired while I am exercising and training, I close my eyes to see that picture, to see that list with my name. This usually motivates me to work again.

***

When I was young, I had to learn the fundamentals of basketball. You can have all the physical ability in the world, but you still have to know the fundamentals.

***

Not every flying hero has a cape.

***

For a competitive junkie like me, golf is a great solution because it smacks you in the face every time you think you've accomplished something. That to me has taken over a lot of the energy and competitiveness for basketball.

✳✳✳

I will not quit this game because of what the media has done to me.

✳✳✳

Playing Sick. That is so hard to do. It has to be a total mental challenge, as well as the physical challenge.

✳✳✳

I like control.

✳✳✳

I want to play for years.

Napoleon Hill

Napoleon Hill (October 26, 1883 – November 8, 1970) was an American author in the area of the new thought movement who was one of the earliest producers of the modern genre of personal-success.

***

The best job goes to the person who can get it done without passing the buck or coming back with excuses.

***

Do not wait; the time will never be just right. Start where you stand, and work with whatever tools you may have at your command, and better tools will be found as you go along.

***

It is always your next move.

***

No one can make you jealous, angry, vengeful, or greedy -- unless you let him.

***

The battle is all over except the shouting when one knows what is wanted and has made up his mind to get it, whatever the price may be.

***

The starting point of all achievement is desire. Keep this constantly in mind. Weak desires bring weak results, just as a small amount of fire makes a small amount of heat.

***

Everyone enjoys doing the kind of work for which he is best suited.

***

It has always been my belief that a man should do his best, regardless of how much he receives for his services, or the number of people he may be serving or the class of people served.

***

When defeat comes, accept it as a signal that your plans are not sound, rebuild those plans, and set sail once more toward your coveted goal.

***

The most common cause of fear of old age is associated with the possibility of poverty.

***

There is one quality which one must possess to win, and that is definiteness of purpose, the knowledge of what one wants, and a burning desire to possess it.

***

Ideas... they have the power...

***

First comes thought; then organization of that thought, into ideas and plans; then transformation of those plans into reality. The beginning, as you will observe, is in your imagination.

***

There is always room for those who can be relied upon to deliver the goods when they say they will.

***

Just as our eyes need light to see, our minds need ideas to conceive.

***

Money without brains is always dangerous.

***

War grows out of the desire of the individual to gain an advantage at the expense of his fellow men.

***

Persistence is to the character of man as carbon is to steel.

***

Reduce your plan for writing. The moment you complete this, you will have given concrete form to the intangible desire.

***

Don't wait. The time will never be just right.

***

Think and grow rich.

***

Every person who wins in any undertaking must be willing to cut all sources of retreat. Only by doing so can one be sure of maintaining that state of mind known as a burning desire to win -- essential to success.

***

The ladder of success is never crowded at the top.

***

All great truths are simple in the final analysis, and easily understood; if they are not, they are not great truths.

***

If you cannot do great things, do small things in a great way.

***

No man can succeed in a line of endeavor which he does not like.

***

What we do not see, what most of us never suspect of existing, is the silent but irresistible power which comes to the rescue of those who fight on in the face of discouragement.

***

The majority of men meet with failure because of their lack of persistence in creating new plans to take the place of those which fail.

***

The most interesting thing about a postage stamp is the persistence with which it sticks to its job.

***

There is always room for those who can be relied upon to deliver the goods when they say they will.

***

Strength and growth come only through continuous effort and struggle...

***

It is true that you can succeed best and quickest by helping others to succeed.

***

No alibi will save you from accepting the responsibility.

***

You might well remember that nothing can bring you success but yourself.

***

Indecision is the seedling of fear.

***

Procrastination is the bad habit of putting off until the day after tomorrow what should have been done the day before yesterday.

***

Big pay and little responsibility are circumstances seldom found together.

Norman Vincent Peale

Norman Vincent Peale (31 May 1898 – 24 December 1993) was an American minister and author known for his work in popularizing the concept of positive thinking.

***

Empty pockets never held anyone back. Only empty heads and empty hearts can do that.

***

Live your life and forget your age.

***

First thing every morning before you arise say out loud, I believe, three times.

***

When you become detached mentally from yourself and concentrate on helping other people with their difficulties, you will be able to cope with your own more effectively. Somehow, the act of self-giving is a personal power-releasing factor.

***

There is real magic in enthusiasm. It spells the difference between mediocrity and accomplishment.

***

One of the greatest moments in anybody's developing experience is when he no longer tries to hide from himself but determines to get acquainted with himself as he is.

***

Stand up to your obstacles and do something about them. You will find that they haven't half the strength you think they have.

***

Every problem has in it the seeds of its solution. If you don't have any problems, you don't get any seeds.

***

It is of practical value to learn to like yourself. Since you must spend so much time with yourself, you might as well get some satisfaction out of the relationship.

***

We struggle with the complexities and avoid the simplicities.

***

The how thinker gets problems solved effectively because he wastes no time with futile ifs.

***

People become quite remarkable when they start thinking that they can do things. When they believe in themselves, they have the first secret of success.

***

Never talk defeat. Use words like hope, belief, faith, victory.

***

Joy increases as you give it, and diminishes as you try to keep it for yourself. In giving it, you will accumulate a deposit of joy greater than you ever believed possible.

***

Those who are fired with an enthusiastic idea and who allow it to take hold and dominate their thoughts find that new worlds open for them. As long as enthusiasm holds out, so will new opportunities.

***

Practice hope. As hopefulness becomes a habit, you can achieve a permanently happy spirit.

***

If you want to get somewhere, you have to know where you want to go and how to get there. Then never, never, never give up.

***

Drop the idea that you are Atlas carrying the world on your shoulders. The world would go on even without you. Don't take yourself so seriously.

***

In every difficult situation is potential value. Believe this, then begin looking for it.

***

The more you lose yourself in something bigger than yourself, the more energy you will have.

***

The how thinker gets problems solved effectively because he wastes no time with futile ifs but goes right to work on the creative how.

***

Resentment or grudges do not harm the person against whom you hold these feelings but every day and every night of your life, they are eating at you.

***

When a problem comes along, study it until you are completely knowledgeable. Then find that weak spot, break the problem apart, and the rest will be easy.

***

Understanding can overcome any situation, however mysterious or insurmountable it may appear to be.

***

The mind, ever the willing servant will respond to boldness, for boldness, in effect, is a command to deliver mental resources.

***

Enthusiasm releases the drive to carry you over obstacles and adds significance to all you do.

***

It's always too soon to quit!

***

Cushion the painful effects of hard blows by keeping the enthusiasm going strong, even if doing so requires struggle.

***

Our happiness depends on the habit of mind we cultivate. So, practice happy thinking every day. Cultivate the merry heart, develop the happiness habit, and life will become a continual feast.

***

Life's blows cannot break a person whose spirit is warmed at the fire of enthusiasm.

***

You can be greater than anything that can happen to you.

***

One way to become enthusiastic is to look for the plus sign. To make progress in any difficult situation, you have to start with what's right about it and build on that.

***

When you wholeheartedly adopt a 'with all your heart' attitude and go all out with the positive principle, you can do incredible things.

***

Watch your manner of speech if you wish to develop a peaceful state of mind. Start each day by affirming peaceful, contented and happy attitudes and your days will tend to be pleasant and successful.

***

To go fast, row slowly.

***

Anybody can do just about anything with himself that he wants to and makes up his mind to do. We are all capable of greater things than we realize.

***

Go forward confidently, energetically attacking problems, expecting favorable outcomes.

***

Yesterday ended last night. Every day is a new beginning. Learn the skill of forgetting. And move on.

***

Believe it is possible to solve your problem. Tremendous things happen to the believer. So, believe the answer will come. It will.

***

The way to happiness: keeps your heart free from hate, your mind from worry. Live, expect little, give much. Fill your life with love. Scatter sunshine. Forget self, think of others. Do as you would be done by. Try this for a week, and you will be surprised.

***

The positive thinker is hard-headed, tough-minded, and factual realism. He sees all the difficulties clearly... which is more than can be said for the average negative thinker. But he sees more than difficulties -- he tries to see the solutions of those difficulties.

***

Practice loving people. It is true that this requires effort and continued the practice, for some are not very lovable, or so it seems - with emphasis on seems. Every person has lovable qualities when you learn to know him.

***

Never react emotionally to criticism. Analyze yourself to determine whether it is justified. If it is, correct yourself. Otherwise, go on about your business.

***

When you are afraid, do the thing you are afraid of, and soon you will lose your fear of it.

***

The more you venture to live greatly, the more you will find within you what it takes to get on top of things and stay there.

***

If you want things to be different, perhaps the answer is to become different yourself.

***

Remember, there is no situation so completely hopeless that something constructive cannot be done about it. When faced with a minus, ask yourself what you can do to make it a plus. A person practicing this attitude will extract undreamed-of outcomes from the most unpromising situations. Realize that there are no hopeless situations; there are only people who take hopeless attitudes.

***

Believe that you are bigger than your difficulties, for you are, indeed.

***

No matter how dark things seem to be or are, raise your sights and see the possibilities -- they're always there.

Paul Sweeney

Paul John **Sweeney** (born 16 January 1989) is a Scottish Labour & Co-operative Party politician.

✳✳✳

You know when you've read a good book when you turn the last page and feel a little as if you have lost a friend.

✳✳✳

True success is overcoming the fear of being unsuccessful.

✳✳✳

A wedding anniversary is the celebration of love, trust, partnership, tolerance, and tenacity. The order varies for any given year.

✳✳✳

True success is overcoming the fear of being unsuccessful.

✳✳✳

How can a society that exists on instant mashed potatoes, packaged cake mixes, frozen dinners, and instant cameras teach patience to its young?

✳✳✳

How often we fail to realize our good fortune in living in a country where happiness is more than a lack of tragedy.

✳✳✳

Self-delusion is pulling in your stomach when you step on the scales.

Paulo Coelho

Paulo Coelho (born on August 24, 1947) is a Brazilian lyricist and novelist. He is best known for his novel The Alchemist

✳✳✳

You have to take risks. We will only understand the miracle of life fully when we allow the unexpected to happen.

✳✳✳

When you are enthusiastic about what you do, you feel this positive energy. It's very simple.

✳✳✳

Be brave. Take risks. Nothing can substitute experience.

✳✳✳

When you find your path, you must not be afraid. You need to have sufficient courage to make mistakes. Disappointment, defeat, and despair are the tools God uses to show us the way.

✳✳✳

If I am a part of your dream, you'll come back one day.

✳✳✳

The secret of life, though, is to fall seven times and to get up eight times.

✳✳✳

One is loved because one is loved. No reason is needed for loving.

***

A child can teach an adult three things: to be happy for no reason, to always be busy with something, and to know how to demand with all his might that which he desires.

***

When a person desires something, all the universe conspires to help that person to realize his dream.

***

There is only one thing that makes a dream impossible to achieve: the fear of failure.

***

When we love, we always strive to become better than we are. When we strive to become better than we are, everything around us becomes better too.

***

Everyone seems to have a clear idea of how other people should lead their lives, but none about his or her own.

***

Everything tells me that I am about to make a wrong decision, but making mistakes is just part of life. What does the world want of me? Does it want me to take no risks, to go back to where I came from because I didn't dare to say 'yes' to life?

***

At every moment of our lives, we all have one foot in a fairy tale and the other in the abyss.

***

Nothing in the world is ever completely wrong. Even a stopped clock is right twice a day.

Ralph Waldo Emerson

Emerson, **Ralph Waldo** (25 May 1803–27 April 1882) was a writer, lecturer, poet, and Transcendentalist thinker.

***

A hero is no braver than an ordinary man, but he is braver five minutes longer.

***

Beware when the great God lets loose a thinker on this planet.

***

The character is higher than intellect... A great soul will be strong to live, as well as to think.

***

Children are all foreigners.

***

Conversation is an art in which a man has all humanity for his competitors, for it is that which all are practicing every day while they live.

***

Do not be too timid and squeamish about your actions. All life is an experiment.

***

Do not go where the path may lead, go instead where there is no path and leave a trail.

***

Don't be too timid and squeamish about your actions. All life is an experiment. The more experiments you make, the better.

✳✳✳

Don't waste yourself in rejection, nor bark against the bad, but chant the beauty of the good.

✳✳✳

Every hero becomes a bore at last.

✳✳✳

Finish each day and be done with it. You have done what you could. Some blunders and absurdities no doubt crept in; forget them as soon as you can. Tomorrow is a new day; begin it well and serenely and with too high a spirit to be cumbered with your old nonsense.

✳✳✳

Give all to love; obey thy heart.

✳✳✳

I awoke this morning with devout thanksgiving for my friends, the old and the new.

✳✳✳

I pack my trunk, embrace my friends, embark on the sea, and at last wake up in Naples, and there beside me is the Stern Fact, the Sad Self, unrelenting, identical, that I fled from.

✳✳✳

If I have lost confidence in myself, I have the universe against me.

***

Insist on yourself; never imitate... Every great man is unique.

***

Let not a man guard his dignity, but let his dignity guard him.

***

Live in the sunshine, swim the sea, drink the wild air...

***

Make the most of yourself, for that, is all there is of you.

***

Nature magically suits a man to his fortunes, by making them the fruit of his character.

***

Nothing can bring you peace but yourself.

***

Nothing is at last sacred but the integrity of your mind.

***

People seem not to see that their opinion of the world is also a confession of their character.

***

Speak what you think today in words as hard as cannon-balls and tomorrow speak what tomorrow thinks in hard words again, though it contradicts everything you said today.

The ancestor of every action is a thought.

✳✳✳

The only way to have a friend is to be one.

✳✳✳

The ornament of a house is the friends who frequent it.

✳✳✳

The world belongs to the energetic.

✳✳✳

We do what we must, and call it by the best names.

✳✳✳

Whoever is open, loyal, true; of humane and affable demeanor; honorable himself, and in his judgment of others; faithful to his word as to law, and faithful alike to God and man.... such a man is a true gentleman.

✳✳✳

Nothing astonishes men so much as common sense and plain dealing.

✳✳✳

He who is in love is wise and is becoming wiser, sees newly every time he looks at the object beloved, drawing from it with his eyes and his mind those virtues which it possesses.

✳✳✳

Trust men and they will be true to you; treat them greatly, and they will show themselves great.

***

The best effect of fine persons is felt after we have left their presence.

***

Every artist was first an amateur.

***

None of us will ever accomplish anything excellent or commanding except when he listens to this whisper which is heard by him alone.

***

A man builds a fine house, and now he has a master and a task for life; he is to furnish, watch, show it, and keep it in repair, the rest of his days.

***

The reward of a thing well done is to have done it.

Robert T. Kiyosaki

Robert T. Kiyosaki (April 8, 1947) is the best-selling author of the Rich Dad books, an educational entrepreneur.

***

Failure defeats losers; failure inspires winners.

***

Your most expensive advice is the free advice you receive from your financially struggling friends and relatives.

***

Average investors are on the outside trying to look into the inside of the company or property they are investing in.

***

It's the investor who is risky, not the investment.

***

The idea of working all your life, saving, and putting money into a retirement account is a very slow plan.

***

If you don't first handle fear and desire, and you get rich, you'll be a high pay slave.

***

To gain more abundance a person needs more skills and needs to be more creative and cooperative.

***

The unique ability to take decisive action while maintaining focus on the ultimate mission is what defines a true leader.

***

Instead of labeling and discriminating against one or the other, we need to learn to blend our gifts and complement our geniuses.

***

By asking the question How can I afford it? Your brain is put to work.

***

One of the main reasons people are not rich is that they worry too much about things that might never happen.

Robert H. Schuller

Robert Harold Schuller (September 16, 1926 – April 2, 2015) was an American Christian televangelist, pastor.

***

Commit yourself to a dream nobody who tries to do something great but fails is a total failure. Why? Because he can always rest assured that he succeeded in life's most important battle -- he defeated the fear of trying.

***

Yes, you can be a dreamer and a doer too, if you will remove one word from your vocabulary: impossible.

***

You can often measure a person by the size of his dream.

***

Build a dream, and the dream will build you.

***

Always look at what you have left. Never look at what you have lost.

***

Commit yourself to a dream... Nobody who tries to do something great but fails is a total failure. Why? Because he can always rest assured that he succeeded in life's most important battle--he defeated the fear of trying.

***

If you listen to your fears, you will die never knowing what a great person you might have been.

***

Impossible situations can become possible miracles.

***

It takes but one positive thought when given a chance to survive and thrive to overpower an entire army of negative thoughts.

***

Let your imagination release your imprisoned possibilities.

***

Every achiever I have ever met says, my life turned around when I began to believe in me.

***

Anyone can count the seeds in an apple, but only God can count the number of apples in a seed.

***

Most people who succeed n the face of seemingly impossible conditions are people who simply don't know how to quit.

***

Life is but a moment; death also is but another.

***

Better to do something imperfectly than to do nothing flawlessly.

***

Again, and again, the impossible problem is solved when we see that the problem is only a tough decision waiting to be made.

***

What great thing would you attempt if you knew you could not fail?

***

The only place where your dream becomes impossible is in your thinking.

***

Never cut a tree down in the wintertime. Never make a negative decision in a low time.

***

What would you attempt to do if you knew you could not fail?

***

Failure doesn't mean you are a failure... it just means you haven't succeeded yet.

***

Goals are not only necessary to motivate us. They are essential to keep us alive.

***

Inch by inch, it's a cinch.

***

When you can't solve the problem, manage it.

***

Never bring the problem-solving stage into the decision-making stage. Otherwise, you surrender yourself to the problem rather than the solution.

***

Problems are not stopped signs; they are guidelines.

***

Doomed are the hotheads! Unhappy are they who lose their cool and are too proud to say, "I'm sorry."

***

Let your hopes, not your hurts, shape your future.

***

Possibilitizing is overcoming while you're undergoing.

***

Always look at what you have left. Never look at what you have lost.

Socrates

Socrates (469-399 B.C.) was a Greek philosopher and is considered the father of western philosophy.

✳✳✳

Employ your time in improving yourself by other men's writings so that you shall come easily by what others have labored hard for.

✳✳✳

Well, I am certainly wiser than this man. It is only too likely that neither of us has any knowledge to boast of; but he thinks that he knows something which he does not know, whereas I am quite conscious of my ignorance. At any rate, it seems that I am wiser than he is to this small extent, that I do not think that I know what I do not know.

✳✳✳

True wisdom comes to each of us when we realize how little we understand about life, ourselves, and the world around us.

✳✳✳

The beginning of wisdom is a definition of terms.

✳✳✳

What a lot of things there are a man can do without.

✳✳✳

I cannot teach anybody anything. I can only make them think.

✳✳✳

Slanderers do not hurt me because they do not hit me.

***

I was afraid that by observing objects with my eyes and trying to comprehend them with each of my other senses I might blind my soul altogether.

***

To find yourself, think for yourself.

***

Know thyself.

***

He who is not contented with what he has, would not be contented with what he would like to have.

***

If a man is proud of his wealth, he should not be praised until it is known how he employs it.

***

Where there is reverence, there is fear, but there is not reverence everywhere that there is fear, because fear presumably has a wider extension than reverence.

***

They are not only idle who do nothing, but they are idle also who might be better employed.

***

One thing only I know, and that is that I know nothing.

***

Our prayers should be for blessings in general, for God knows best what is good for us.

***

I only wish that ordinary people had an unlimited capacity for harming; then they might have unlimited power for doing good.

***

How many are the things I can do without!

***

I was too honest a man to be a politician and live.

***

Ordinary people seem not to realize that those who apply themselves in the right way to philosophy are directly and of their own accord preparing themselves for dying and death.

***

The hottest love has the coldest end.

***

See one promontory, one mountain, one sea, one river and see all.

***

A system of morality which is based on relative emotional values is a mere illusion, a thoroughly vulgar conception which has nothing sound in it and nothing true.

***

By all means, marry. If you get a good wife, you will become happy, and if you get a bad one, you will become a philosopher.

***

When desire, having rejected reason and overpowered judgment which leads to right, is set in the direction of the pleasure which beauty can inspire, and when again under the influence of its kindred desires it is moved with violent motion towards the beauty of corporeal forms, it acquires a surname from this very violent motion, and is called love.

***

I pray Thee, O God, that I may be beautiful within.

***

The way to gain a good reputation is to endeavor to be what you desire to appear.

***

Nature has given us two ears, two eyes, and but one tongue-to the end that we should hear and see more than we speak.

***

In childhood be modest, in youth temperate, in adulthood just, and in old age prudent.

***

The end of life is to be like God, and the soul following God will be like Him.

***

We are convinced that if we are ever to have pure knowledge of anything, we must get rid of the body and contemplate things by themselves with the soul by itself. It seems, to judge from the argument, that the wisdom which we desire and upon which we profess to have set our hearts will be attainable only when we are dead and not in our lifetime.

***

Nothing is to be preferred before justice.

***

Death may be the greatest of all human blessings.

***

Let him that would move the world, first move.

***

The comic and the tragic lie inseparably close, like light and shadow.

***

I am not an Athenian, nor a Greek, but a citizen of the world.

***

Call no man unhappy until he is married.

***

Happiness is an unrepentant pleasure.

***

The unexamined life is not worth living.

***

Wars and revolutions and battles are due simply and solely to the body and its desires. All wars are undertaken for the acquisition of wealth, and the reason why we have to acquire wealth is the body because we are slaves in its service.

***

No man undertakes a trade he has not learned, even the meanest; yet everyone thinks himself sufficiently qualified for the hardest of all trades, that of government.

***

The only good is knowledge, and the only evil is ignorance.

***

The nearest way to glory is to strive to be what you wish to be thought to be.

***

Be slow to fall into friendship; but when thou art in, continue firm and constant.

***

Enjoy yourself — it's later than you think.

***

Worthless people live only to eat and drink; people of worth eat and drink only to live.

***

Once made equal to man, a woman becomes his superior.

***

Crito, I owe a cock to Asclepius; will you remember to pay the debt?

***

Fame is the perfume of heroic deeds.

***

The envious person grows lean with the fatness of their neighbor.

***

From the deepest desires often come the deadliest hate.

***

An education obtained with money is worse than no education at all.

***

Whom do I call educated? First, those who manage well the circumstances they encounter day by day. Next, those who are decent and honorable in their intercourse with all men, bearing easily and good naturedly what is offensive in others and being as agreeable and reasonable to their associates as is humanly possible to be... those who hold their pleasures always under control and are not ultimately overcome by their misfortunes... those who are not spoiled by their successes, who do not desert their true selves but hold their ground steadfastly as wise and sober-minded men.

***

False words are not only evil in themselves, but they infect the soul with evil.

***

The fewer our wants, the more we resemble the Gods.

***

Life contains but two tragedies. One is not to get your heart's desire; the other is to get it.

***

A multitude of books distracts the mind.

***

Whenever, therefore, people are deceived and form opinions wide of the truth, it is clear that the error has slid into their minds through the medium of certain resemblances to that truth.

***

If I tell you that I would be disobeying the god and, on that account, it is impossible for me to keep quiet, you won't be persuaded by me, taking it that I am ionizing. And if I tell you that it is the greatest good for a human being to have discussions every day about virtue and the other things you hear me talking about, examining myself and others and that the unexamined life is not livable for a human being, you will be even less persuaded.

***

The hour of departure has arrived, and we go our ways; I to die, and you to live. Which is better? Only God knows.

***

To fear death, my friends is only to think ourselves wise, without being wise: for it is to think that we know what we do not know. For anything that men can tell, death may be the greatest good that can happen to them: but they fear it as if they knew quite well that it was the greatest of evils. And what is this but that shameful ignorance of thinking that we know what we do not know?

***

Think not those faithful who praise all thy words and actions, but those who kindly reprove thy faults.

***

Contentment is natural wealth; luxury is artificial poverty.

***

Give me beauty in the inward soul; may the outward and the inward man be at one.

***

He is rich who is content with the least; for contentment is the wealth of nature.

***

Remember, no human condition is ever permanent. Then you will not be overjoyed in good fortune nor too scornful in misfortune.

***

Beauty is a short-lived tyranny.

***

The only true wisdom is in knowing you know nothing.

***

There is only one good, knowledge, and one evil, ignorance.

***

Wonder if the beginning of wisdom.

***

Be kind; for everyone you meet is fighting a hard battle.

***

Every action has its pleasures and its price.

***

Remember what is unbecoming to do is also unbecoming to speak of.

***

Be as you wish to seem.

***

Do not do to others what angers you if done to you by others.

***

Beware the barrenness of a busy life.

***

Bad men live that they may eat and drink, whereas good men eat and drink that they may live.

***

I know that I am intelligent because I know that I know nothing.

***

Are you not ashamed of heaping up the greatest amount of money and honor and reputation, and caring so little about wisdom and truth and the greatest improvement of the soul?

***

Remember that there is nothing stable in human affairs; therefore, avoid undue elation in prosperity, or undue depression in adversity.

***

We cannot live better than in seeking to become better.

***

The secret of change is to focus all of your energy, not on fighting the old, but on building the new.

***

Smart people learn from everything and everyone, average people from their experiences, stupid people already have all the answers.

***

Education is the kindling of a flame, not the filling of a vessel.

* * *

The shortest and surest way to live with honor in the world is to be in reality what we would appear to be; and if we observe, we shall find, that all human virtues increase and strengthen themselves by the practice of them.

* * *

No man has the right to be an amateur in the matter of physical training. It is a shame for a man to grow old without seeing the beauty and strength of which his body is capable.

* * *

I know nothing except the fact of my ignorance.

* * *

Silence is a profound melody, for those who can hear it above all the noise.

* * *

If you don't get what you want, you suffer; if you get what you don't want, you suffer; even when you get exactly what you want, you still suffer because you can't hold on to it forever. Your mind is your predicament. It wants to be free of change. Free of pain, free of the obligations of life and death. But change is law, and no amount of pretending will alter that reality.

* * *

There are two kinds of disease of the soul, vice and ignorance.

* * *

Sometimes you put walls up not to keep people out, but to see who cares enough to break them down.

***

Strong minds discuss ideas, average minds discuss events, weak minds discuss people.

***

The secret of happiness, you see, is not found in seeking more, but in developing the capacity to enjoy less.

***

When the debate is lost, slander becomes the tool of the loser.

***

Having the fewest wants, I am nearest to the gods.

***

The children now love luxury. They have bad manners, contempt for authority; they show disrespect for elders and love chatter in place of exercise.

***

Falling is not a failure. Failure comes when you stay where you have fallen.

***

Prefer knowledge to wealth, for the one is transitory, the other perpetual.

***

Get not your friends by bare compliments, but by giving them sensible tokens of your love.

***

Be nicer than necessary to everyone you meet. Everyone is fighting some battle.

***

All wars are fought for the acquisition of wealth.

***

Thou shouldst eat to live; not live to eat.

***

If you want to be a good saddler, saddle the worst horse; for if you can tame one, you can tame all.

***

One should never do wrong in return, nor mistreat any man, no matter how he has mistreated one.

***

Be the kind of person that you want people to think you are.

***

Understanding a question is half the answer.

***

The greatest way to live with honor in this world is to be what we pretend to be.

***

If all our misfortunes were laid in one common heap whence everyone must take an equal portion; most people would be content to take their own and depart.

***

We can easily forgive a child who is afraid of the dark; the real tragedy of life is when men are afraid of the light.

***

Children nowadays are tyrants. They contradict their parents, gobble their food, and tyrannize their teachers.

***

The greatest blessing granted to humanity come by way of madness, which is a divine gift.

***

There is no possession more valuable than a good and faithful friend.

***

The years wrinkle our skin, but lack of enthusiasm wrinkles our soul.

***

The highest realms of thought are impossible to reach without first attaining an understanding of compassion.

***

The easiest and noblest way is not to be crushing others, but to be improving yourselves.

***

When you want wisdom and insight as badly as you want to breathe, it is then you shall have it.

***

To move the world, we must move.

***

Through your rags, I see your vanity.

Steve Jobs

Steven Paul Jobs (February 24, 1955 – October 5, 2011) was an American business magnate and investor. Jobs is widely recognized as a pioneer of the microcomputer revolution of the 1970s and 1980s, along with Apple co-founder Steve Wozniak.

***

Stay hungry, stay foolish.

***

It's really hard to design products by focus groups. A lot of times, people don't know what they want until you show it to them.

***

Sometimes I believe in God; sometimes I don't. I think it's 50-50 maybe. But ever since I've had cancer, I've been thinking about it more. And I find myself believing a bit more. I kind of – maybe it's 'because I want to believe in an afterlife. That when you die, it doesn't just all disappear. The wisdom you've accumulated. Somehow it lives on, but sometimes I think it's just like an on-off switch. Click, and you're gone. And that's why I don't like putting on-off switches on Apple devices.

***

I was worth about over a million dollars when I was twenty-three and over ten million dollars when I was twenty-four, and over a hundred million dollars when I was twenty-five, and it wasn't that important because I never did it for the money.

***

Do you want to spend the rest of your life selling sugared water or do you want a chance to change the world?

***

I'm the only person I know that's lost a quarter of a billion dollars in one year.... It's very character-building.

***

Picasso had a saying: Good artists copy, great artists steal, and we have always been shameless about stealing great ideas.

***

It's more fun to be a pirate than to join the navy.

***

You can't connect the dots looking forward; you can only connect them looking backward. So, you have to trust that the dots will somehow connect in your future. You have to trust in something — your gut, destiny, life, karma, whatever. This approach has never let me down, and it has made all the difference in my life.

***

The ones who are crazy enough to think that they can change the world, are the ones who do.

***

The only problem with Microsoft is they have no taste. They have absolutely no taste. And I don't mean that in a small way, I mean that in a big way, in the sense that they don't think of original ideas, and they don't bring much culture into their products.

***

Our friends up north spend over five billion dollars on research and development, and all they seem to do is copy Google and Apple.

***

I wish developing great products was as easy as writing a check. If that were the case, Microsoft would have great products.

***

Every once in a while, a revolutionary product comes along that changes everything. It's very fortunate if you can work on just one of these in your career. ... Apple's been very fortunate in that it's introduced a few of these.

***

When you first start off trying to solve a problem, the first solutions you come up with are very complex, and most people stop there. But if you keep going, and live with the problem and peel more layers of the onion off, you can often arrive at some very elegant and simple solutions.

***

No one wants to die. Even people who want to go to heaven don't want to die to get there. And yet death is the destination we all share. No one has ever escaped it. And that is as it should be because Death is very likely the single best invention of Life. It is Life's change agent. It clears out the old to make way for the new. Right now, the new is you, but someday not too long from now; you will gradually become the old and be cleared away. Sorry to be so dramatic, but it is quite true.

✳✳✳

Nobody has tried to swallow us since I've been here. I think they are afraid of how we would taste.

✳✳✳

My model for business is The Beatles. They were four guys who kept each other's kind of negative tendencies in check. They balanced each other, and the total was greater than the sum of the parts. That's how I see business: great things in business are never done by one person; they're done by a team of people.

✳✳✳

It's not a faith in technology. It's faith in people.

✳✳✳

I would trade all of my technology for an afternoon with Socrates.

✳✳✳

The most compelling reason for most people to buy a computer for the home will be to link it into a nationwide communications network. We're just in the beginning stages of what will be a remarkable breakthrough for most people–as remarkable as the telephone.

✳✳✳

It's hard to tell with these Internet startups if they're interested in building companies or if they're just interested in the money. I can tell you, though: If they don't want to build a company, they won't luck into it. That's because it's so hard that if you don't have a passion, you'll give up.

**

We made the buttons on the screen look so good you'll want to lick them.

**

The problem with the Internet startup craze isn't that too many people are starting companies; it's that too many people aren't sticking with it.

**

We believed that if we kept putting great products in front of customers, they would continue to open their wallets.

**

And it comes from saying no to 1,000 things to make sure we don't get on the wrong track or try to do too much. We're always thinking about new markets we could enter, but it's only by saying no that you can concentrate on the really important things.

**

That's been one of my mantras — focus and simplicity. Simple can be harder than complex: You have to work hard to get your thinking clean to make it simple. But it's worth it in the end because once you get there, you can move mountains.

***

Your time is limited, so don't waste it living someone else's life. Don't be trapped by dogma – which is living with the results of other people's thinking. Don't let the noise of other's opinions drown out your inner voice. And most important, dare to follow your heart and intuition. They somehow already know what you truly want to become. Everything else is secondary.

***

I've always been attracted to the more revolutionary changes. I don't know why. Because they're harder. They're much more stressful emotionally. And you usually go through a period where everybody tells you that you've completely failed.

***

I think we're having fun. I think our customers like our products. And we're always trying to do better.

***

Innovation has nothing to do with how many R&D dollars you have. It's about the people you have, how you're led, and how much you get it.

***

Older people sit down and ask, 'What is it?' but the boy asks, 'What can I do with it?'.

***

Sometimes when you innovate, you make mistakes. It is best to admit them quickly, and get on with improving your other innovations.

***

Being the richest man in the cemetery doesn't matter to me … Going to bed at night saying we've done something wonderful… that's what matters to me.

***

Creativity is just connecting things. When you ask creative people how they did something, they feel a little guilty because they didn't do it, they just saw something. It seemed obvious to them after a while.

***

My favorite things in life don't cost any money. It's really clear that the most precious resource we all have is time.

***

Let's invent tomorrow rather than worrying about what happened yesterday.

***

Your work is going to fill a large part of your life, and the only way to be truly satisfied is to do what you believe is great work. And the only way to do great work is to love what you do. If you haven't found it yet, keep looking. Don't settle. As with all matters of the heart, you'll know when you find it. And, like any great relationship, it just gets better and better as the years roll on. So keep looking until you find it. Don't settle.

***

If you are working on something exciting that you care about, you don't have to be pushed. The vision pulls you.

***

The design is a funny word. Some people think design means how it looks. But of course, if you dig deeper, it's really how it works.

***

An iPod, a phone, and an Internet communicator. An iPod, a phone ... are you getting it? These are not three separate devices, this is one device, and we are calling it iPhone.

***

Quality is more important than quantity. One home run is much better than two doubles.

***

I think if you do something and it turns out pretty good, then you should do something else wonderful, not dwell on it for too long. Just figure out what's next.

***

We're gambling on our vision, and we would rather do that than make, too products. Let some other companies do that. For us, it's always the next dream.

***

We're not going to be the first to this party, but we're going to be the best.

***

Innovation distinguishes between a leader and a follower.

***

Start small, think big. Don't worry about too many things at once. Take a handful of simple things, to begin with, and then progress to more complex ones. Think about not just tomorrow, but the future. Put a ding in the universe.

***

We're just enthusiastic about what we do.

***

You've got to start with the customer experience and work back toward the technology – not the other way around.

***

Be a yardstick of quality. Some people aren't used to an environment where excellence is expected.

***

Real artists ship.

***

We don't get a chance to do that many things, and everyone should be excellent. Because this is our life. Life is brief, and then you die, you know? And we've all chosen to do this with our lives. So, it better be damn good. It better be worth it.

✳✳✳

People think focus means saying yes to the thing you've got to focus on. But that's not what it means at all. It means saying no to the hundred other good ideas that there are. You have to pick carefully.

✳✳✳

You have to be burning with an idea, or a problem, or a wrong that you want to right. If you're not passionate enough from the start, you'll never stick it out.

✳✳✳

Remembering that I'll be dead soon is the most important tool I've ever encountered to help me make the big choices in life. Because almost everything — all external expectations, all pride, all fear of embarrassment or failure — these things fall away in the face of death, leaving only what is truly important. Remembering that you are going to die is the best way I know to avoid the trap of thinking you have something to lose. You are already naked. There is no reason not to follow your heart. ... Stay hungry. Stay foolish.

✳✳✳

When I was 17, I read a quote that went something like: If you live each day as if it was your last, someday you'll most certainly be right. It made an impression on me, and since then, for the past 33 years, I have looked in the mirror every morning and asked myself: If today were the last day of my life, would I want to do what I am about to do today? And whenever the answer has been no for too many days in a row, I know I need to change something.

✳✳✳

The computer is the most remarkable tool we've ever come up with. It's the equivalent of a bicycle for our minds.

***

I don't care about being right; I care about success. I don't mind being wrong, and I'll admit that I'm wrong a lot. It doesn't matter to me too much. What matters to me is that we do the right thing.

***

Getting fired from Apple was the best thing that could have ever happened to me. The heaviness of being successful was replaced by the lightness of being a beginner again. It freed me to enter one of the most creative periods of my life.

***

The bottom line is, I didn't return to Apple to make a fortune. I've been very lucky in my life and already have one. When I was 25, my net worth was $100 million or so. I decided then that I wasn't going to let it ruin my life. There's no way you could ever spend it all, and I don't view wealth as something that validates my intelligence.

***

What is Apple, after all? Apple is about people who think 'outside the box,' people who want to use computers to help them change the world, to help them create things that make a difference, and not just to get a job done.

I'm as proud of many of the things we haven't done as the things we have done. Innovation is saying no to a thousand things.

***

When you're a carpenter making a beautiful chest of drawers, you're not going to use a piece of plywood on the back, even though it faces the wall and nobody will ever see it. You'll know it's there, so you're going to use a beautiful piece of wood on the back. For you to sleep well at night, the aesthetic, the quality, has to be carried all the way through.

***

I hate the way people use slide presentations instead of thinking. People would confront a problem by creating a presentation. I wanted them to engage, to hash things out at the table, rather than show a bunch of slides. People who know what they're talking about don't need PowerPoint.

***

I'm convinced that about half of what separates the successful entrepreneurs from the non-successful ones is pure perseverance. It is so hard.

***

Sometimes life hits you in the head with a brick. Don't lose faith. I'm convinced that the only thing that kept me going was that I loved what I did.

***

You've got to find what you love. And that is as true for your work as it is for your lovers.

* * *

You always have to keep pushing to innovate.

* * *

My job is to not be easy on people. My job is to make them better.

* * *

When you grow up, you tend to get told that the world is the way it is and your life is to live your life inside the world. Try not to bash into the walls too much. Try to have a nice family, have fun, save a little money. That's a very limited life. Life can be much broader once you discover one simple fact: Everything around you that you call life was made up by people that were no smarter than you and you can change it, you can influence it, you can build your things that other people can use.

Thomas Edison

Thomas Alva **Edison** (February 11, 1847 – October 18, 1931) was an American inventor and businessman. He invented many useful items including the practical light bulb and phonograph.

✳✳✳

Genius is one percent inspiration and ninety-nine percent perspiration. Accordingly, a 'genius' is often merely a talented person who has done all of his or her homework.

✳✳✳

Opportunity is missed by most people because it is dressed in overalls and looks like work.

The first requisite for success is to develop the ability to focus and apply your mental and physical energies to the problem at hand - without growing weary. Because such thinking is often difficult, there seems to be no limit to which some people will go to avoid the effort and labor that is associated with it...

✳✳✳

I never did anything worth doing entirely by accident... Almost none of my inventions came about totally by accident. They were achieved by having trained me to endure and tolerate hard work.

✳✳✳

I enjoy working for about 18 hours a day. Besides the short catnaps I take each day, I average about four to five hours of sleep per night.

✳✳✳

My main purpose in life is to make money so I can afford to go on creating more inventions...

***

My principal business is giving commercial value to the brilliant - but misdirected ideas of others...

***

I am quite correctly described as 'more of a sponge than an inventor....'

***

Because I readily absorb ideas from every source - frequently starting where the last person left off - I never pick up an item without thinking of how I might improve it.

***

I am not overly impressed by the great names and reputations of those who might be trying to beat me to an invention... It's their 'ideas' that appeal to me.

***

Because ideas have to be original only about their adaptation to the problem at hand, I am always extremely interested in how others have used them...

***

A good idea is never lost. Even though its originator or possessor may die, it will someday be reborn in the mind of another...

***

I never perfected an invention that I did not think about in terms of the service it might give others... I find out what the world needs, then I proceed to invent...

$$***$$

The dove is my emblem... I want to save and advance human life, not destroy it... I am proud of the fact that I never invented weapons to kill...

$$***$$

Most of the exercise I get is from standing and walking around laboratory tables all day. I derive more benefit and entertainment from this than some of my friends, and competitors get from playing games like golf.

$$***$$

If we all did the things, we are capable of doing; we would astound ourselves...

$$***$$

Our schools and are not teaching students to think. It is astonishing how many young people have difficulty in putting their brains definitely and systematically to work...

$$***$$

The three things that are most essential to achievement are common sense, hard work, and stick-to-it-iv-ness...

$$***$$

I have far more respect for the person with a single idea who gets there than for the person with a thousand ideas who does nothing...

***

Many of life's failures are experienced by people who did not realize how close they were to success when they gave up.

***

Pretty much everything will come to him who hustles while he waits. I believe that restlessness is discontent, and discontent is merely the first necessity of progress. Show me a thoroughly satisfied man and I will show you a failure.

***

Unfortunately, there seems to be far more opportunity out there than ability... We should remember that good fortune often happens when opportunity meets with preparation.

***

Sometimes, all you need to invent something is a good imagination and a pile of junk...

Just because something doesn't do what you planned it to do in the first place doesn't mean it's useless...

***

Results? Why, man, I have gotten lots of results! If I find 10,000 ways something won't work, I haven't failed. I am not discouraged, because every wrong attempt discarded is often a step forward...

***

Surprises and reverses can serve as an incentive for great accomplishment. There are no rules here; we're just trying to accomplish something.

***

As a cure for worrying, work is far better than whiskey. I always found that, if I began to worry, the best thing I could do was focus upon doing something useful and then work very hard at it. Soon, I would forget what was troubling me.

***

Barring serious accidents, if you are not preoccupied with worry and you work hard, you can look forward to a reasonably lengthy existence... It's not the hard work that kills; it's the worrying that kills.

***

The only time I become discouraged is when I think of all the things I would like to do and the little time I have in which to do them.

***

The thing I lose patience with the most is the clock. Its hands move too fast.

***

Time is the only capital that any human being has and the thing that he can least afford to waste or lose...

***

From his neck down a man is worth a couple of dollars a day, from his neck up he is worth anything that his brain can produce.

***

The doctor of the future will give no medicine but will interest his patients in the care of the human body, in diet, and the cause and prevention of disease.

***

Whatever the mind of man creates, should be controlled by man's character.

***

Even though I am nearly deaf, I seem to be gifted with a kind of inner hearing which enables me to detect sounds and noises which the ordinary person does not hear.

***

I love great music and art, but I think 'cubist' songs and paintings are hideous.

***

Someday, man will harness the rise and fall of the tides, imprison the power of the sun, and release atomic power.

***

I am both pleased but astonished by the fact that humankind has not yet begun to use all the means and devices that are available for destruction. I hope that such weapons are never manufactured in quantity.

***

The United States and other advanced nations will someday be able to produce instruments of death so terrible the world will be in abject terror of itself and its ability to end civilization... Such war-making weapons should be developed - but only for purposes of discovery and experimentation

***

The dove is my emblem... I want to save and advance human life, not destroy it... I am proud of the fact that I never invented weapons to kill...

To me, the idea and expectation that the day is slowly and surely coming when we will be able to honestly say we are our brother's keeper and not his oppressor is very beautiful.

***

Until man duplicates a blade of grass, nature can laugh at his so-called scientific knowledge...

***

It's obvious that we don't know one-millionth of one percent about anything.

***

I believe that the science of chemistry alone almost proves the existence of an intelligent creator.

***

We have merely scratched the surface of the store of knowledge which will come to us. I believe that we are now, a-tremble on the verge of vast discoveries - discoveries so wondrously important they will upset the present trend of human thought and start it along completely new lines.

***

Be courageous! Whatever setbacks America has encountered, it has always emerged as a stronger and more prosperous nation... Be as brave as your fathers before you. Have faith and go forward!

***

If parents pass enthusiasm along to their children, they will leave them an estate of incalculable value...

***

The memory of my mother will always be a blessing to me...

***

Life's most soothing things are a child's goodnight and sweet music....

***

Great music and art are earthly wonders, but I think 'cubist' songs and paintings are hideous.

***

Even though I am nearly deaf, I seem to be gifted with a kind of inner hearing which enables me to detect sounds and noises which the ordinary listener does not hear.

Thomas Jefferson

Thomas Jefferson (1743-1826), the author of the Declaration of Independence and the third U.S. president, was a leading figure in America's early development.

✳✳✳

I believe that every human mind feels pleasure in doing good to another.

✳✳✳

The energy, the faith, the devotion which we bring to this endeavor will light our country and all who serve it, and the glow from that fire can truly light the world.

✳✳✳

The most valuable of all talents is that of never using two words when one will do.

✳✳✳

Merchants have no country. The mere spot they stand on does not constitute so strong an attachment as that from which they draw their gains.

✳✳✳

A coward is much more exposed to quarrels than a man of spirit.

✳✳✳

Enlighten the people generally, and tyranny and oppressions of body and mind will vanish like evil spirits at the dawn of day.

***

Friendship is precious, not only in the shade but in the sunshine of life.

***

It is my principle that the will of the majority should always prevail.

***

Peace and friendship with all humankind is our wisest policy, and I wish we may be permitted to pursue it.

***

When a man assumes a public trust, he should consider himself as public property.

***

The man who fears no truths has nothing to fear from lies.

***

Nothing can stop the man with the right mental attitude from achieving his goal; nothing on earth can help the man with the wrong mental attitude.

***

Determine never to be idle...It is wonderful how much may be done if we are always doing.

***

Do not bite at the bait of pleasure till you know there is no hook beneath it.

***

I do not take a single newspaper, nor read one a month, and I feel myself infinitely the happier for it.

***

I'm a great believer in luck, and I find the harder I work the more I have of it.

***

Never fear the want of business. A man who qualifies himself well for his calling never fails of employment.

***

Never spend your money before you have it.

***

Never trouble another for what you can do for yourself.

***

Nothing gives one person so much advantage over another as to remain always cool and unruffled under all circumstances.

***

The advertisement is the most truthful part of a newspaper.

***

Walking is the best possible exercise. Habituate yourself to walk very far.

***

Nothing can stop the man with the right mental attitude from achieving his goal; nothing on earth can help the man with the wrong mental attitude.

***

Honesty is the first chapter in the book of wisdom.

***

When angry count to ten before you speak. If very angry, count to one hundred.

***

We hold these truths to be self-evident: that all men are created equal; that they are endowed by their Creator with certain unalienable rights; that among these are life, liberty, and the pursuit of happiness.

***

Rightful liberty is unobstructed action according to our will within limits drawn around us by the equal rights of others. I do not add 'within the limits of the law' because the law is often but the tyrant's will, and always so when it violates the rights of the individual.

***

The care of human life and happiness, and not their destruction, is the first and only object of good government.

***

Nothing gives one person so much advantage over another as to remain always cool and unruffled under all circumstances.

***

Nothing gives one person so much advantage over another as to remain always cool and unruffled under all circumstances.

✳✳✳

Experience hath shewn, that even under the best forms of government those entrusted with power have, in time, and by slow operations, perverted it into tyranny.

✳✳✳

The tree of liberty must be refreshed from time to time with the blood of patriots and tyrants.

✳✳✳

Every government degenerate when trusted to the rulers of the people alone. The people themselves are its only safe depositories.

✳✳✳

I never considered a difference of opinion in politics, in religion, in philosophy, as a cause for withdrawing from a friend.

✳✳✳

Good wine is a necessity of life for me.

✳✳✳

But friendship is precious, not only in the shade, but in the sunshine of life, and thanks to a benevolent arrangement the greater part of life is sunshine.

✳✳✳

A Bill of Rights is what the people are entitled to against every government, and what no just government should refuse, or rest on inference.

***

I believe that every human mind feels pleasure in doing good to another.

***

Do not bite at the bait of pleasure, till you know there is no hook beneath it.

***

He who knows best knows how little he knows.

***

The question with boldness even the existence of a God; because, if there be one, he must more approve of the homage of reason, than that of blind-folded fear.

***

I'm a greater believer in luck, and I find the harder I work the more I have of it.

***

We in America do not have government by the majority. We have government by the majority who participate.

***

History, in general, only informs us what bad government is.

***

Determine never to be idle. No person will have occasion to complain of the want of time, who never loses any. It is wonderful how much may be done if we are always doing.

✳✳✳

I had rather be shut up in a very modest cottage with my books, my family and a few old friends, dining on simple bacon, and letting the world roll on as it liked than to occupy the most splendid post, which any human power can give.

✳✳✳

If a nation expects to be ignorant and free, in a state of civilization, it expects what never was and never will be.

✳✳✳

There is nothing more unequal than the equal treatment of unequal people.

✳✳✳

When injustice becomes law, resistance becomes a duty.

✳✳✳

Do you want to know who you are? Don't ask. Act! Action will delineate and define you.

✳✳✳

Every day is lost in which we do not learn something useful. The man has no nobler or more valuable possession at that time.

✳✳✳

Be polite to all, but intimate with few.

***

I believe that banking institutions are more dangerous to our liberties than standing armies.

***

Our liberty depends on the freedom of the press, and that cannot be limited without being lost.

***

I like the dreams of the future better than the history of the past.

***

I hold it that a little rebellion now and then is a good thing, and as necessary in the political world as storms in the physical.

***

Enlighten the people generally, and tyranny and oppression of the body and mind will vanish like evil spirits at the dawn of day.

***

He who permits himself to tell a lie once finds it much easier to do it the second time.

***

It is error alone which needs the support of the government. Truth can stand by itself.

***

The man who reads nothing at all is better educated than the man who reads nothing but newspapers.

***

An honest man can feel no pleasure in the exercise of power over his fellow citizens.

***

Pride costs us more than hunger, thirst, and cold.

***

Peace and friendship with all humankind is our wisest policy, and I wish we may be permitted to pursue it.

***

An enemy generally says and believes what he wishes.

***

I cannot live without books.

***

Where the press is free and every man able to read, all is safe.

***

The dead should not rule the living.

***

Experience demands that man is the only animal which devours his kind, for I can apply no milder term to the general prey of the rich on the poor.

***

I prefer dangerous freedom over peaceful slavery.

***

In matters of style, swim with the current; in matters of principle, stand like a rock.

***

No man will ever bring out of that office the reputation which carries him into it. The honeymoon would be as short in that case as in any other, and its moments of ecstasy would be ransomed by years of torment and hatred.

***

Always take hold of things by the smooth handle.

***

Ignorance is preferable to error, and he is less remote from the truth who believes nothing than he who believes what is wrong.

***

The most valuable of all talents is that of never using two words when one will do.

***

The laws that forbid the carrying of arms... disarm only those who are neither inclined nor determined to commit crimes.

***

We confide in our strength, without boasting of it, we respect that of others, without fearing it.

***

Everything yields to diligence.

***

Too old to plant trees for my gratification, I shall do it for my posterity.

***

Books constitute capital. A library book lasts as long as a house, for hundreds of years. It is not, then, an article of mere consumption but fairly of capital, and often in the case of professional men, setting out in life, it is their only capital.

***

Whenever you do a thing, act as if all the world were watching.

***

As discoveries are made, new truths discovered and manners and opinions change with the change of circumstances; institutions must also advance to keep pace with the times.

***

The happiest moments of my life have been the few which I have passed at home in the bosom of my family.

***

I find friendship to be like wine, raw when new, ripened with age, the true old man's milk and restorative cordial.

***

Whiskey claims to itself alone the exclusive office of sot-making.

✳✳✳

I predict future happiness for Americans if they can prevent the government from wasting the labors of the people under the pretense of taking care of them.

✳✳✳

Delay is preferable to error.

✳✳✳

It is my rule never to take a side in any part in the quarrels of others, nor to inquire into them. I generally presume them to flow from the indulgence of too much passion on both sides, & always find that each party thinks all the wrong was in his adversary. These bickerings, which are always useless, embitter human life more than any other cause...

✳✳✳

Half a loaf is better than no bread.

✳✳✳

A great deal of love given to a few is better than a little too many.

✳✳✳

Never spend your money before you have it.

✳✳✳

The policy of the American government is to leave its citizens free, neither restraining them nor aiding them in their pursuits.

***

Leave all the afternoon for exercise and recreation, which are as necessary as reading. I will rather say more necessary because health is worth more than learning.

***

The art of life is the art of avoiding pain; and he is the best pilot, who steers clearest of the rocks and shoals with which it is beset.

***

Don't talk about what you have done or what you are going to do.

***

With your talents and industry, with science, and that steadfast honesty, which eternally pursues right, regardless of consequences, you may promise yourself everything but health, without which there is no happiness.

***

Never trouble another for what you can do yourself.

***

Laws and institutions must go hand in hand with the general progress of the human mind.

***

But whether I retire to bed early or late, I rise with the sun.

**

I hope our wisdom will grow with our power, and teach us, that the less we use our power, the greater it will be.

**

No instance exists of a person's writing two languages perfectly.

**

That will always appear to be his native language which was most familiar to him in his youth.

**

Nothing is troublesome that we do willingly.

**

The spirit of resistance to government is so valuable on certain occasions that I wish it always to be kept alive.

**

But every difference of opinion is not a difference of principle.

**

But this momentous question. Like a fire bell in the night, awakened and filled me with terror.

**

Perfect happiness, I believe, was never intended by the Deity to be the lot of one of his creatures in this world; but that he has very much put in our power the nearness of our approaches to it, is what I have steadfastly believed.

***

When the government fears the people, there is liberty. When the people fear the government, there is tyranny.

***

I would rather be exposed to the inconveniencies attending too much liberty than those attending too small a degree of it.

***

It is neither wealth nor splendor, but tranquility and occupation which give you happiness.

***

How much pain have cost us the evils which have never happened?

***

If our house is on fire, without inquiring whether it was fired from within or without, we must try to extinguish it.

***

No occupation is so delightful to me as the culture of the earth, and no culture comparable to that of the garden...But though an old man, I am but a young gardener.

***

Advertisements... contain the only truths to be relied on in a newspaper.

***

May I never get too busy in my affairs that I fail to respond to the needs of others with kindness and compassion.

***

The glow of one warm thought is to be worth more than money.

***

A strict observance of the written laws is doubtless one of the high virtues of a good citizen, but it is not the highest. The laws of necessity, of self-preservation, of saving our country when in danger, are of higher obligation.

***

I never submitted the whole system of my opinions to the creed of any party of men whatever in religion, in philosophy, in politics, or in anything else where I was capable of thinking for myself. Such an addiction is the last degradation of a free and moral agent.

***

Walking is the very best exercise. Habituate yourself to walk very far.

***

Christianity neither is nor ever was a part of the common law.

***

If I am to meet with a disappointment, the sooner I know it, the more of life I shall have to wear it off.

✳✳✳

Was the government to prescribe us our medicine and diet, our bodies would be in such keeping as our souls are now.

✳✳✳

There is not a truth existing which I fear, or would wish unknown to the whole world.

✳✳✳

Dispositions of the mind, like limbs of the body, acquire strength by exercise.

✳✳✳

No ignorant people can be truly free.

✳✳✳

Man is an imitative animal. This quality is the germ of all education in him. From his cradle to his grave he is learning to do what he sees others do.

✳✳✳

Everything is useful which contributes to fix in the principles and practices of virtue.

✳✳✳

Self-love is no part of morality. Indeed, it is exactly its counterpart. It is the sole antagonist of virtue leading us constantly by our propensities to self-gratification in violation of our moral duties to others.

✳✳✳

That government is best which governs the least because its people discipline themselves.

***

Freedom, the first-born of science.

***

Follow the truth wherever it may lead you.

***

Nature intended me for the tranquil pursuits of science, by rendering them my supreme delight. But the enormities of the times in which I have lived, have forced me to take part in resisting them, and to commit myself on the boisterous ocean of political passions.

***

Of all machines, the human heart is the most complicated and inexplicable.

***

A machine for making revolutions is doing precisely the wrong thing at just the right time.

***

The object of walking is to relax the mind. You should therefore not permit yourself even to think while you walk. But divert your attention by the objects surrounding you.

***

Nobody is better than you and remember, you are better than nobody.

***

Every American citizen must take part in a vigorous debate on the issues of the day.

***

Every generation needs a new revolution.

***

Ridicule is the only weapon which can be used against unintelligible propositions.

Tupac Shakur

Tupac Amaru Shakur (**born** June 16, 1971-died September 13, 1996) also known by his stage names 2Pac and Makaveli, was an American rapper and actor.

***

Reality is wrong. Dreams are for real.

***

A coward dies a thousand deaths. A soldier dies but once.

***

During your life, never stop dreaming. No one can take away your dreams.

***

There's going to be some stuff you are going to see what's going to make it hard to smile in the future, but through whatever you see, through all the rain and the pain, you have to keep your sense of humor. You have to be able to smile through all this bullshit...remember that.

***

I don't see myself being special; I see myself having more responsibilities than the next man. People look to me to do things for them, to have answers.

***

It's the game of life. Do I win or do I lose? One day they're going to shut the game down. I have to have as much fun and go around the board as many times as I can before it's my turn to leave.

✳✳✳

I think I'm a natural-born leader. I know how to bow down to authority if it's an authority that I respect.

✳✳✳

For every night, there's a brighter day.

✳✳✳

I know it seems hard sometimes but remember one thing. Through every night, there's a bright day after that. So, no matter how hard it gets, stick your chest out, keep your head up and handle it.

✳✳✳

It's a struggle for every young Black man. You know how it is, only God can judge us.

✳✳✳

I don't know how to deal with so many people giving me that much affection. I never had that in my life.

✳✳✳

All I'm trying to do is survive and make good out of the dirty, nasty, unbelievable lifestyle that they gave me.

tupac-quotes-wheel

✳✳✳

Life's a wheel of fortune, and it's my chance to spin it.

✳✳✳

When you do rap albums, you got to train yourself. You got to be in character constantly.

***

Somebody help me, tell me where to go from here cause even thugs cry, but do the Lord care?

***

We wouldn't ask why a rose that grew from the concrete for having damaged petals; in turn, we would all celebrate its tenacity, we would all love its will to reach the sun. Well, we are the roses, this is the concrete, and these are my damaged petals. Don't ask me why to thank God, and ask me how.

***

Everybody's at war with different things. I'm at war with my own heart sometimes.

***

Would I rather have been shot straight-up in cold blood-but to be set up? By people who you trusted? That's bad.

***

Let the Lord judge the criminals.

***

The only thing that comes to a sleeping man is dreams.

***

What I learned in jail is that I can't change. I can't live a different lifestyle – this is it. This is the life that they gave, and this is the life that I made.

***

I'm a reflection of the community.

***

We all going to die; we bleed from similar veins.

***

I'd rather die like a man than live like a coward.

***

I feel like role models today are not meant to be put on a pedestal. But more like angels with broken wings.

***

My mama always used to tell me: 'if you can't find somethin' to live for, you best find somethin' to die for.'

***

If God wanted me to be quiet, he would've never shown me what he does.

***

I'll probably be punished for hard living.

***

I am society's child. This is how they made me, and now I'm sayin' what's on my mind, and they don't want that. This is what you made me, America.

***

Though things change, the future's still inside of me.

***

I don't have any fear of death. My only fear is coming back reincarnated.

***

I'm 23 years old. I might be my mother's child, but in all reality, I'm everybody's child. Nobody raised me; I was raised in this society.

***

There's nobody in the business strong enough to scare me.

***

In my mind, I'm a blind man doin' time.

***

With all my fans I got a family again.

***

I believe that everything that you do bad comes back to you. So, everything that I do that's bad, I'm going to suffer from it. But in my mind, I believe what I'm doing is right. So, I feel like I'm going to heaven.

***

It seems like every time you come up something happens to bring you back down.

***

Of course, I'm going to say   I'm a thug, that's because I came from the gutter and I'm still here!

***

I've been shot five times, but I'm still breathing, living proof there a God if you need a reason.

***

I don't want to be a role model. I want to be someone who says; this is who I am, this is what I do, I say what's on my mind.

***

If we are saying that rap is an art form, then we got to be more responsible for our lyrics. If you see everybody dying because of what you are saying, it doesn't matter that you didn't make them die. It just matters that you didn't save them.

***

Death is not the greatest loss in life. The greatest loss is what dies inside while still alive. Never surrender.

***

I'm not sayin' I'm going to rule the world, or that I'm going to change the world, but I guarantee that I will spark the brain that will change the world.

***

That which does not kill me can only make me stronger. I don't see why everybody feel as though they must tell me how to live my life.

***

Forgive but don't forget, girl keep your head up. And when he tells you-you are nothing, don't believe him. And if he can't learn to love you, you should leave him.

***

Can't close my eyes cause all I see is a terror. I hate the man in the mirror cause his reflection makes the pain turn more real.

***

Fear is stronger than love, remember that. Fear is stronger than love. All that love I gave didn't mean anything when it came to fear.

***

One day I'm going to bust, blow up on this society. Why did you lie to me? I couldn't find a trace of equality.

***

The seed must grow even though it's planted in stone.

***

Every day, I'm standing outside trying to sing my way in: We are hungry, please let us in We are hungry, please let us in. After about a week that song is going to change to We hungry, we need some food. After two, three weeks, it's like: Give me the food Or I'm breaking down the door. After a year you're like: I'm picking the lock. Coming through the door blasting.

***

I have not brought violence to you. I have not brought 'thug life' to America. I didn't create 'thug life;' I diagnosed it.

***

If I were white, I would be like John Wayne. I feel like a tragic hero in a Shakespeare play. Somebody who pulled himself up by his bootstraps, from poverty.

✳✳✳

Behind every sweet smile, there is a bitter sadness that no one can see and feel.

✳✳✳

I said, I'm going to write a song about the women like my mom, women like my sister, who I think to represent the strong black women, and I did that. Now I'm writing about the women I see every day, and that was '[I] Get Around.' If I write songs like 'Keep Ya Head Up,' it will make me seem more than what I am, but I'm just a normal man.

✳✳✳

Don't live to fight, fight to live.

✳✳✳

Hip Hop when it started it was supposed to be this new thing that had no boundaries and was so different from everyday music. Now it seems like I was starting to get caught up in the mode of what made hip hop come about. As long as the music has the true to the heart soul, it can be hip hop. As long it has a soul to it, hip hop can live on.

✳✳✳

Why can't [the President] take some of those people off the street and put them in his White House? Then he'll have people from the street to help him with his ideas. They haven't been homeless forever; they've done things for society.

✳✳✳

I want to grow. I want to be better. You grow. We all grow. We're made to grow. You either evolve or you disappear.

✳✳✳

Until it happened, I did believe that no Black person would ever shoot me. I believed that I didn't have to fear my community, you know, I was like I represent them. I'm their ambassador to the world; they will never do me wrong.

✳✳✳

Every time I speak, I want the truth to come out. Every time I speak, I want a shiver. I don't want them to be like they know what I'm going to say because it's polite. I'm not saying I'm going to rule the world, or I'm going to change the world, but I guarantee you that I will spark the brain that will change the world.

✳✳✳

I set goals, take control, drink out my bottle. I make mistakes but learn from everyone. And when it's said and done, I bet this brother be a better one. If I upset you don't stress; never forget, that God isn't finished with me yet.

✳✳✳

If you let a person talk long enough, you'll hear their true intentions! Listen twice; speak once.

✳✳✳

We can never go anywhere unless we share.

✳✳✳

You can spend minutes, hours, days, weeks, or months over-analyzing a situation; trying to put the pieces together, justifying what could've, would've happened...or you can leave the pieces on the floor and move the f*** on.

✳✳✳

Never surrender, it's all about the faith you got; don't ever stop, push it 'till you hit the top, and if you drop, at least you know you gave your all to be true to you, that way you can never fail.

✳✳✳

Even the genius asks questions.

✳✳✳

The same crime element that white people are scared of black people is scared of. While they are waiting for legislation to pass, we next door to the killer. All them killers they let out, they're in that building. Just because we black, we get along with the killers? What is that?

✳✳✳

I shall not fear man but God, though I walk through the valley of death.

✳✳✳

I am not a perfectionist, but still, I seek perfection. I am not a great romantic, but yet I yearn for affection.

✳✳✳

Even warriors put their spears down on Sundays.

✳✳✳

There's no way I could pay you back, but I plan to show you that I understand, you are appreciated.

***

You just can't be calling us fakers and pretenders and non-creative and say we can't freestyle.

***

No matter who committed the crime, they all yell at me. And the media is greedier than most. You could sell them your soul, and they'll be on you till a nigga's a ghost.

***

I feel like Black Jesus got his hands on me and guided me through life to put me where I'm supposed to be.

***

You can never be friends with someone you fall in love with.

***

Follow your heart, but take your brain with you.

***

It takes skill to be real. Time to heal each other.

***

Out of anger comes controversy, out of controversy comes conversation, out of conversation comes to action.

***

America wants its respect.

***

I worked hard all my life as far as this music business. I dreamed of the day when I could go to New York and feel comfortable, and they could come out here and be comfortable.

***

The only time I have problems is when I sleep.

***

If you could walk a mile in my shoes, you'd be crazy too.

***

I didn't choose the thug life; the thug life chose me.

***

No matter what these people say about me, my music doesn't glorify any image. My music is spiritual when you listen to it. It's all about emotion; I tell my innermost, darkest secrets.

***

Don't change on me. Don't extort me unless you intend to do it forever.

***

They got money for the war but can't feed the poor.

***

What people do for the struggle of power is madness.

***

Imperfection is inherited, therefore we all sin, but fighting the war of sin is the greatest war of all because we all die in the end, no matter how hard we fight.

***

I'm not perfect. But I'll always be real.

***

I know death follows me, but I murder him first.

***

Ain't a woman alive that can take my momma's place.

***

This fast life soon shatters, cause after all the lights and screams, nothing but my dreams matter.

***

Unconditional love. Talking about, the stuff that doesn't wear off, it doesn't fade. It'll last for all these crazy days, these crazy nights. Whether you wrong or you right, I'ma still love you, still feel you, still there for you. No matter what, you will always be in my heart with unconditional love.

***

I know what good morals are, but you're supposed to disregard good morals when you're living in a crazy, bad world. If you're in hell, how can you live like an angel? You're surrounded by devils, trying to be an angel? That's like suicide.

***

I don't want it if it's that easy.

It doesn't stop 'til the casket drop.

I am a hard person to love, but when I love, I love hard.

Is it a crime to fight for what is mine?

Many dreams are what we had and plenty wishes.

Walt Disney

Walter Elias **Disney** (December 5, 1901— December 15, 1966), was an American entrepreneur, animator, voice actor, and film producer. A pioneer of the American animation industry.

***

Laughter is America's most important export.

***

There is more treasure in books than in all the pirate's loot on Treasure Island.

***

The era we are living in today is a dream of coming true.

***

Somehow, I can't believe that any heights can't be scaled by a man who knows the secrets of making dreams come true. This special secret, it seems to me, can be summarized in four Cs. They are curiosity, confidence, courage, and constancy.

***

There are great comfort and inspiration in the feeling of close human relationships and its bearing on our mutual fortunes – a powerful force, to overcome the tough breaks which are certain to come to most of us from time to time.

***

A man should never neglect his family for business.

***

The worst of us is not without innocence, although buried deeply it might be.

***

Leadership means that a group, large or small, is willing to entrust authority to a person who has shown judgment, wisdom, personal appeal, and proven competence.

***

Fantasy and reality often overlap.

***

Laughter is timeless; imagination has no age, dreams are forever.

***

The important thing is the family. If you can keep the family together — and that's the backbone of our whole business, catering to families — that's what we hope to do.

***

There's nothing funnier than the human animal.

***

Our heritage and ideals, our code and standards – the things we live by and teach our children – are preserved or diminished by how freely we exchange ideas and feelings.

***

You reach a point where you don't work for money.

***

For every laugh, there should be a tear.

***

You can't just let nature run wild.

***

The way to get started is to quit talking and begin doing.

***

I always like to look on the optimistic side of life, but I am realistic enough to know that life is a complex matter.

***

If you can dream it, you can do it.

***

Do a good job. You don't have to worry about the money; it will take care of itself. Just do your best work — then try to trump it.

***

The more you like yourself, the less you are like anyone else, which makes you unique.

***

A person should set his goals as early as he can and devote all his energy and talent to getting there. With enough effort, he may achieve it. Or he may find something that is even more rewarding. But in the end, no matter what the outcome, he will know he has been alive.

***

When you believe in a thing, believe in it all the way, implicitly and unquestionable.

***

All our dreams can come true if we dare to pursue them.

***

All the adversity I've had in my life, all my troubles and obstacles, have strengthened me... You may not realize it when it happens, but a kick in the teeth may be the best thing in the world for you.

***

Why worry? If you've done the very best you can, worrying won't make it any better.

***

First, think. Second, believe. Third, dream. And finally, dare.

***

Get a good idea and stay with it. Dog it, and work at it until it's done right.

***

The difference between winning and losing is most often not quitting.

***

Whatever you do, do it well.

***

All you've got to do is own up to your ignorance honestly, and you'll find people who are eager to fill your head with information.

***

Everyone falls. Getting back up is how you learn how to walk.

***

Never get bored or cynical. Yesterday is a thing of the past.

***

Courage is the main quality of leadership, in my opinion, no matter where it is exercised. Usually, it implies some risk —, especially in new undertakings. Courage to initiate something and to keep it going, pioneering and adventurous spirit to blaze new ways, often, in our land of opportunity.

***

Doing the impossible is fun.

***

People often ask me if I know the secret of success and if I could tell others how to make their dreams come true. My answer is, you do it by working.

***

When you're curious, you find lots of interesting things to do. And one thing it takes to accomplish something is courage.

***

That's the real trouble with the world, too many people grow up. They forget.

✳✳✳

Crowded classrooms and half-day sessions are a tragic waste of our greatest national resource – the minds of our children.

✳✳✳

Adults are interested if you don't play down to the little 2 or 3-year olds or talk down. I don't believe in talking down to children. I don't believe in talking down to any certain segment. I like to just talk in a general way to the audience. Children are always reaching.

✳✳✳

Children are people, and they should have to reach to learn about things, to understand things, just as adults have to reach if they want to grow in mental stature.

✳✳✳

Childishness? I think it's the equivalent of never losing your sense of humor. I mean, there's a certain something that you retain. It's the equivalent of not getting so stuffy that you can't laugh at others.

✳✳✳

Our greatest natural resource is the minds of our children.

✳✳✳

I do not make films primarily for children. I make them for the child in all of us, whether he be six or sixty. Call the child innocence.

I don't believe in playing down to children, either in life or in motion pictures. I didn't treat my youngsters like fragile flowers, and I think no parent should.

***

I have long felt that the way to keep children out of trouble is to keep them interested in things.

***

Why do we have to grow up? I know more adults who have children's approach to life. They're people who don't give a hang what the Jones' do. You see them at Disneyland every time you go there. They are not afraid to be delighted with simple pleasures, and they have a degree of contentment with what life has brought – sometimes it isn't much, either.

***

You're dead if you aim only for kids. Adults are only kids grown up, anyway.

***

Every child is born blessed with a vivid imagination. But just as a muscle grows flabby with disuse, so the bright imagination of a child pales in later years if he ceases to exercise it.

***

It's a mistake not to give people a chance to learn to depend on themselves while they are young.

***

Animation offers a medium of storytelling and visual entertainment which can bring pleasure and information to people of all ages everywhere in the world.

***

The animation is different from other parts. Its language is the language of caricature. Our most difficult job was to develop the cartoon's unnatural but seemingly natural anatomy for humans and animals.

***

All cartoon characters and fables must be an exaggeration, caricatures. It is the very nature of fantasy and fable.

***

Animation can explain whatever the mind of man can conceive. This facility makes it the most versatile and explicit means of communication yet devised for quick mass appreciation.

***

In our animation, we must show only the actions and reactions of a character, but we must also picture with the action. . . the feeling of those characters.

***

I try to build a full personality for each of our cartoon characters – to make them personalities.

***

I think a good study of music would be indispensable to the animators — a realization on their part of how primitive music is, how natural it is for people to want to go to music — a study of rhythm, the dance — the various rhythms enter into our lives every day.

***

Until a character becomes a personality, it cannot be believed. Without personality, the character may do funny or interesting things, but unless people can identify themselves with the character, its actions will seem unreal. And without personality, a story cannot ring true to the audience.

***

I think you have to know these fellows definitely before you can draw them. When you start to caricature a person, you can't do it without knowing the person. Take Laurel and Hardy for example; everybody can see Laurel doing certain things because they know Laurel.

***

Of all of our inventions for mass communication, pictures still speak the most universally understood language.

Warren Buffett

Warren Edward Buffett (born August 30, 1930) is an American business magnate, investor, speaker, and philanthropist. He is considered one of the most successful investors in the world.

***

We will have another bubble, but usually, you don't get it the same way you got it before.

***

Never invest in a business you cannot understand.

***

Always invest for the long term.

***

No matter how great the talent or efforts, some things take time. You can't produce a baby in one month by getting nine women pregnant.

***

Cash combined with courage in a time of crisis is priceless.

***

Whether we're talking about socks or stocks, I like buying quality merchandise when it is marked down.

***

What we learn from history is that people don't learn from history.

***

Buy a business, don't rent stocks.

***

A climate of fear is your friend when investing; a euphoric world is your enemy.

***

You don't need to be a rocket scientist. Investing is not a game where the guy with the 160 IQ beats the guy with 130 IQ.

***

We don't have to be smarter than the rest. We have to be more disciplined than the rest.

***

We have long felt that the only value of stock forecasters is to make fortune-tellers look good.

***

A prediction about the direction of the stock market tells you nothing about where stocks are headed, but a whole lot about the person doing the predicting.

***

Someone's sitting in the shade today because someone planted a tree a long time ago.

***

I like my life. I've arranged my life so that I can do what I want.

***

We will only do with your money what we would do with our own.

***

If you don't feel comfortable owning something for ten years, then don't own it for 10 minutes.

***

I am a better investor because I am a businessman and a better businessman because I am an investor.

***

Price is what you pay. Value is what you get.

***

Opportunities come infrequently. When it rains gold, put out the bucket, not the thimble.

***

All there is to invest is picking good stocks at good times and staying with them as long as they remain good companies.

***

The Stock Market is designed to transfer money from the Active to the Patient.

***

Stop trying to predict the direction of the stock market, the economy, interest rates, or elections.

***

I never attempt to make money on the stock market. I buy on the assumption that they could close the market the next day and not reopen it for ten years.

***

By periodically investing in an index fund, the know-nothing investors can outperform most investment professionals.

***

I have pledged... to always run Berkshire with more than ample cash... I will not trade even a night's sleep for the chance of extra profits.

***

The best business returns are usually achieved by companies that are doing something quite similar today to what they were doing five or ten years ago.

***

Investing is laying out money now to get more money back in the future.

***

The stock market is a no-called-strike game. You don't have to swing at everything – you can wait for your pitch.

***

Never count on making a good sale. Have the purchase price be so attractive that even a mediocre sale gives good results.

***

I don't look to jump over 7-foot bars: I look around for 1-foot bars that I can step over.

***

What the wise man does in the beginning, the fool does in the end.

***

The chains of habit are too light to be felt until they are too heavy to be broken.

***

For some reason, people take their cues from price action rather than from values. What doesn't work is when you start doing things that you don't understand or because they worked last week for somebody else. The dumbest reason in the world to buy a stock is because it's going up.

***

Never give up searching for the job that you're passionate about. Try to find the job you'd have if you were independently rich. Forget about the pay. When you're associating with the people that you love, doing what you love, it doesn't get any better than that.

***

We don't get paid for activity, just for being right. As to how long we will wait, we'll wait indefinitely.

***

As Buffet said in the speech, He's not looking at quarterly earnings projections, he's not looking at next year's earnings, he's not thinking about what day of the week it is, he doesn't care what investment research from any place says, he's not interested in price momentum, volume or anything. He's simply asking: What is the business worth?

***

Buy companies with strong histories of profitability and with a dominant business franchise.

***

Most people get interested in stocks when everyone else is. The time to get interested is when no one else is. You can't buy what is popular and do well.

***

Our approach is very much profiting from lack of change rather than from change. With Wrigley chewing gum, it's the lack of change that appeals to me. I don't think it is going to be hurt by the Internet. That's the kind of business I like.

***

When asked how he became so successful in investing, Buffett answered: 'we read hundreds and hundreds of annual reports every year.

***

When a management team with a reputation for brilliance joins a business with poor fundamental economics, it is the reputation of the business that remains intact.

✳✳✳

I try to buy stock in businesses that are so wonderful that an idiot can run them. Because sooner or later, one will.

✳✳✳

Only those who will be sellers of equities shortly should be happy at seeing stocks rise. Prospective purchasers should much prefer sinking prices.

✳✳✳

Diversification is a protection against ignorance. It makes very little sense for those who know what they're doing.

✳✳✳

Wide diversification is only required when investors do not understand what they are doing.

✳✳✳

You're neither right nor wrong because other people agree with you. You're right because your facts are right and your reasoning is right – that's the only thing that makes you right. And if your facts and reasoning are right, you don't have to worry about anybody else.

✳✳✳

It takes 20 years to build a reputation and five minutes to ruin it. If you think about that, you'll do things differently.

***

The first rule is not to lose. The second rule is not to forget the first rule.

***

Only buy something that you'd be perfectly happy to hold if the market shut down for ten years.

***

I will tell you how to become rich. Close the doors. Be fearful when others are greedy. Be greedy when others are fearful.

***

Why not invest your assets in the companies you like? As Mae West said, 'Too much of a good thing can be wonderful.

***

Our favorite holding period is forever.

***

Investing is laying out money now to get more money back in the future.

***

The most important thing to do if you find yourself in a hole is to stop digging.

***

Money is not everything. Make sure you earn a lot before speaking such nonsense.

When a management with a reputation for brilliance tackles a business with a reputation for bad economics, it is the reputation of the business that remains intact.

***

Risk comes from not knowing what you're doing.

***

Volatility is not the same thing as risk, and anyone who thinks it is will cost themselves money.

***

Unless you can watch your stock holding decline by 50% without becoming panic-stricken, you should not be in the stock market.

***

The critical investment factor is determining the intrinsic value of a business and paying a fair or bargain price.

***

Investors making purchases in an overheated market need to recognize that it may often take an extended period for the value of even an outstanding company to catch up with the price they paid.

***

It's better to hang out with people better than you. Pick out associates whose behavior is better than yours, and you'll drift in that direction.

***

Risk can be greatly reduced by concentrating on only a few holdings.

***

It is not necessary to do extraordinary things to get extraordinary results.

***

An investor should ordinarily hold a small piece of an outstanding business with the same tenacity that an owner would exhibit if he owned all of that business.

***

Diversification may preserve wealth, but concentration builds wealth.

***

You won't keep control of your time unless you can say 'no.' You can't let other people set your agenda in life.

***

In the business world, the rearview mirror is always clearer than the windshield.

***

If a business does well, the stock eventually follows.

***

Cash never makes us happy, but it's better to have the money burning a hole in Berkshire's pocket than resting comfortably in someone else's.

***

Wall Street is the only place that people ride to in a Rolls-Royce to get advice from those who take the subway.

***

A public-opinion poll is no substitute for thought.

***

I never buy anything unless I can fill out on a piece of paper my reasons. I would know the answer to that ... *I'm paying $32 billion today for the Coca Cola Company because...* If you can't answer that question, you shouldn't buy it. If you can answer that question, and you do it a few times, you'll make a lot of money.

***

The investor of today does not profit from yesterday's growth.

***

I knew a lot about what I did when I was 20. I had read a lot, and I aspired to learn everything I could about the subject.

You only have to do very few things right in your life so long as you don't do too many things wrong.

***

It's far better to buy a wonderful company at a fair price than a fair company at a wonderful price.

***

You ought to be able to explain why you're taking the job you're taking, why you're making the investment you're making, or whatever it may be. And if it can't stand applying pencil to paper, you'd better think it through some more. And if you can't write an intelligent answer to those questions, don't do it.

***

Look at market fluctuations as your friend rather than your enemy; profit from folly rather than participate in it.

***

An investor needs to do very few things right as long as he or she avoids big mistakes.

***

Do a lot of reading. – *on how to determine the value of a business*

***

Somebody once said that in looking for people to hire, you look for three qualities: integrity, intelligence, and energy. And if you don't have the first, the other two will kill you.

You think about it; it's true. If you hire somebody without [integrity], you want them to be dumb and lazy.

***

Only when the tide goes out, do you discover who's been swimming naked?

***

The fact that people will be full of greed, fear, or folly is predictable. The sequence is not predictable.

***

Time is the friend of the wonderful company, the enemy of the mediocre.

***

I do not like debt and do not like to invest in companies that have too much debt, particularly long-term debt. With long-term debt, increases in interest rates can drastically affect company profits and make future cash flows less predictable.

***

We will reject interesting opportunities rather than over-leverage our balance sheet.

***

I always knew I was going to be rich. I don't think I ever doubted it for a minute.

***

Turnarounds seldom turn.

***

If at first, you do succeed, quit trying on investing.

***

I don't measure my life by the money I've made. Other people might, but certainly, don't.

***

Anything can happen in stock markets and you ought to conduct your affairs so that if the most extraordinary events happen, that you're still around to play the next day.

***

You shouldn't own common stocks if a 50 percent decrease in their value in a short period caused you acute distress.

***

With few exceptions when a manager with a reputation for brilliance tackles a business with a reputation for poor economics, it is the reputation of the business which remains intact.

***

It's not debt per se that overwhelms an individual corporation or country. Rather it is a continuous increase in debt about income that causes trouble.

A great investment opportunity occurs when a marvelous business encounters a one-time huge, but solvable problem.

***

You do not adequately protect yourself by being half awake when others are sleeping.

***

We like to buy businesses, but we don't like to sell them.

***

Money to some extent sometimes let you be in more interesting environments. But it can't change how many people love you or how healthy you are.

***

It's our fun being gorse when the tractor comes along, or the blacksmith when the car comes along.

***

Enjoy your work and work for whom you admire.

***

With enough insider information and a million dollars, you can go broke in a year.

***

Read Ben Graham, and Phil Fisher read annual reports, but don't do equations with Greek letters in them.

***

In a commodity business, it's very hard to be smarter than your dumbest competitor.

***

A hyperactive stock market is the pickpocket of enterprise.

***

Valuing a business is part art and part science.

***

Chains of habits are too light to be felt until they are too heavy to be broken.

Winston Churchill

Sir Winston Leonard Spencer-Churchill (November 30, 1874 - January 24, 1965) was a British politician, military officer, and writer who served as the prime minister of Great Britain from 1940 to 1945 and from 1951 to 1955.

✱✱✱

The whole history of the world is summed up in the fact that, when nations are strong, they are not always, and when they wish to be, they are no longer strong.

✱✱✱

Politics is more dangerous than war, for in war you are only killed once.

✱✱✱

We shape our dwellings, and afterward, our dwellings shape us.

✱✱✱

It has been said that Democracy is the worst form of government except for all those other forms that have been tried from time to time.

✱✱✱

It is a mistake to try to look too far ahead. The chain of destiny can only be grasped one link at a time.

✱✱✱

When I am abroad, I always make it a rule never to criticize or attack the government of my own country. I make up for lost time when I come home.

***

I have nothing to offer but blood, toil, tears, and sweat.

***

Dictators ride to and fro on tigers from which they dare not dismount. And the Tigers are getting hungry.

***

A fanatic is one who can't change his mind and won't change the subject.

***

Employ your time in improving yourself by other men's writings so that you shall come easily by what others have labored hard for.

***

I have never accepted what many people have kindly said, namely that I have inspired the nation. It was the nation and the race dwelling all around the globe that had the lion heart. I had the luck to be called upon to roar.

***

Without a measureless and perpetual uncertainty, the drama of human life would be destroyed.

***

Never in the field of human conflict was so much owed by so many to so few.

***

An appeaser is one who feeds a crocodile – hoping it will eat him last.

***

I am easily satisfied with the very best.

***

Solitary trees, if they grow at all, grow strong.

***

Say what you have to say and the first time you come to a sentence with a grammatical ending – sit down.

***

It is no use saying 'we are doing our best.' You have got to succeed in doing what is necessary.

***

Let us, therefore, brace ourselves to our duties, and so bear ourselves that, if the British Empire and its Commonwealth last for a thousand years, men will still say: This was their finest hour.

***

Do not let us speak of darker days; let us speak rather of sterner days. These are not dark days: these are great days – the greatest days our country has ever lived.

***

The English know how to make the best of things. Their so-called muddling through simply skills at dealing with the inevitable.

***

Continuous efforts – not strength or intelligence – is the key to unlocking our potential.

***

War is mainly a catalog of blunders.

***

In war, as in life, it is often necessary, when some cherished scheme has failed, to take up the best alternative open, and if so, it is folly not to work for it with all your might.

***

No one can guarantee success in war but only deserve it.

***

If one has to submit, it is wasteful not to do so with the best grace possible.

***

All the great things are simple, and many can be expressed in a single word: freedom; justice; honor; duty; mercy; hope.

***

Without courage, all other virtues lose their meaning.

***

Curse ruthless time! Curse our mortality. How cruelly short is the allotted span for all we must cram into it!

***

We must beware of needless innovations, especially when guided by logic.

One ought never to turn one's back on a threatened danger and try to run away from it. If you do that, you will double the danger. But if you meet it promptly and without flinching, you will reduce the danger by half. Never run away from anything. Never!

**

Success is never found. Failure is never fatal. Courage is the only thing.

**

Victory at all costs, victory in spite of all terror, victory however long and hard the hard may be; for without victory there is no survival.

**

We shall draw from the heart of suffering itself the means of inspiration and survival.

**

History is written by the victors.

**

The problems of victory are more agreeable than those of defeat, but they are no less difficult.

**

My most brilliant achievement was my ability to be able to persuade my wife to marry me.

***

I am prepared to meet my Maker. Whether my Maker is prepared for the ordeal of meeting me is another matter.

***

The English never draw a line without blurring it.

***

It is a good thing for an uneducated man to read books of quotations.

***

The price of greatness is responsibility.

***

There are a terrible lot of lies going about the world, and the worst of it is that half of them are true.

***

To may have to be the slow and laborious task of years. To can be the thoughtless act of a single day.

***

The farther backward you can look, the farther forward you are likely to see.

***

Do you have enemies? Good. It means you've stood up for something, sometime in your life.

In finance, everything agreeable is unsound, and everything sound is disagreeable.

✳✳✳

If you're going through hell, keep going.

✳✳✳

A state of society where men may not speak their minds cannot long endure.

✳✳✳

This is the lesson: never give in, never give in, never, never, never, never — in nothing, great or small, large or petty — never give in except to convictions of honor and good sense. Never yield to force; never yield to the overwhelming might of the enemy.

✳✳✳

There is only one duty, only one safe course, and that is to try to be right and not to fear to do or say what you believe to be right.

✳✳✳

It is a fine thing, to be honest, but it is also very important to be right.

✳✳✳

I like pigs. Dogs look up to us. Cats look down on us. Pigs treat us as equals.

✳✳✳

Never hold discussions with the monkey when the organ grinder is in the room.

***

Attitude is a little thing that makes a big difference.

***

The best argument against democracy is a five-minute conversation with the average voter.

***

We shall defend our island, whatever the cost may be, we shall fight on the beaches, we shall fight on the landing grounds, we shall fight in the fields and the streets, we shall fight in the hills; we shall never surrender.

***

Never, never, never believe any war will be smooth and easy, or that anyone who embarks on the strange voyage can measure the tides and hurricanes he will encounter. The statesman who yields to war fever must realize that once the signal is given, he is no longer the master of policy but the slave of unforeseeable and uncontrollable events.

***

What is adequacy? Adequacy is no standard at all.

***

Socialism is a philosophy of failure, the creed of ignorance, and the gospel of envy, its inherent virtue is the equal sharing of misery.

***

We make a living by what we get, but we make a life by what we give.

***

Those who can win a war well can rarely make a good peace, and those who could make a good peace would never have won the war.

***

It's not enough that we do our best; sometimes we have to do what's required.

***

Healthy citizens are the greatest asset any country can have.

***

We shall not fail or falter. We shall not weaken or tire. Neither the sudden shock of battle nor the long-drawn trials of vigilance and exertion will wear us down. Give us the tools, and we will finish the job.

***

Men occasionally stumble over the truth, but most of them pick themselves up and hurry off as if nothing ever happened.

***

It is wonderful what great strides can be made when there is a resolute purpose behind them.

***

I never worry about action, but only inaction.

***

We are stripped bare by the curse of plenty.

***

If you do not fight for right when you can easily win without bloodshed; if you will not fight when your victory is sure and not too costly; you may come to the moment when you will have to fight with all the odds against you and only a precarious chance of survival. There may even be a worse case. You may have to fight when there is no hope of victory because it is better to perish than to live as slaves.

***

Great and good are seldom the same man.

***

I always seem to get inspiration and renewed vitality by contact with this great novel land of yours which sticks up out of the Atlantic.

***

We shall show mercy, but we shall not ask for it.

***

Success is not final; failure is not fatal; it is the courage to continue that counts.

***

All the greatest things are simple, and many can be expressed in a single word: freedom; justice; honor; duty; mercy; hope.

***

Everyone has his day and some days last longer than others.

✳✳✳

I'm always ready to learn, although I do not always like being taught.

✳✳✳

The first duty of the university is to teach wisdom, not a trade; character, not technicalities. We want a lot of engineers in the modern world, but we do not want a world of engineers.

✳✳✳

The inherent vice of capitalism is the unequal sharing of blessings; the inherent virtue of socialism is the equal sharing of miseries.

✳✳✳

When the eagles are silent, the parrots begin to chatter.

✳✳✳

History will be kind to me for I intend to write it.

✳✳✳

Christmas is a season not only of rejoicing but of reflection.

✳✳✳

If we open a quarrel between the past and the present, we shall find we have lost the future.

✳✳✳

Politics is the ability to foretell what is going to happen tomorrow, next week, next month and next year. And to have the ability afterward to explain why it didn't happen.

***

If you have an important point to make, don't try to be subtle or clever. Use a pile driver. Hit the point once. Then come back and hit it again. Then hit it a third time-a tremendous whack.

***

Do not let spacious plans for a new world divert your energies from saving what is left of the old.

***

Success is the ability to go from one failure to another with no loss of enthusiasm.

***

All I can say is that I have taken more out of alcohol than alcohol has taken out of me.

***

Out of intense complexities, intense simplicities emerge.

***

I may be drunk, miss, but in the morning I will be sober, and you will still be ugly.

***

Courage is rightly esteemed the first of human qualities because it has been said, it is the quality which guarantees all others.

Every man should ask himself each day whether he is not too readily accepting negative solutions.

***

The power of man has grown in every sphere, except over himself.

***

The greatest lesson in life is to know that even fools are right sometimes.

***

Writing a book is an adventure. To begin with, it is a toy than an amusement. Then it becomes a mistress, and then it becomes a master, and then it becomes a tyrant and, in the last stage, just as you are about to be reconciled to your servitude, you kill the monster and fling him to the public.

***

To improve is to change, so to be perfect is to change often.

***

The truth is incontrovertible. Malice may attack it, ignorance may deride it, but in the end, there it is.

***

Broadly speaking short words are best and the old words when short, are best of all.

***

I am never going to have anything more to do with politics or politicians. When this war is over, I shall confine myself entirely to writing and painting.

***

Courage is what it takes to stand up and speak; it's also what it takes to sit down and listen.

***

There is always much to be said for not attempting more than you can do and for making a certainty of what you try. But this principle, like others in life and war, has its exceptions.

***

Success is going from failure to failure without loss of enthusiasm.

***

Every day you may make progress. Every step may be fruitful. There will stretch out before you an ever-lengthening, ever-ascending, ever-improving path. You know you will never get to the end of the journey. But this, so far from discouraging, only adds to the joy and glory of the climb.

***

If you have ten thousand regulations, you destroy all respect for the law.

***

In the course of my life, I have often had to eat my words, and I must confess that I have always found it a wholesome diet.

***

Everyone has his day, and some days last longer than others.

***

In wartime, the truth is so precious that she should always be attended by a bodyguard of lies.

***

The empires of the future are the empires of the mind.

***

I have never developed indigestion from eating my words.

***

Two things are more difficult than making an after-dinner speech: climbing a wall which is leaning toward you and kissing a girl who is leaning away from you.

***

Difficulties mastered are opportunities won.

***

I am certainly not one of those who needs to be prodded. If anything, I am the prod.

***

There is no time for ease and comfort. It is time to dare and endure.

***

A pessimist sees the difficulty in every opportunity; an optimist sees the opportunity in every difficulty.

***

We are masters of the unsaid words, but slaves of those we let slip out.

***

Nothing in life is so exhilarating as to be shot at without result.

***

Let our advance worrying become advance thinking and planning.

***

No crime is so great as daring to excel.

***

A lie gets halfway around the world before the truth has a chance to get its pants on.

***

Play the game for more than you can afford to lose. Only then will you learn the game.

***

Ending a sentence with a preposition is something up with which I will not put.

W. Clement Stone

William Clement Stone (May 4, 1902 - September 3, 2002) was a prominent businessman, philanthropist, and self-help book author.

***

Aim for the moon. If you miss, you may hit a star.

***

Be careful the environment you choose for it will shape you; be careful the friends you choose for you will become like them.

***

Everyone who achieves success in a great venture solves each problem as they came to it. They helped themselves. And they were helped through powers known and unknown to them at the time they set out on their voyage. They keep going regardless of the obstacles they met.

***

Have the courage to say no. Have the courage to face the truth. Do the right thing because it is right. These are the magic keys to living your life with integrity.

***

I think there is something, more important than believing: Action! The world is full of dreamers; there aren't enough who will move ahead and begin to take concrete steps to actualize their vision.

***

If there is something to gain and nothing to lose by asking, by all means, ask!

***

If you employed study, thinking, and planning time daily, you could develop and use the power that can change the course of your destiny.

***

Self-suggestion makes you master of yourself.

***

Tell everyone what you want to do, and someone will want to help you do it.

***

Thinking will not overcome fear but action will.

***

The truth will always be the truth, regardless of lack of understanding, disbelief or ignorance.

***

Try, try, try, and keep on trying is the rule that must be followed to become an expert in anything.

***

When we direct our thoughts properly, we can control our emotions...

***

When you discover your mission, you will feel its demand. It will fill you with enthusiasm and a burning desire to get to work on it.

＊＊＊

When you do the wrong thing, knowing it is wrong, you do so because you haven't developed the habit of effectively controlling or neutralizing strong inner urges that tempt you, or because you have established the wrong habit and don't know how to eliminate them effectively.

＊＊＊

You affect your subconscious mind by verbal repetition.

＊＊＊

So many fail because they don't get started -- they don't go. They don't overcome inertia. They don't begin.

＊＊＊

There is little difference in people, but that little difference makes a big difference. That little difference is attitude. The big difference is whether it is positive or negative.

＊＊＊

You are a product of your environment. So, choose the environment that will best develop you toward your objective. Analyze your life in terms of its environment. Are the things around you helping you toward success -- or are they holding you back?

＊＊＊

You affect your subconscious mind by verbal repetition.

***

Definiteness of purpose is the starting point of all achievement

***

Success is achieved and maintained by those who try and keep trying.

***

We have a problem. "Congratulations." But it's a tough problem. "Then double congratulations."

***

To solve a problem or to reach a goal, you don't need to know all the answers in advance. But you must have a clear idea of the problem or the goal you want to reach.

***

You. Too, can determine what you want. You can decide on your major objectives, targets, aims, and destination.

Vince Lombardi

Vincent Thomas **Lombardi** (June 11, 1913 – September 3, 1970) was an American football player, coach, and executive in the National Football League (NFL).

***

The price of success is hard work, dedication to the job at hand, and the determination that whether we win or lose, we have applied the best of ourselves to the task at hand.

***

Winning isn't everything, but wanting to win is.

***

The quality of a person's life is in direct proportion to their commitment to excellence, regardless of their chosen field of endeavor.

***

Individual commitment to a group effort that is what makes a team work.

***

After the cheers have died down and the stadium is empty after the headlines have been written and after you are back in the quiet of your room and the championship ring has been placed on the dresser, and all the pomp and fanfare has faded, the end.

***

In great attempts, it is glorious even to fail.

***

It's not whether you get knocked down, it's whether you get up.

***

Football is like life – it requires perseverance, self-denial, hard work, sacrifice, dedication and respect for authority.

***

Once a man has committed to a way of life, he puts the greatest strength in the world behind him. It's something we call heart power. Once a man has made this commitment, nothing will stop him short of success.

***

Leaders are made; they are not born. They are made by hard effort, which is the price which all of us must pay to achieve any worthwhile goal.

***

I firmly believe that any man's finest hour, the greatest fulfillment of all that he holds dear, is the moment when he has worked his heart out in a good cause and lies exhausted on the field of battle, victorious.

***

The only place success comes before work is in the dictionary.

***

Leadership rests not only upon ability, not only upon capacity; having the capacity to lead is not enough. The leader must be willing to use it. His leadership is then based on truth and character. There must be truth in the purpose and will power in character.

***

Inches make champions.

***

If you can accept losing you can't win. If you can walk, you can run. No one is ever hurt. Hurt is in your mind.

***

The greatest accomplishment is not in never falling, but in rising again after you fall.

***

Once you learn to quit, it becomes a habit.

***

Every time a football player goes to ply his trade, he's got to play from the ground up — from the soles of his feet right up to his head. Every inch of him has to play. Some guys play with their heads. That's OK. You've got to be smart to be number one in any business. But more importantly, you've got to play with your heart, with every fiber of your body. If you're lucky enough to find a guy with a lot of head and a lot of heart, he's never going to come off the field second.

***

Practice does not make perfect. Only perfect practice makes perfect.

***

The real glory is being knocked to your knees and then coming back. That's real glory. That's the essence of it.

***

If you aren't fired up with enthusiasm, you'll be fired with enthusiasm.

***

Life's battles don't always go to the stronger or faster man. But sooner or later, the man who wins is the man who thinks he can.

***

Confidence is contagious; so is lack of confidence.

***

Winning is a habit. Unfortunately, so is losing.

***

The achievements of an organization are the results of the combined effort of each.

***

Fatigue makes cowards of us all.

***

There's only one way to succeed in anything, and that is to give it everything. I do, and I demand that my players do.

***

Winning is not a sometime thing; it's an all-time thing. You don't win once in a while; you don't do things right once in a while, you do them right all the time. Winning is a habit. Unfortunately, so is losing.

***

There is only one way to succeed in anything, and that is to give it everything.

***

Some of us will do our jobs well and some will not, but we will be judged by only one thing-the result.

***

The measure of who we are is what we do with what we have.

***

People who work together will win, whether it be against complex football defenses or the problems of modern society.

***

Coaches who can outline plays on a blackboard are a dime a dozen. The ones who win get inside their player and motivate.

***

Leaders aren't born; they are made. And they are made just like anything else, through hard work. And that's the price we'll have to pay to achieve that goal or any goal.

***

Leadership is based on a spiritual quality; the power to inspire, the power to inspire others to follow.

***

People who work together will win, whether it be against complex football defenses or the problems of modern society.

***

Show me a good loser, and I'll show you a loser.

***

The spirit, the will to win, and the will to excel are the things that endure. These qualities are so much more important than the events that occur.

***

It's easy to have faith in yourself and have discipline when you're a winner when you're number one. What you've got to have is faith and discipline when you're not yet a winner.

***

Unless a man believes in himself and makes a total commitment to his career and puts everything, he has into it – his mind, his body, his heart – what's a life worth to him?

***

I would say that the quality of each man's life is the full measure of that man's commitment of excellence and victory – whether it be football, whether it be business, whether it be politics or government or what have you.

***

The difference between a successful person and others is not a lack of strength, not a lack of knowledge, but rather in a lack of will.

***

Football is a great deal like life in that it teaches that work, sacrifice, perseverance, competitive drive, selflessness and respect for authority is the price that every one of us must pay to achieve any worthwhile goal.

✳✳✳

Success is like anything worthwhile. It has a price. You have to pay the price to win, and you have to pay the price to get to the point where success is possible. Most importantly, you must pay the price to stay there.

✳✳✳

Once you agree upon the price you and your family must pay for success, it enables you to ignore the minor hurts, the opponent's pressure, and the temporary failures.

✳✳✳

A man can be as great as he wants to be. If you believe in yourself and have the courage, the determination, the dedication, the competitive drive, and if you are willing to sacrifice the little things in life and pay the price for the worthwhile things, it can be done.

✳✳✳

It is essential to understand that battles are primarily won in the hearts of men.

✳✳✳

After all the cheers have died down, and the stadium is empty, after the headlines have been written, and after you are back in the quiet of your room and the championship ring has been placed on the dresser and after all the pomp and fanfare have faded, the enduring thing that is left is the dedication to doing with our lives the very best we can to make the world a better place in which to live.

***

If you do not settle for anything less than your best, you will be amazed at what you can accomplish in your lives.

***

Most important of all, to be successful in life demands that a man make a personal commitment to excellence and victory, even though the ultimate victory can never be completely won. That victory might be pursued and wooed with every fiber of our body, with every bit of our might and all our effort. And each week, there is a new encounter; each day, there is a new challenge.

***

Obstacles are what you see when you take your eyes off of the goal.

***

Morally, the life of the organization must be exemplary. This is one phase where the organization must not have criticism.

***

To succeed, this group will need a singleness of purpose, they will need dedication, and they will have to convince all of their prospects of the willingness to sacrifice.

***

Once you have established the goals you want and the price, you're willing to pay; you can ignore the minor hurts, the opponent's pressure, and the temporary failures.

***

Mental toughness is Spartanism, with all its qualities of self-denial, sacrifice, dedication, fearlessness, and love.

***

There is no substitute for work.

***

Faithfulness and truth are the most sacred excellences and endowments of the human mind.

***

Teams do not go physically flat; they go mentally stale.

***

When we place our dependence on God, we are unencumbered, and we do not worry. We may even be reckless, insofar as our part in the production is concerned. This confidence, this sureness of action, is both contagious and an aid to the perfect action. The rest is in the hands of God – and this is the same God, gentlemen, who have won all His battles up to now.

***

I've never known a man worth his salt who, in the long run, deep down in his heart, didn't appreciate the grind, the discipline.

***

The good Lord gave you a body that can stand most anything. It's your mind you have to convince.

***

Three things are important to every man in this locker room. His God, his family, and the Green Bay Packers. In that order.

***

To achieve success, whatever the job we have, we must pay the price.

***

Mental toughness is many things and rather difficult to explain. Its qualities are sacrifice and self-denial. Also, most importantly, it is combined with a perfectly disciplined will that refuses to give in. It's a state of mind – you could call it a character in action.

***

Leadership is not just one quality, but rather a blend of many qualities; and while no one individual possesses all of the needed talents that go into leadership, each man can develop a combination to make him a leader.

***

Success is based upon a spiritual quality, a power to inspire others.

***

We would accomplish many more things if we did not think of them as impossible.

***

There is only one kind of discipline, and that is the perfect discipline. As a leader, you must enforce and maintain that discipline; otherwise, you will fail at your job.

***

A leader must identify himself with the group, must back up the group, even at the risk of displeasing superiors. He must believe that the group wants from him a sense of approval. If this feeling prevails, production, discipline, morale will be high, and in return, you can demand the cooperation to promote the goals of the community.

***

Perfection is not attainable. But if we chase perfection, we can catch excellence.

***

Second place is meaningless. You can't always be first, but you have to believe that you should have been – that you were never beaten – that time just ran out on you.

***

No leader, however great, can long continue unless he wins battles. The battle decides all.

***

To the winner, there is 100-percent elation, 100-percent fun, 100-percent laughter; and yet the only thing left to the loser is resolution and determination.

***

Winning is a habit. Watch your thoughts; they become your beliefs. Watch your beliefs; they become your words. Watch your words; they become your actions. Watch your actions; they become your habits. Watch your habits; they become your character.

***

You defeat defeatism with confidence.

***

You never win a game unless you beat the guy in front of you. The score on the board doesn't mean a thing. That's for the fans. You've got to win the war with the man in front of you. You've got to get your man.

***

If you don't think you're a winner, you don't belong here.

***

At many a moment on many a day, I am convinced that pro football must be a game for madmen, and I must be one of them.

***

Before I can embrace freedom, I should be aware of what duties I have.

***

If it doesn't matter who wins or loses, then why do they keep score?

***

Individual commitment to a group effort – that is what makes a team work, a company work, a society work, a civilization work.

∗∗∗

The harder you work, the harder it is to surrender.

∗∗∗

It is and has always been an American zeal to be first in everything we do, and to win...

∗∗∗

I derived my strength from daily mass and communion.

∗∗∗

To be successful, a man must exert an effective influence upon his brothers and his associates, and the degree in which he accomplishes this depends on the personality of the man. The incandescence of which he is capable of. The flame of fire that burns inside of him. The magnetism which draws the heart of other men to him.

∗∗∗

Live as if you were living already for the second time and as if you had acted the first time as wrongly as you are about to act now!

∗∗∗

Winning is not everything – but making an effort to win is.

∗∗∗

∗∗∗

Mental toughness is essential to success.

***

Running a football team is no different than running any other kind of organization...

***

The objective is to win: fairly, squarely, decently, win by the rules, but still, win.

***

Don't succumb to excuses. Go back to the job of making the corrections and forming the habits that will make your goal possible.

***

Teamwork is what the Green Bay Packers were all about. They didn't do it for individual glory. They did it because they loved one another.

***

The leader can never close the gap between himself and the group. If he does, he is no longer what he must be. He must walk a tightrope between the consent he must win and the control he must exert.

***

Winning isn't everything; it's the only thing.

***

Getting to the final is everything, and winning is icing on the cake.

***

Brains without competitive hearts are rudderless.

***

A team that thinks it's going to lose is going to lose.

***

When you've got the momentum in a football game, that is a time to keep going and get it into the end zone. We want to score for America's families.

***

Some people try to find things in this game that don't exist, but football is only two things – blocking and tackling.

***

Confidence is contagious and so is lack of confidence, and a customer will recognize both.

***

We know how rough the road will be, how heavy here the load will be, we know about the barricades that wait along the track, but we have seen our soul ahead upon a certain goal ahead, and nothing left from hell to sky shall ever turn us back.

***

It is time for us all to stand and cheer for the doer, the achiever — the one who recognizes the challenges and does something about it.

***

A school without football is in danger of deteriorating into a medieval study hall.

Run for daylight.

All right Mister, let me tell you what winning means... you're willing to go longer, work harder, give more than anyone else.

Build for your team a feeling of oneness, of dependence on one another and of strength to be derived by unity.

I'm not afraid to die – it's just that I had so much left to do in this world.

A disciplined person is one who follows the will of the one who gives the orders.

We didn't lose the game; we just ran out of time.

I've been accused of lacking compassion. But that shows I'm not without compassion.

Zig Ziglar

Zig Ziglar (November 6, 1926.—November 28, 2012) was a motivational speaker, teacher, and trainer who traveled the world over delivering his messages of humor, hope, and encouragement.

***

You are the only person on earth who can use your ability.

***

When you put faith, hope, and love together, you can raise positive kids in a negative world.

***

There has never been a statue erected to honor a critic.

***

Failure is a detour, not a dead-end street.

***

What you get by achieving your goals is not as important as what you become by achieving your goals.

***

Happiness is not pleasure; it is a victory.

***

Every sale has five basic obstacles: no need, no money, no hurry, no desire, no trust.

***

It's not what you've got; it's what you use that makes a difference.

✳✳✳

Success is the maximum utilization of the ability that you have.

✳✳✳

Winning is not everything, but the effort to win is.

✳✳✳

Efficiency is doing things right. Effectiveness is doing the right thing.

✳✳✳

The person who will not stand for something will fall for anything.

✳✳✳

You are what you are, and you are where you are because of what has gone into your mind. You change what you are, and you change where you are by changing what goes into your mind.

✳✳✳

It's your attitude, not your aptitude that determines your altitude.

✳✳✳

You do not pay the price of success; you enjoy the price of success.

✳✳✳

The real test in golf and life is not in keeping out of the rough, but in getting out after you are in.

***

All resources are not obvious; great managers find and develop available talent.

***

A goal properly set is halfway reached.

***

Success is dependent upon the glands - sweat glands.

***

Go as far as you can see, and when you get there, you will always be able to see farther.

***

If you want to reach a goal, you must 'see the reaching' in your mind before you arrive at your goal.

***

Positive thinking will let you do everything better than negative thinking will.

***

If you can dream it, then you can achieve it. You will get all you want in life if you help enough other people get what they want.

***

Success means doing the best we can with what we have. Success is the doing, not the getting; in the trying, not the triumph. Success is a personal standard, reaching for the highest that is in us, becoming all that we can be.

The most important persuasion tool you have in your entire arsenal is integrity.

Expect the best. Prepare for the worst. Capitalize on what comes

Made in the USA
Columbia, SC
20 September 2020